Luminos is the Open Access monograph publishing program from UC Press. Luminos provides a framework for preserving and reinvigorating monograph publishing for the future and increases the reach and visibility of important scholarly work. Titles published in the UC Press Luminos model are published with the same high standards for selection, peer review, production, and marketing as those in our traditional program. www.luminosoa.org

D1711467

The Stains of Imprisonment

GENDER AND JUSTICE
Edited by Claire M. Renzetti

This University of California Press series explores how the experiences of offending, victimization, and justice are profoundly influenced by the intersections of gender with other markers of social location. Cross-cultural and comparative, series volumes publish the best new scholarship that seeks to challenge assumptions, highlight inequalities, and transform practice and policy.

The Stains of Imprisonment

*Moral Communication and Men Convicted
of Sex Offenses*

Alice Ievins

UNIVERSITY OF CALIFORNIA PRESS

University of California Press
Oakland, California

Suggested citation: Ievins, A. *The Stains of Imprisonment: Moral Communication and Men Convicted of Sex Offenses*. Oakland: University of California Press, 2023. DOI: https://doi.org/10.1525/luminos.143

Cataloging-in-Publication Data is on file at the Library of Congress.
ISBN 978-0-520-38371-5 (pbk. : alk. paper)
ISBN 978-0-520-38372-2 (ebook)

32 31 30 29 28 27 26 25 24 23
10 9 8 7 6 5 4 3 2 1

CONTENTS

CONTENTS

ACKNOWLEDGMENTS

I write these acknowledgments as I come to the end of fourteen years based at the University of Cambridge, for eleven of which I have been affiliated with the Institute of Criminology. I have been so fortunate in finding this academic home and am endlessly grateful to Ben Crewe for supervising me as a student, mentoring me as a postdoc, and encouraging me as a friend. I am also grateful to him and the rest of the Comparative Penology team (especially Julie Laursen, Kristian Mjåland, and Anna Schliehe) for embodying what I hoped academic life would be like: scholarly, supportive, and funny. I would also like to thank all the academic and nonacademic members of the Prisons Research Centre for all sorts of help over the years. Particular gratitude goes to Borah Kant, who has always picked up the pieces and who I would trust with anything. I am also grateful to many other colleagues at the Institute: Bethany Schmidt, Loraine Gelsthorpe, Alison Liebling, everyone at the CCGSJ, Eliza Preece, Kathy Oswald, Claire Bonner, Sarah Rosella, Matt Skipper, everyone in the library and on reception and in accounts, Sarah Doxat-Pratt, Antony Orchard and Arnel Badayos, Magda Bergman and Anna Zofka, Sophie Ellis (for helping with the Brown Bag seminars especially), everyone from the PhD Writing Group, the yoga group, the Reading Aloud Group, the PRC Book Group, the Ethics Reading Group, and the Criminal Jurisprudence and Philosophy Reading Group. I am excited to make new friends and build new connections at the University of Liverpool, but I am so grateful for what has come before.

I was the lucky recipient of financial support from the Dawes Trust, who funded my PhD and the open access publication of this book. I would also like to thank the Institute of Criminology and Pembroke College, Cambridge, for funding some of my fieldwork expenses. After finishing my PhD, I worked for the Comparative

Penology project (funded by the European Research Council) and then on two grants funded by the ESRC, both of which allowed me the financial security to write this book. This journey started because of the financial support of my grandmother, Moira Bambrough, who paid for me to do my Masters. I was so lucky, and am thankful for my Grannie's generosity and seriousness about education.

I am grateful to all the staff of HMP Stafford for their welcome, in particular those who worked on the wings I worked on: I showed up one day and said I'd be hanging around at your workplace for five months, and you never let me feel guilty or intrusive. I would especially like to thank Bridie Oakes-Richards, Deborah Butler, PJ Butler, Anne Cherriman, Claud Lofters, Paddy Keane, Steve Paice, Donna Insull, Jody Roberts, Caroline Jones, Davina Shelley, Alex Preston, Ralph Lubkowski, Ian West, and Andy Holmes. I would also like to thank Kam Sarai for meeting with me and discussing this project, and Kate Gooch and David Sheldon for facilitating feedback sessions a few years later. I am also grateful to Ruth Mann, who gave me useful advice in the project's early days, and who was an extraordinarily inspiring figure. And, of course, this book would have been impossible had the men held in Stafford not been generous and gracious enough to let me talk to them. I am honored by the trust you placed in me, and grateful for every conversation. I hope that I have done you justice.

Developing the PhD project into a book was a difficult task. I am grateful to the editors and publishers of book chapters in which I trialed some of the ideas more fully developed here; for more details, see the following:

- Ievins, Alice. 2019. "Finding Victims in the Narratives of Men Imprisoned for Sex Offences." In *The Emerald Handbook of Narrative Criminology*, edited by Jennifer Fleetwood, Lois Presser, Sveinung Sandberg, and Thomas Ugelvik, 279–300. Bingley, UK: Emerald.
- Ievins, Alice. 2019. "Prison Officers, Professionalism and Moral Judgement." In *Sexual Crime and the Experience of Imprisonment*, edited by Nicholas Blagden, Belinda Winder, Kerensa Hocken, Richard Lievesley, Phil Banyard, and Helen Elliott, 85–108. London: Palgrave Macmillan.
- Ievins, Alice. 2022. "The Society of 'Sex Offenders.'" In *Power and Pain in the Modern Prison: The Society of Captives Revisited*, edited by Ben Crewe, Andrew Goldsmith, and Mark Halsey, 175–92. Oxford: Clarendon Press.
- Ievins, Alice. Forthcoming. "Taking the Long View: The Role of Shame and Guilt in Desistance." In *Criminology as a Moral Science*, edited by Anthony E. Bottoms and Jonathan Jacobs. Oxford: Hart.

I was very fortunate in my examiners, Thomas Ugelvik and Shadd Maruna, who championed the work in its early days, and I thank Shadd for suggesting that I try US publishers, introducing me to the Gender and Justice series, and coming up with the title. Thanks to Claire Renzetti, for being open to a manuscript about one prison in England, and to Maura Roessner, Madison Wetzell and Sam Warren, not only for their efficient, wise, and practical support of this book, but for never making me feel stupid for asking questions. I am also grateful to Linda Gorman for copyediting the manuscript so beautifully—no doubt a lengthy task as I had not used American spellings—and to Paige MacKay for her patience in the final stages of the submission. Thanks to everyone who reviewed the proposal and the manuscript, whose comments have enhanced it greatly: Yvonne Jewkes, Fergus McNeill, Rose Ricciardelli, and those whose names I don't know. Thanks also to those who read drafts of the proposal or chapters, sent resources, or had conversations with me that gave me ideas, including but not limited to Ruth Armstrong, Charlotte Barrington, Jessica Bird, Tony Bottoms, Rob Canton, Ben Crewe, Sophie Ellis, Gareth Evans, Aya Gruber, Guy Hamilton-Smith, Tom Hawker-Dawson, David Hayes, Susie Hulley, Ben Jarman, Borah Kant, Anja Kruse, Julie Laursen, Amy Ludlow, Shadd Maruna, Kristian Mjåland, Nicky Padfield, Victoria Pereyra, Beth Phillips, Thea Reimer, Anna Schliehe, Rita Shah, Kanupriya Sharma, Miriam Shovel, Ted Smyth, Rachel Tynan, and Ryan Williams. Special thanks go to Bethany Schmidt, for answering my many questions about "what Americans say," and Joe Ashmore, for proofing the manuscript at very short notice when he had COVID-19.

I would like to thank my friends and family for too much to describe here. Much of this book manuscript was written during the pandemic, under conditions I never expected. Many people made this time bearable—Peter and Catherine Ievins, John Ievins, David, Jane, and Eddie Ievins, Pippa Carter, Borah Kant, Barry Colfer, Tom Zawisza, Gareth Evans, Julie Laursen, and Susie Hulley among them. I am beyond grateful to Joe Ashmore, for unwavering faith and trust through all stages of the process. Writing this while learning to share a workspace has been a treat.

I wrote this book in the years after the November 29, 2019, terrorist attack at Fishmongers' Hall, London. The attack took place at a Learning Together celebration event. Learning Together is a national initiative which seeks to bring together criminal justice and higher education institutions to provide settings for people to study alongside each other. The initiative started at my department, and I had been involved in Learning Together since I was a PhD student and had run courses with them as a postdoc, but I couldn't attend the celebration event as I was supposed to be going on holiday. During the event, Usman Khan, a former Learning Together student, attacked other attendees at the event, and killed Jack Merritt, Course Coordinator for Learning Together, and Saskia Jones, a former student. Usman was then shot dead by the police. He, Jack, and Saskia were all in their twenties. I didn't know Usman or Saskia, but I was friends and colleagues with Jack. In the time since the attack, I have questioned things I never thought I would, and it has been sometimes disorienting and sometimes helpful to be writing a book about what we should do in the aftermath of serious crime. I am beyond grateful to those who have asked questions alongside me, even when that has been hard and even when we have disagreed. I haven't found the answers, but I drink a cup of coffee every morning from a mug I have with a photo of Jack on it, and we keep going.

Punishing Rape

Feminisms and the Carceral Conversation

In May 2011, UK Minister of Justice Kenneth Clarke appeared on popular British current affairs radio program *Victoria Derbyshire*.[1] A long-standing and widely respected Conservative MP and former criminal barrister, he was there to discuss his plan to cut the prison population by halving the sentences of all people who pleaded guilty early (already, people received a "sentencing discount" of up to a third for an early guilty plea, and this plan would have increased the discount). The prison population had almost doubled in the previous twenty years (Ministry of Justice 2013), and Clarke saw cutting it as the first step of a reforming agenda which would facilitate a "rehabilitation revolution," and also lead to cost savings at a time of widespread financial austerity.[2] By appearing on Derbyshire's show, Clarke hoped to sell his policy as one which both served the interests of victims, who would not need to testify at trials, and the taxpayer, who would not need to pay for them. Derbyshire, however, had other ideas. She opened the segment by asking whether it was appropriate that this policy be applied to those convicted of serious sex offenses: "Many people believe you should make an exception for rapists. Why aren't you?" She said that under these proposals, someone convicted of rape could serve just over a year in prison; such a short sentence would not just be an "insult" to victims, she argued, it would actively disincentivize them from reporting the crime. Clarke contested both the figure Derbyshire reached and the implications she drew from it, but listeners to the program seemed to agree with her. After pausing the interview for a brief break, Derbyshire returned and told Clarke that a number of people had phoned in to say that the proposal showed that the government cared more about "saving money than justice for victims."

In his attempt to argue that sentences were not as light as Derbyshire implied, Clarke suggested that not all rapes were equally "serious," a claim which Derbyshire contested:

DERBYSHIRE: If I had been raped, why would I be encouraged to go to the police when I know full well that the rapist could get just over a year
in jail? Why would I put myself through the trauma, the exami-
nations, the hell of it, when he might be out in fifteen months?

CLARKE: Well, I must stop you repeating this total nonsense . . . Assuming
you and I are talking about rape in the ordinary conversational
sense. Some man has forcefully, with a bit of violence—

DERBYSHIRE: Rape is rape, with respect.

CLARKE: No, it's not, and if an eighteen-year-old has sex with a
fifteen-year-old and she's perfectly willing, that is rape. That's
'cause she's underage, can't consent. Anybody has sex with a fifteen-year-old, it's rape. So what you and I are talking about, we're
talking about a man forcibly having sex with a woman and she
doesn't want to. That is rape. Serious crime, of course it's a serious
crime. And I'm very glad that people do now go to the police and
report it. There used to be a taboo against it, in a crazy way.

Like much of the popular discourse around sexual violence, the conversation centered on a disputed definition and highlighted the many different meanings and
functions which the word *rape* has in contemporary discourse. It is a term with a
legal sense, as Clarke recognized, one which categorizes multiple different sorts of
incidents.[3] It also means something "in the ordinary conversational sense," raising
the question of who is participating in this conversation and under what conditions. Most importantly, the word serves as a marker of moral seriousness. To
name an act as "rape" is, in most cases, to denounce it. It is for this reason that the
phrase "rape is rape," as used by Derbyshire, is both tautological and politically
significant, a sign that the speaker understands the gravity of the act.

The incident is remembered regretfully by many in England and Wales who
would like the prison population to be significantly lower.[4] Clarke's comments
proved controversial, and were attacked by political opponents and women's
groups, ultimately resulting in the proposal being dropped. Over the subsequent months, the rehabilitation revolution stalled, and the next year Clarke was
replaced as Secretary of State for Justice by Chris Grayling, a politician with a
populist edge and a "tough justice" agenda. Under Grayling's leadership, significant cuts were made to legal aid and to prison staffing, without any accompany-
ing reductions in the prison population. As a result, according to Her Majesty's
(HM) Chief Inspector of Prisons (2015), rates of violence, suicide, and self-harm
in prisons increased drastically. I have described this incident at length, however,
because it is illustrative of penal trends which extend far beyond the jurisdiction of
England and Wales. In discourse about punishment throughout the Global North,
sexual violence functions as either a warning against, or a "silent exception" (Gruber
2020, 171) within, any calls for penal reform, reduction, or abolition. In this incident, Derbyshire positioned sexual offenses as the most serious of crimes, and

the idea of those who commit such offenses being helped by a policy designed to make the legal system operate more smoothly was enough to delegitimize its wider application.

Derbyshire's response to Clarke's proposal provides a good example of mainstream feminist thought about the ideal response to sexual violence: that more punishment, more generously distributed, is the best route to justice. This position (sometimes known as "carceral feminism"; Bernstein 2007) has been heavily influenced by the desire of second-wave and radical feminists to reconstruct the state so that it protects women and children from the scourge of the patriarchy and of rape as its corollary and its weapon, and the position has had numerous victories in England and Wales, as well as elsewhere in the Global North.[5] These legal successes include expanding the definition of rape so that it includes (for example) marital rape and date rapes, and introducing new offenses like the sexual grooming of children (McAlinden 2007a).[6] Significant effort has also been expended on altering procedures in criminal trials, for instance, by tightly restricting the admissibility of sexual history evidence, removing the requirement for judges to warn juries against convicting on the basis of a woman's uncorroborated evidence, and securing anonymity for complainants. In part, these changes resulted from the recognition that trials can be extremely painful and invasive for victims, as is reflected in the widespread use of terms like "second rape" (Madigan and Gamble 1991), "judicial rape" (Lees 1993), and "secondary victimization" (Adler 1987) to describe how the process is experienced. These changes were also intended to alter judicial outcomes by making it more likely that victims would report their experiences and stay involved in the legal process, that offenders would be charged by the Crown Prosecution Service (CPS), and that convictions would be secured. Feminist campaigners have also fought to ensure that sexual offending is met by tougher punishments, both in order to persuade victims to follow through with prosecutions and in order to send a message about the cruelty of the crime (Goodmark 2018a; Martin 1998).

The attempt to achieve sexual and gender justice by increasing the state's power to punish sexual violations has been considerably successful on its own terms, as is illustrated by the increasing number of men convicted of sex offenses in prison and the lengthening sentences they serve. The prison population in England and Wales has more than doubled since 1970 (Sturge 2020), and at the same time the proportion of prisoners convicted of sex offenses has also increased. In 1980 in England and Wales, there were 1,100 people convicted of sex offenses in prison, making them 4 percent of the sentenced population; by 1990 there were over three thousand (7 percent) and by 2000 they were 10 percent of the prison population (R. Mann 2016).[7] Following the passing of the Sexual Offences Act 2003, which introduced new offenses and extended sentence lengths, numbers increased even further, and the Ministry of Justice (2013) found that between 2004 and 2011, the number of people being sentenced for sex offenses increased by 31 percent and the average custodial sentence length increased by thirteen months. The population therefore expanded significantly, and by its peak in 2018, 19 percent of all men in prison were serving a sentence for a sex offense (Ministry of Justice 2018). Numbers since then have dropped very slightly, but there are still significant numbers of people in prison for sex offenses: on December 31, 2021, there were 12,130 people serving an immediate custodial sentence for a sex offense, and they constituted just under 19 percent of the sentenced prison population (Ministry of Justice 2022a).

Nevertheless, campaigners continue to raise concerns about the proportion of rape offenses being prosecuted. Between 2007–8 and 2016–17, the number of convictions for rape in England and Wales rose by 48 percent, and over the same time period the proportion of the CPS caseload accounted for by violence against women and girls increased from 7 percent to 19 percent. In 2016–17, 5,190 rape prosecutions were recorded and 2,991 convictions were secured—both the highest numbers ever (CPS 2017). Since then, the number of prosecutions has fallen by 71 percent, reaching just 1,490 in the year to December 2020, and the number of convictions has more than halved to 1,074 (Topping and Barr 2021).[8] A recent annual report published by the Victims' Commissioner stated that less than 3 percent of rapes in England and Wales lead to someone being charged, let alone convicted, and warned that this "justice gap" hurts current victims and creates future ones:[9]

> In effect, what we are witnessing is the de-criminalisation of rape. In doing so, we are failing to give justice to thousands of complainants. In some cases, we are enabling persistent predatory sex offenders to go on to reoffend in the knowledge that they are highly unlikely to be held to account. This is likely to mean we are creating more victims as a result of our failure to act. (Baird 2020, 16)

Cognizant of the reduction in prosecutions and convictions, the government published an end-to-end review of the criminal justice system response to rape which found that changes in prosecution practices mean that "too many rape victims do not receive the justice they deserve" (HM Government 2021, 3). Prime Minister Boris Johnson drew on similar rhetoric when he was questioned on *The Andrew Marr Show* on October 3, 2021, about the kidnap, rape, and murder of Sarah Everard by serving police officer Wayne Couzens: "What I want you to know is that we will stop at nothing to make sure that we get more rapists behind bars and that we have more successful prosecutions for rape and for sexual violence, because that is where I think things are going wrong."

The feminist demand for punishment which Baird, Derbyshire, and Johnson echo has been criticized from many different angles. Liberals have argued that it damages due process and, in its desire to increase the rate of convictions, risks people's right to a fair trial (McGlynn 2010, 2011).[10] Sex positive and queer theorists have suggested that strengthening the regulatory power of the state risks criminalizing nonharmful but nonnormative sexual behavior (Butler 1997; Levine 2002).

Abolition feminists, informed by critical race theory and intersectionality, have argued against shackling the feminist movement to the carceral state (Davis 2013, 2017; Goodmark 2018a; Gruber 2020; Levine and Meiners 2020). Many restorative justice advocates argue that the retributive framework is limited and damaging, even in the cases of sex offenses (Ackerman and Levenson 2019; Zehr 1990). Finally, criminologists have highlighted that there is a limited evidence base for the ability of imprisonment to reduce reoffending, calling into question Baird's casual assumption that imprisonment reduces crime (Bales and Piquero 2012).

There are three strands to the most legitimate of these critiques. The first focuses on the power which the feminist push for punishment cedes to the state. Activists of the left assert that the state is an illegitimate, racist, (cis)sexist, and classist institution and is thus the wrong mechanism to use when dealing with the aftermath of sexual violence. They argue that the history of lynching in the United States and the racialized concerns about Asian grooming gangs in the United Kingdom reveal "the centrality of race to the political history of rape" (Freedman 2013, 2), and suggest that incarceration is concerned more with making money and controlling the racialized poor than it is with repairing harm.[11] Political liberals, who do not share this radical doubt in the state, nevertheless argue that its legitimacy is not a given and its punitive operations are unequally distributed. They question the self-professed benevolence of state intervention and argue that strong due process rights are necessary to protect people from excessive or biased state power, and they fear that the push to increase the numbers of convictions for sexual offenses risks skewing the balance too far in the opposite direction. Advocates of restorative justice argue that the state is preoccupied by its own bureaucratic functioning, and it takes the requirements of efficiency more seriously than it does the demands of justice (Zehr 1990). What matters is that it meets its own targets by ensuring that enough people are arrested, enough convictions are achieved, enough people are unlocked during the prison day, and enough money is saved, and it is much less invested in meeting the needs or respecting the desires of those more personally affected by the crime. (Ironically, the belief that the state was subordinating the needs of victims to its own bureaucratic requirements was at the core of Derbyshire's criticism of Clarke's money-saving proposal, but it led her to call for more punishment, not less state intervention.)

The second, related, strand is that criminalizing and punishing sexual violations allows the state to police the most personal part of our lives, and in so doing it takes something intimate and uses it for its own purposes. Many of these criticisms come from feminists, who are concerned about the state wresting something that happened to women from their control and using their stories as evidence but not allowing them to have a voice (McGlynn and Westmarland 2019). This is not a tender way to treat something painful, and it often involves twisting and simplifying a complex event so that it fits legalistic categories. Much is obscured when calculating which acts are illegal and merit punishment, and when sifting people into the binary classes of victim and offender. Convictions are harder to achieve when those who are hurt do not fit the limiting criteria of the "ideal victim" (Christie 1986; Hohl and Stanko 2015), leaving the harm which has been done to them unrecognized by the state. At the same time, being convicted has permanent labeling effects on men who are found guilty of committing wrongs.[12] As restorative justice theorist Howard Zehr (1990, 69) argues, legal guilt has a "'sticky,' indelible quality," and it is hard for people whose wrongdoing has been publicly recorded to wash themselves clean.

The third strand is in many ways the simplest. It critiques the urge to punish. Criminologist and abolitionist Nils Christie (1981) famously called punishment a "pain delivery system," and he alongside a great many other abolitionists and advocates of restorative justice argued that deliberately inflicting pain is always wrong. In their eyes, retributive punishment is simply legally sanctioned revenge, and it contributes neither to accountability nor to justice (Sered 2019).

Advocates of retributivism, however, would argue that many of these alleged problems with punishment are in fact its virtues. They would say that it is right that punishment should be ceded to the state, as the most authoritative institution we have and as one which acts on behalf of the community with the impartiality which comes from distance (Hampton 1991, 1693–94). They would say that the application of a condemnatory label to a complex event is the point of criminalization and punishment. To them, one function of punishment is to denounce, and denunciation necessarily involves placing something into the category of wrongness (Duff 2011). Finally, they would say that the infliction of pain adds both a symbolic and a material emphasis to this denunciation (Feinberg 1965; Von Hirsch 1993). Their logic is simple. If we want to respond to sexual violence in a way that shows that it is serious, and if the way we deal with serious crimes is through state imprisonment, it follows that people who commit sexual violence should be imprisoned (Martin 1998). In Derbyshire's straightforward language, "Rape is rape," and it is by imprisoning people that we send that condemnatory message.

The simplicity of this logic has enabled a lack of curiosity about the nature and experience of punishment. Feminist advocates have tended to stop at the gates of the prison and have paid very little attention to what happens inside it. This is a mistake. Simply replicating established methods of moral communication does not mean that we are sending the message that we intend to, and we need to understand the form a message takes if we want to understand what it says. Furthermore, those who advocate for more punishment have a special responsibility to understand the effects this punishment has, and the worlds it creates. To argue that those who push for more imprisonment have a responsibility to understand prisons is not to say that modern prisons are what people involved in the feminist movement wanted. Current forms of imprisonment are a product of many historical phenomena—the growth of mass incarceration, shifts in criminal justice policy and practice, the local histories of individual prisons, recent budget and staffing cuts, to name but a few—but if the goal of your activism is to send more people to prison for longer, and you do this in a world in which prisons look like they currently do, then it is unsurprising that this form of imprisonment is the outcome. Prisons are part of our communities, and they are also, sometimes, the products of our political engagement. For both reasons, it is incumbent on us as citizens and as feminists to understand, critique, and intervene in them.

The purpose of this book is therefore to offer a rich empirical account of one of the worlds created by the feminist push for punishment—HMP Stafford, an English prison for men convicted of sex offenses—and to describe what it communicated to prisoners about their offending and their moral status. While it is based on ethnographic work conducted in one medium-sized prison in one country, the argument which this book presents—that we should pay more attention to the messages which prisons send—has relevance wherever imprisonment is used as a denunciatory technique. My aim in presenting this ethnography is not to evaluate Stafford's contribution to justice, nor do I intend to take an explicit position in the debate among feminists about the role punishment should play in their worldmaking. Instead, the goal is to provide a thick description of one of the worlds produced by the deliberate attempt to punish people for sexual violence in a way which speaks to and is informed by literature on the messages we send through punishment, and which hopes to inform and engage with all sides of the debate.

· · ·

From the very beginning of my fieldwork in Stafford, it was evident that this was a world which was saturated by an overriding consciousness of prisoners' criminal convictions and their moral implications. When I stood on wings, trying to talk to prisoners about their life in prison, they would often tell me, unprompted, that they weren't a "real sex offender"—because they said that what had happened was more nuanced than the totalizing label implied, or because they said they weren't guilty, or because they said they had done it but they would never do anything like it again. Others told me about the devastating feelings of guilt and shame which had accompanied their offending, but they also spoke of their hope that people might be able to see beyond their pasts and recognize them for the good men they believed themselves to be now. Almost everyone I spoke to feared that they would be judged seriously on release and would struggle to escape the legal and social repercussions of their conviction. Many talked with emotion about having been abandoned by families and friends following their arrest and trial; others said that their families had stood by them but been harassed by members of the public or targeted by Social Services as a result. Almost all prisoners felt that at least some prison staff judged them for their offenses, and the few who detected no judgment praised staff for their superhuman compassion.

But prisoners' deep reflections on justice were knottier than this implied account of unmerited punishment. In some cases, they struggled to balance their belief that they deserved some form of punishment with their insistence that the form their actual punishment had taken was excessive and unjust. Even those who resisted the moral condemnation which directly targeted them demonstrated similar condemnation toward others, frequently telling me that other prisoners were dangerous, irredeemable, or "creepy," and sometimes bemoaning that these other monsters had not received a more severe punishment. Nestled within these contradictory instincts about the condemnation which different people deserved was a complex ongoing conversation about what it means, and what it should mean, to have been convicted of causing sexual harm. This conversation permeated the prison and seeped into every corner of prisoners' lives within it. This is not to say that prisoners only talked about their convictions and their resulting stigmatized identities as "sex offenders"; in fact, the men in Stafford were often at pains to tell me that their interests and preoccupations were "normal," and certainly much of what people discussed on a day-to-day basis—television shows, pool games, exercise regimes—was prosaic and familiar. Nevertheless, prisoners' shaming convictions were ever-present on the wings of Stafford. They shaped how prisoners thought about their lives, how they interacted with their peers and with prison officers, and how they talked to me, a young female researcher.

This book argues that Stafford functioned as a morally communicative institution—that is, as an institution which said something to prisoners about who they were and what they had done. It argues that being punished in Stafford imparted an exclusionary and stigmatizing message—that you are an inherent sexual offender, a bad person, a dangerous object—with the effect that most prisoners focused their energy on challenging the label rather than engaging with the moral connotations, meaning, and effect of the offense. This is not to say that anyone intended to send this message. Staff in Stafford were reluctant to acknowledge the criminal convictions which lay at the heart of the prison and worked hard to avoid displaying punitive or judgmental impulses. Nevertheless, (almost) everyone in Stafford was there because they had been convicted of a sexual crime, and this unavoidably shaped how they thought about and adapted to their sentence.

The concept of moral communication is properly introduced in chapter 2, "Communicating Badly." This chapter argues that we need to understand imprisonment's condemnatory functions and effects and draws together literature by sociologists of imprisonment and penal theorists to explore the potential messages which Stafford could send to its prisoners. It then briefly describes HMP Stafford and the fieldwork for this project, with a particular focus on the experience of being a young female ethnographer conducting research in a prison for men convicted of sex offenses. Chapter 3, "Distorting Institutions," is the first properly empirical chapter, and it argues that there was a gap between the offenses (most) prisoners had committed, the convictions they had received, and the stories they told about their offenses. It is well known that many men convicted of sex offenses maintain that they are not guilty of their convictions, and this was also the case for a third of the men I interviewed (a proportion consistent with other research on the categorical claims of innocence of men convicted of sex offenses; Hood et al. 2002; Kennedy and Grubin 1992). However, even the men who believed that they were guilty rarely felt that their convictions properly accounted for what they had done. Researchers have normally considered the gap between prisoners' convictions and their narratives to be a product of individual cognitive distortions, but this chapter describes three ways in which it was produced by the institutional context—by the legal system which selected them for admission into the prison, the staining label which it placed on them, and the rehabilitative regime which tried to reshape them. Not all prisoners responded to the context in the same way, however. In chapters 4 and 5, "Managing Guilt" and "Maintaining Innocence," I outline how prisoners tried to "do their time" while also adjusting to the shame of their convictions, and I do this by offering a typology of adaptive styles. In so doing, I show the intimate connections between the messages the prison sent and the way it used power over prisoners, and argue that the resulting moral conversation was confusingly framed.

Chapter 6, "Moralizing Boundaries," shifts to describe what prison officers, as the group of prison staff with the most contact with and power over prisoners, communicated to them. It argues that officers' vision of professional behavior discouraged them from talking to prisoners about their offenses, but it also led them to maintain strict moral and relational barriers which sent their own exclusionary message. Chapter 7, "Denying Community," moves to describe social relationships among prisoners, and it argues that the pressures of living among people convicted of deeply staining offenses, while also being convicted of similar offenses, pushed people to try to ignore them. If one goal of imprisonment is to show that offenses matter, it is a great irony that they produce environments which pressure people not to acknowledge them. Finally, chapter 8, "Judging Prisons," concludes by pulling together the book's arguments about the effectiveness of imprisonment as a communicative response to sexual violence, and suggesting both alternatives to imprisonment and ways of improving it.

The book's empirical focus is everyday life in prison, and it focuses mostly on the dimensions of prison life which prison sociology has deemed most significant: prisoners' adaptations to the sentence and relationships with prison officers and their fellow prisoners. Some readers may find it surprising that it pays less attention to the sorts of ritualized spaces (treatment programs, courtrooms, or meetings with probation officers) in which penal actors engage in deliberate and vocalized forms of moral training. My reasons for this are threefold. First, other work has already considered the ways in which these spaces shape how people, including people convicted of sex offenses, feel about themselves (e.g., Digard 2010; Hawker-Dawson forthcoming; K. Hudson 2005; Lacombe 2008; Waldram 2012), whereas much less research has been conducted on the more prosaic dimensions of moral communication (although a significant exception is Schinkel 2014a, 2014b).

Second, one goal of this book is to bring the questions of justice raised by feminist scholars and penal theorists into conversation with prison sociology, and to do this it seems most effective to focus on the areas already explored by prison sociologists. Third, and most importantly, everyday life matters hugely to those in prison, and ritualized interactions are not the only ones which communicate meaning. While many people in prison complete some sort of treatment during their sentence, many do not, and even those who complete it most intensively spend much more time on the wings talking to officers and other prisoners than they do in treatment programs formally reflecting on their moral identities. In arguing for the significance of the everyday, I am following in the footsteps of Gresham Sykes, the father of prison sociology, with whose words I finish the chapter:

> [P]resent knowledge of human behavior is sufficient to let us say that whatever the influence of imprisonment on the man held captive may be, it will be a product of the pattern of social interaction which the prisoner enters into day after day, year after year, and not of the details of prison architecture, brief exhortations to reform, or sporadic attacks on the "prison problem." The particular pattern of social interaction into which the inmate enters is, in turn, part of a complex social system with its own norms, values, and methods of control; and any attempt to reform the prison—and thus to reform the criminal—which ignores this social system of the prison is as futile of the labors of Sisyphus. The extent to which the existing social system works in the direction of the prisoner's deterioration rather than his rehabilitation; the extent to which the system can be changed; the extent to which we are willing to change it—these are the issues which confront us and not the recalcitrance of the individual inmate. ([1958] 2007, 134)

2

Communicating Badly

Prisons as Morally Communicative Institutions

Sociologists from Durkheim onward have acknowledged the morally communicative function of punishment.[1] They argue that it signifies and reinforces moral boundaries, trying to fashion the community into one which does not accept the punished acts. In constructing this official moral regime, punishment imprints a vision of the world the state imagines should exist; as David Garland (1990, 265) argues, it serves as "a dramatic, performative demonstration of the way things officially are and ought to be, whatever else the deviant would make of them." In so doing, punishment has multiple possible audiences. It seeks to operate as a warning and an exhortation to those who might otherwise be tempted to stray. It also addresses the person who has been harmed and seeks to "vindicate the value of the victim" (Hampton 1991, 1686) by showing a willingness to do something about the wrong that has been done. Finally, it speaks to the person being punished, and it is this moral conversation which is the focus of this book. In this chapter, I introduce the relationship between punishment and moral expression, first by arguing that prisons should be seen as morally communicative institutions, and then by briefly sketching theoretical, empirical, and normative work on the messages prisons could send and the mechanisms by which they might do this. I conclude the chapter by describing HMP Stafford and the fieldwork on which this book is based.

The morally communicative role which punishment plays takes different forms depending on the punitive technology being used. In the late-modern Global North, imprisonment has become the culturally dominant instrument of punishment, and the moral messages which prisons send are impacted by the fundamental structure of imprisonment. At their most foundational, prisons sort people into categories, using their walls to render literal the moral boundary between criminals and the law-abiding, and constructing further moralized distinctions between prisoners and prison officers. They also impose restrictions and demands on prisoners based on moralized judgments about what they need and deserve. Membership of criminalized categories continues to have a significant effect after people are released from prison. Being marked as a former prisoner has material and moral effects for years afterward (LeBel 2012), restricting people's ability to gain employment, housing, and trust.

Prisons' moralizing foundations are evident in their history. The penitentiary, which emerged as a response to crime in Britain and the United States in the eighteenth century, and which was the precursor to modern prisons, has its ideological roots in nonconformist Christian doctrine, and it was advocated for by early reformers who hoped to use this form of incarceration as a mechanism of salvation and reform.[2] Their aims were high-minded and didactic, and they hoped to impose discipline and to nurture feelings of guilt, remorse, and the desire for reacquaintance with God, and promoted ways of living which accorded with their middle-class Christianity. The methods prescribed by the reformers were, on the one hand, rational and scientific, and on the other, religious and educative. They were preoccupied by the physical and moral risks of disorder, and established regimes of daily chapel services and regular Bible reading, as well as work and order. Chaplains were to play a significant role, trying to persuade prisoners of the justice of their punishment and the wrongness of their actions. Fearing that prisoners would morally and physically contaminate each other, they sought to fragment the prisoner society and thereby enhance the authority of prison staff. They segregated prisons by sex for the first time, preventing much of the sexual activity which had been widespread in earlier institutions. They also encouraged either solitary confinement, to prevent prisoners from infecting one another with immorality, or silence, to focus prisoners' minds on hearing the voices of God and of their consciences.[3] They were aware that such isolation would induce profound suffering, but they considered it the best way to foster remorse. John Brewster (1792, quoted in Ignatieff 1989, 78), an early advocate of solitary confinement, put it clearly:

> To be abstracted from a world where he has endeavoured to confound the order of society, to be buried in a solitude where he has no companion but reflection, no counsellor but thought, the offender will find the severest punishment he can receive. The sudden change of scene that he experiences, the window which admits but a few rays of light, the midnight silence which surrounds him, all inspire him with a degree of horror which he never felt before. The impression is greatly heightened by his being obliged to think. No intoxicating cup benumbs his senses, no tumultuous revel dissipates his mind. Left alone and feelingly alive to the strings of remorse, he revolves on his present situation and connects it with that train of events which has banished him from society and placed him there.

Other early reformers were concerned less with the generation of personal guilt as a prompt to reformation than with the performance of public shame as an act of deterrence. Jeremy Bentham's Panopticon, the apparently ideal prison he designed but which was never built, is mostly remembered as a model of disciplinary power (Foucault 1991), but Bentham also imagined it as a space for punitive spectacle. During religious services, members of the public would be allowed to enter the prison to gaze upon the inmates, all of whom would be wearing grimacing masks. These masks would directly refer to prisoners' offenses, but the desired effect was to be on the observer:

> The masks may be made more or less tragical, in proportion to the enormity of the crimes of those who wear them. The air of mystery which such a contrivance will throw over the scene will contribute in a great degree to fix the attention by the curiosity it will excite, and the terror it will inspire. (Bentham 1830, 135)

The power of the masks would lie in their capacity to render visible an otherwise imperceptible conviction, but the mask would also protect the prisoner by allowing guilt to "be pilloried in the abstract, without the exposure of the guilty" (Bentham [1791] 1995, 100)—that is, without prompting unnecessarily excessive *feelings* of shame which may have distracted the prisoner from reforming themselves, and without permanently branding them in a way which would damage them after their release from prison. The effect would be that of "a masquerade," albeit one of "a serious, affecting, and instructive" (100) nature.

Brewster's and Bentham's recommendations highlight two possible messages which imprisonment could send: one directed at the soul of the prisoner, which seeks to generate guilt and prompt personal reflection, and one aimed at the mind and heart of the public, which seeks to deter them from committing crime by stirring up fear and disgust. But these recommendations also underscore some of the difficulties associated with using imprisonment to send moral messages. To do this properly would be a precise science, but pain is an inexact tool. Early advocates of the penitentiary wanted the prisoner to focus on their own guilt and not be distracted by questioning the justice of their situation, and so they thought it was important that prisoners respect the authority of those who punished them. Too much pain, too brutally administered, would delegitimize the punisher in the eyes of the punished, working against the aim of redemption by allowing prisoners to escape into feelings of anger and contempt against "the system." Sentences were to be relatively short, then, and physical conditions to be austere but not cruel. John Howard, a highly influential British prison reformer, maintained that "gentle discipline [was] commonly more efficacious than severity" (1777, quoted in Ignatieff 1989, 74). Brewster agreed: "There are cords of love as well as fetters of iron" (1792, quoted in Ignatieff 1989, 74).

Imprisonment's explicitly moralizing foundations have been obscured by the institutional architecture which has grown over them, and thus they are rarely acknowledged by those who work in and run prisons. In the years since the penitentiary was established, prisons have been bureaucratized and have come to prioritize their own organizational objectives (Christie 1981).[4] Where once those who ran these penal institutions were driven by a reforming zeal and saw themselves as radicals saving souls, they now see themselves as professionals running prisons, a change in motivation described by Rothman (1980) as a shift from "conscience" to "convenience." In the twenty-first century, the administration of prisons in England and Wales has become further influenced by managerialism (J. Bennett 2016). Prisons have increasingly prioritized utilitarian over moralistic goals, in some cases identified as running safe and decent prisons, and in others as running cheap and efficient ones (Liebling and Crewe 2013). When prisons do aim at transformation and pursue goals of rehabilitation or reduced reoffending, they prioritize psychologically altering individuals over directly addressing the crime as a moral act (McNeill 2012).[5]

As a result of this rationalizing process, "penal professionals have been able to redefine the social meaning of punishment" (Garland 1990, 184). A moral division of labor has emerged between institutions of punishment allocation, such as the courts, and institutions of punishment delivery, such as prisons. Punishment has been removed from the public view and hidden behind closed walls, and the moral dialogue in which punishment engages has become an "oblique communication carried out in institutions which give little expression to the public voice" (186–87). Unable to see the delivery of the penalty on the person convicted of the crime, all that is left to symbolize justice to victims and to the community is the number of years to which people are sentenced—a brute communicative tool about which members of the public tend to know very little (Hough and Roberts 2017). Meanwhile, penal professionals have sought to keep daily life in prisons uncorrupted by open discussions of the crimes for which people have been convicted and the emotions which they engender. They see themselves as administrators, not condemners, a self-identity reflected in the frequently quoted aphorism that people go to prison *as* punishment, and not to be punished further.

Despite the rationalized prison's attempts to obscure its moralizing foundations, those foundations persist.[6] As some penologists are beginning to acknowledge, the artificial distinction between the allocation and delivery of punishment falls apart when we consider how punishment is experienced by those subjected to it (Hall 2016; Hayes 2018; Schinkel 2014a, 2014b; Sexton 2015). Existing research on the capacity of prisons to send specific moral messages has not been promising (Ievins and Mjåland 2021; Schinkel 2014b), but prisoners still know that their imprisonment is a condemnatory response to a crime they've been convicted of, and this knowledge shapes the meaning they find in the regimes to which they are subjected and the deprivations which they endure. Even if those who work in prisons try to envelop their knowledge with professionalism, they still know that imprisonment signals condemnation, as do members of the public to whom most prisoners will be released. It is in the punishment of people imprisoned for sex offenses that the moral questions at the heart of imprisonment pierce with the most violence through the bureaucratic veil (Digard 2014; Simon 1998). Prison officers often express high levels of disgust and judgment toward people convicted of sex offenses (Hogue 1993; Kjelsberg and Loos 2008; Ricciardelli and Spencer 2018), and other prisoners sometimes enact forms of punitive violence against them (Crewe 2009; Ugelvik 2014). Furthermore, as this book shall argue, people imprisoned for sex offenses are themselves aware that their convictions have stained them as morally unacceptable, and this stain seeps through their experience of incarceration.

Sociologists of imprisonment have replicated the moral division of labor and have rarely analyzed the prison as a producer of guilt or a site of moral communication. Instead, they have imagined the prison as a total institution, an institution of domination, a disciplinary institution, or even as an organization.[7] They see the prison's primary tool as power and its primary goal as the control of prisoners' bodies and time. This conceptual framing has shaped the questions they have tended to ask of their sites of research. How do prisons achieve, or seek to achieve, order (Skarbek 2014; Sparks, Bottoms, and Hay 1996)? What sort of social world develops within them, and what causes the prisoner society to take this shape (Crewe 2009; Sykes [1958] 2007)? How do people adapt to the restrictions which prisons place on them (Cohen and Taylor 1972; Crewe, Hulley, and Wright 2019)? What forms of gendered power do prisons rely on, and what gendered identities do they produce (Bosworth 1999; Sloan 2016)? How do they discipline people, and how do prisoners experience being subjected to disciplinary power (Crewe 2011a; Crewe and Ievins 2021)? The accounts produced by this body of research have been insightful and detailed, and have helped to build an increasingly clear picture of how imprisonment's regimes and practices intervene in people's lives.

However, this conception of the prison as an institution of domination and discipline, and the attendant focus on the shape and effect of power within the prison, means that its other, more morally expressive dimensions have generally been overlooked.[8] In particular, prison sociologists have rarely discussed the fact that, in most cases, a criminal conviction is the justification for and instigator of the prison sentence, and instead have rendered the offense barely visible in their accounts of prison life. When they have discussed prisoners' convictions, they have described them as either a resource in or a marker of prisoner hierarchies (Åkerström 1986; Crewe 2009) or as a symptom of orientations to authority which are perpetuated within the prison (Cohen and Taylor 1972; Irwin and Cressey 1962), and have rarely depicted them as a direct target of penal intervention.[9] On the whole, this reluctance to discuss people's offenses has been for sensible methodological and moral reasons. Prison researchers prefer to think of their subjects as prisoners, as people subjected to an intrusive and oppressive form of power and control, rather than as criminals, as people who have done wrong.[10] To do otherwise would often feel like a betrayal, like either uncritically supporting the unjust social and moral systems which produce prisoners, or like further stigmatizing and condemning them.

But thinking of prisoners in this way—and, as a corollary, thinking of prisons as institutions of domination—means that descriptions of the experience of imprisonment ignore one significant component of these experiences: that people are sent there because society told them they did wrong. It leaves mainstream prison sociology unable to account for the desire of many people in prison to talk to researchers about their offenses, trials, or convictions. It makes it harder for prison scholars to engage in public discussions about the functions and effects of imprisonment, in which questions of guilt, remorse, and condemnation are prominent. It also deprives prison scholars of one challenge to prison privatization: if instead of being a morally imbued task, imprisonment is reducible to "the delivery of penal 'services'" (Sparks, Bottoms, and Hay 1996, 22), there is no reason why it needs to be the sole prerogative of the state.[11] Finally, overlooking the offense and its reverberations throughout the prison also means that prison sociologists struggle to evaluate the effectiveness of prisons as morally communicative institutions, and the extent to which they take us closer to or further from justice.

"THE VERY WALLS OF HIS CELL CONDEMN HIM": WHAT MESSAGES COULD PRISONS SEND?

Prison sociologists may have overlooked the expressive dimension of imprisonment, but penal theorists have put it at the center of many of their attempts to justify punishment.[12] Joel Feinberg's (1965) article "The Expressive Function of Punishment" is often credited with founding the "moral communication" tradition in penal theory.[13] In this article, the legal philosopher argues against conventional retributive justifications of punishment, rebuking as irrational the idea that punishment can somehow offset wrongdoing. Instead, he says that punishment is justified because of its "reprobative symbolism" (400)—that is, he argues that punishment is necessary because it expresses that the offense was wrong. Feinberg argues that the two aspects of punishment—the infliction of pain, which penal theorists term "hard treatment," and the condemnatory content—are in theory distinguishable. In practice, however, they are hard to pull apart. To some extent, this indivisibility is simply an experiential reality: condemnation is a form of hard treatment because it is painful to know that we are judged. But the connection between hard treatment and condemnation is, Feinberg argues, also a matter of habit. Just as "champagne is the alcoholic beverage traditionally used in celebration of great events," and just as "black is the color of mourning" (402), so punishment is the "conventional device" (400) by which we tend to express our serious disapproval. This means that "[t]he problem of justifying punishment . . . may really be that of justifying our particular symbols of infamy" (421).[14]

Recognizing the contingency of our methods of communication opens a space in which we can criticize our current devices. In the middle section of this chapter, I draw on literature in the moral communication tradition to sketch out what these penal theorists suggest punishment could and should say, with a particular focus on the messages which imprisonment could send to men imprisoned for sex offenses.[15] (I briefly return to penal theorists' reflections on what imprisonment could communicate to victims and members of the public in the book's conclusion, "Judging Prisons.") To take advantage of the critical space allowing us to analyze our methods of communication, I also draw on empirical evidence which speaks to the desirability and feasibility of these messages and which raises questions which the research conducted in this book will begin to answer.

The penal theory literature suggests that punishment could send three broad categories of message to people convicted of a crime: "what you did was wrong," "you should feel guilty about what you have done," and "you should be ashamed of yourself."[16] The first message, which moral education theorists believe should be the goal of punishment, accords with the moral instinct we often have that those who do wrong must, on some level, know not what they do. It certainly seems tempting in a world in which rape myths, "prejudicial, stereotyped or false beliefs about rape, rape victims, or rapists" (Burt 1980, 217), are widespread and are particularly likely to be believed by men who commit sexual violence (Johnson and Beech 2017). However, it is not feasible to suggest that most people convicted of a sex offense require such an education, nor is it clear that doing so would necessarily reduce reoffending. Even though people accused of sexual violence in England and Wales plead guilty at a lower rate than those accused of other types of offenses, more than half of all people charged with a sex offense plead guilty (The Lammy Review 2017). Even if some of these plead guilty because they hope it will get them a lower sentence, a significant number of people sentenced for sex offenses must believe that they have committed a crime. Those who do not, however, would not necessarily benefit from having their minds changed. While there is evidence that having offense-supportive *attitudes* (that is, beliefs that excuse or justify sexual offending in general) makes sexual reoffending more likely (Mann, Hanson, and Thornton 2010), denying, excusing, or justifying one's own past offending does not seem to increase the likelihood of reoffending, and may in some circumstances make it *less* likely (Hood et al. 2002; Maruna and Mann 2006; Ware and Blagden 2020; Yates 2009).

Furthermore, theorists who advocate for the moral education approach rarely explain how punishment in general, or imprisonment more specifically, is supposed to teach quite complex moral lessons. Hampton (1984), the leading moral education theorist, offers a metaphoric model which inadvertently highlights many of the weaknesses of her approach. She suggests that punishment should be compared to an electric fence bordering a field, which shocks people whenever they stray. At the very least, this shock should deter them from straying again, but ideally the pain should push them to reflect on why the fence is there. But her idealistic strategy raises questions about the eloquence of pain and the extent to which we can control how people respond to it. There is a difference between what punishment is supposed to say and what it actually says, and the medium carries its own message (Skillen 1980). The person who put up the fence might have done so to get people to think about why what is beyond it is forbidden, but fenced-in people might hear it tell them that the person who put it up hates them, or that they are trying to keep whatever is beyond it to themselves, or that you should hurt people to get what you want. Rather than reflecting on the reasons for the fence's existence, they might focus their individual and collective energies on tearing it down or soothing their pain. They might even, as Howard and Brewster feared, be in such agony that they cannot think beyond their own sufferings.

If we are to believe that punishment in general, and imprisonment in particular, can send the message that people have done something wrong, we will require a specific model of how this message could be sent. The fact that those who run and work in prisons claim to see them as rationalized spaces within which the offense has little relevance is not a strong basis for such a model. One possibility is that imprisonment could exist alongside formal treatment programs which teach the moral lesson more clearly (Robinson 2008), and there is certainly evidence to suggest that offense-specific treatment programs can reduce recidivism for people convicted of sex offenses (Gannon et al. 2019; Hanson et al. 2002), although they seem to be less effective when delivered in custody (Schmucker and Lösel 2015). However, in recognition of the fact that the way prisoners talk about their previous crimes does not seem to affect whether they reoffend, modern treatment programs in England and Wales focus on how to avoid future offending and do not discuss people's past crimes.

The practical difficulty of using punishment to tell people that they have done wrong, combined with liberal questions about the right of the state to rewire people's moral frameworks, has led most moral communication theorists to argue that punishment should aim to send the second message: "You should feel guilty about what you have done."[17] They imagine that punishment should appeal to a preexisting sense of wrongness and prompt people to recognize the gravity of what they have done and the extent of their responsibility for it.[18] Penal theorists disagree about the mechanism by which punishment in general, and imprisonment in particular, should seek to send this message. One way of pushing people to realize the gravity of their offending would be to penalize them in a way that balanced the severity of the initial crime ("What you did was wrong, and its wrongness was equivalent to five years in prison").[19] A more promising alternative, and one which echoes the desire of early developers of the penitentiary for prisoners to spend their days communing with God, the chaplains, and their consciences, is that punishment should force people to reflect on their actions, encouraging repentance and reform ("What you did was wrong, and I want you to spend the next five years thinking about it").[20] According to this framework, imprisonment is not a reeducation but an opportunity to engage the better angels of people's nature and push them toward contemplation and deeper understanding. This could lead to what Duff (2001), a leading theorist in this tradition, calls the three Rs: remorse, reform, and reconciliation. Realizing what they have done (remorse) could lead them to the pained recognition of the need to change (reform). Being punished in such a way could also operate as a form of "secular penance" (Duff 2001), or a ritualized apology (C. Bennett 2008), allowing punished people to perform their remorse, willingness to change, and improved moral understanding of the past to their victims and to the wider community.[21] This performance could, Duff argues, make it easier for them to be reconciled with the community after their release.

There is some dispute among penal theorists as to whether it is appropriate or possible for the state to use punishment to peer into our souls, to try to shape our moral characters, or to ask us to repent for what we have done.[22] While these critics accept that the state should censure wrongdoing, they suggest that the liberal state does not have a close enough relationship with us to do anything more invasive. While our friends and families may have the right to ask us to be sorry, the state does not because, in Von Hirsch's (1993, 10) words, "[t]he condemnor's role is not that of the mentor or priest." Furthermore, they argue that it is not possible for a coercive institution like the state or the prison to generate authentic repentance, and any attempt to do so will push people toward straightforward dishonesty, manipulated regret, or even outraged defiance.[23] This may appear to be a pessimistic vision, but accounts of contemporary penal power have described how it wraps itself around people's beings and their behaviors, demanding them to act in particular ways and sometimes twisting their thinking so that they conflate demands and desires (Crewe 2011a), and it is certainly possible to see how this invasive form of power could also work on people's feelings about their offense. At the same time, existing empirical research suggests that at least some imprisoned people do feel profound regret and remorse about their crimes, and that they want their punishment to give shape to their repentance (Crewe and Ievins 2020; Ievins and Mjåland 2021). Hidden within the normative question of whether the state can legitimately ask its citizens to repent, then, lies an empirical question about the nature of penal power and its relationship to feelings of remorse.[24]

There is a real risk that the message "you should feel guilty about what you have done" could blur into the third message: "you should be ashamed of yourself." Penal theorists rarely consider this message to be a justifiable goal of punishment, but it was described by criminologist John Braithwaite (1989) as the message which state punishment most commonly sends. The emotional goal of the second message is guilt, an emotion with a complicated empirical and theoretical relationship to shame.[25] Guilt is the word we tend to give to the negative feeling we have when we think that we have done something wrong, and when this knowledge troubles us. It is empirically correlated with rule-following behavior (Trivedi-Bateman 2019), empathy (Van Stokkom 2002), the desire to confess the wrongdoing and change our behavior (Baumeister, Stillwell, and Heatherton 2001), and the desire to repair the harm (Tangney, Stuewig, and Hafez 2011). Shame, on the other hand, is the word we tend to give to the negative feeling we have when we think we are not the person we want to be. It often constitutes a fundamental threat to our sense of self and can therefore be experienced as physical and devastating. It is empirically correlated with depression (Nussbaum 2004), distress, psychological problems, substance abuse (Tangney, Stuewig, and Hafez 2011), low self-esteem (Velotti et al. 2017), and anger (Scheff and Retzinger 1991).

The differences between the two emotions mean that guilt is often described as morally constructive and shame as morally destructive.[26] In practice, we do not always distinguish well between a bad person and a person who has done a bad thing, and it is easy to see how an attempt to elicit guilt could end up producing shame. The emotions themselves blur into each other, and scholars have often struggled to distinguish them empirically (for reviews, see Elison 2005; Tangney and Dearing 2002; Tracy and Robins 2006). If a distinction exists, it probably lies in how the person experiencing the emotion *interprets* it (Elison 2005). Shame can be so overwhelming that it is difficult to acknowledge, and it is often twisted (or "managed") into different forms. Some people guard against shame through denial, defensiveness, and excuse-making (Tangney and Dearing 2002), and others by hiding away or by developing a new identity which more proudly absorbs that which shames them and thus enables them to reject their rejectors (Sykes and Matza 1957). In its most extreme forms, shame turns into rage, and the experience of being shamed can lead people to commit serious acts of violence (Gilligan 2003). When we do acknowledge it, we tend to think responsibility for the thing that shames us lies in internal and stable causes which we cannot control, such as our laziness, stupidity, or sexuality. When we feel guilty, we place the blame for whatever is wrong in internal but unstable causes, which we can therefore control, like an error of judgment or a failure to manage our temper (Tracy and Robins 2006). When we feel guilty, we are therefore able to place a distance between ourselves and our faults.

The difference between constructive guilt and destructive shame therefore lies in how people make sense of the emotion, but social conditions play a significant role in shaping this process of moral sense-making. Empirical research by criminologist Nathan Harris (2001) suggests that other people's expressions of displeasure about our wrongful actions can predict feelings of constructive guilt, but this is much more likely when the people expressing these emotions are people we respect, when we agree that we have done wrong, when we feel reintegrated, and when we do not feel stigmatized. People are more likely to feel destructive shame, however, when they feel stigmatized, when they do not agree that they have done wrong, and when they feel that important issues have not been addressed by the people shaming them.[27] In a related project, Eliza Ahmed (2001) argues that how people experience the emotion closely links to what they do with it (or in her language, how they discharge it). Feelings of constructive guilt can be discharged by taking responsibility and trying to set things right. Destructive shame, on the other hand, is less likely to be acknowledged, and is either internalized or displaced by blaming or being angry at others.[28] Taken together, these studies suggest that when we have moral clarity about what we have done wrong, when we do not feel that our identities and social positions have been overwhelmed or destroyed by it, and when we feel that there is a way we can fix the problem, we are more likely to accept responsibility for what we have done wrong and feel guilty about it. In other words, if morally communicative punishment focuses clearly on what we have done wrong and does not threaten our membership of the group, it can encourage us to engage in self-evaluation and, perhaps, moral transformation. If, however, it claims that *we* are wrong, if it threatens our most meaningful social bonds, and if it offers us no options for repair, it is more likely to lead to resistance, denial, and anger.

FROM THE ABSTRACT TO THE CONCRETE: HOW DO PRISONS SEND MORAL MESSAGES?

These three messages—"what you did was wrong," "you should feel guilty about what you have done," and "you should be ashamed of yourself"—provide a useful framework for thinking about what imprisonment could or should communicate. However, the penal theory literature from which they derive rarely engages with empirical findings about prisons and their effects. If we want to understand what imprisonment actually communicates—what real prisons say to real people about who they are and what they have done—it is necessary to step inside the belly of the beast.[29] That is the goal of this book, which will argue that incarceration in a prison which holds men convicted of sex offenses speaks more effectively about the shamefulness of the wrongdoer than about the wrongfulness of the act. It communicates the third message much more clearly than it does the first or second. In part, this results from the very structure of imprisonment. At their most fundamental, prisons hold some people apart from other people for reasons related to their alleged wrongdoing, and thus at their most basic they imply a moral difference between those they imprison and the rest of society. They also deliberately remove prisoners from the people they love and care about, who the shaming research I have discussed suggests should most effectively be able to discuss their wrongdoing with them. They also remove people from those whom they have harmed, and thus from the opportunity to redress the harm and make amends. Through their imprisonment, people are therefore subjected to a form of shaming which is both stigmatizing and difficult to discharge. The result is an institution which, despite its best efforts, pushes people to deny and minimize their offenses and discourages them from making amends.

However, sixty years of prison sociology have warned against making grandiose claims about what *the prison* does, explaining life inside solely with structural arguments about the fundamental nature of imprisonment.[30] Instead, prison sociologists say that we should also pay attention to how differences between prisons (institutional factors) and in prisoners' biographies (imported factors) affect the experience of incarceration, as well as to social relationships among imprisoned people. Being convicted of a sex offense is an imported factor which is likely to significantly deepen the shame prisoners feel. In England and Wales, as in most other countries in the Global North, sex offenses are the most despised category of crimes. They are believed to cause extreme harm, paralleled only with that caused by murder and some extreme forms of physical violence, and to be committed by those who are pathologically sexually deviant. Public attitude surveys indicate that people massively overstate the danger which people convicted of sex offenses pose, and therefore support socially and legally excluding them (Lussier and Healey 2009; McAlinden 2007b). The public distaste is ossified by the numerous legal restrictions which apply to people convicted of sex offenses after release, including the Sex Offenders' Register (which is not publicly available in England and Wales). It is therefore no exaggeration to say that being convicted of a sex offense fundamentally changes your status as a citizen and your position in society, in a way which must alter both the tone and content of the message communicated by a prison sentence. Despite this, very little systematic research has been conducted on their experiences of imprisonment, with a few exceptions (e.g., Blagden and Perrin 2016; Blagden et al. 2017; Blagden et al. 2019; N. Mann 2012; Priestley 1980; Ricciardelli and Spencer 2018; Schwaebe 2005; Sheldon 2021).

The nature of the moral message is also shaped by the specific character and culture of each penal institution. A significant body of sociological research has demonstrated that different prisons operate in ways which are informed by different moral values and are guided by different criminologies of the "offender"—that is, different ways of thinking about who the "offender" is and what motivates them (Garland 2001; Liebling and Kant 2018). Some prisons treat those they hold with more humanity and respect and leave more room for hope, while other prisons, and other sentences, make the possibility of progress seem impossible (Liebling, Arnold, and Straub 2011; Liebling et al. 2019). Prisons rely on several forms of power, create diverse types of order, and place varying amounts of weight on risk assessments when making decisions. Taken together, these small contrasts can make a big difference to how prisons are experienced, and evidence suggests that they can affect how survivable a prison is (Liebling et al. 2005) as well as the levels of reoffending after someone is released (Auty and Liebling 2020). As I will go on to argue in this book, these differences also impact what each institution says to and about the people it holds. This does not mean that these different messages are intentionally sent. The growing bureaucratization and managerialism of prisons, as well as the belief in the difference between institutions of punishment allocation and those of punishment delivery, mean that people who work in prisons do not tend to acknowledge them as morally communicative institutions. This does

COMMUNICATING BADLY   23

not mean that they do not accidentally communicate through their actions and demeanor, as well as through their reluctance to address the offense more directly: shame festers in silence, and the reluctance to acknowledge its presence makes it more likely that it will take its most damaging forms.

The moral conversation also operates on a horizontal plane, through the ways prisoners talk and think about their peers and in the relationships they form with each other. The metaphor of "communication," as well as the existing scholarship on punishment and moral communication, focuses our attention on the messages sent by the state as though they are the only condemner. In reality, prisons are made up of many different interlocutors, and the cacophonous conversations on the wings are made up of them speaking to, over, at, and about each other. Previous ethnographies of imprisonment have argued that the prisoner society can be a refuge from the power of the institution, and that prisoners can work to collectively resist what penal authorities try to impose (Cohen and Taylor 1972), offering them ways of thinking about themselves which resist the dishonoring labels applied to them. However, just as other studies have described the ways in which prisoners can exert painful and damaging forms of power over each other (Crewe 2009), so too can prisoners shame each other. Indeed, one of the most widely known and casually stated facts about imprisonment is that those convicted of sex offenses, particularly against children, are socially excluded, verbally abused, and often physically beaten while they are in prison. Research suggests that the shame and fear which this produces encourage many people imprisoned for sex offenses to deny that they are guilty (Blagden et al. 2011; Vaughn and Sapp 1989).

Prisons are morally communicative institutions, then, and what they communicate is shaped by a combination of structural, imported, and institutional factors, as well as by the shape of the prisoner society. In this book, I follow in the footsteps of other prison sociologists by conducting an ethnographic study of one institution, and I use this study to describe how these different entangled factors shaped what this prison said to the people it held about who they were and what they had done. First, however, I offer a description of the history and culture of HMP Stafford and of the fieldwork I conducted there. I include a brief description of my experiences as a woman conducting research in a prison for men convicted of sex offenses, both so that readers can better evaluate my findings, and for the benefit of other women who may do similar work.

HMP STAFFORD

The argument that prisons are morally communicative institutions is reinforced by the fact that violence is a cross-jurisdictional reality for prisoners convicted of sex offenses.[31] Previous ethnographies of "mainstream" prisons—that is, those that do not primarily hold men convicted of sex offenses—have highlighted that men in such prisons see "sex offenders" as "fundamentally and essentially different from the proper, normal prisoners" (Ugelvik 2014, 214), and that they idealize, and sometimes enact, violence against them as a way of reinforcing this moral distance. In England and Wales, this distance has been institutionalized. In an attempt to protect a steadily increasing population of men imprisoned for sex offenses, the Prison Service in England and Wales has historically tried to hold men convicted of sex offenses separately from "mainstream" prisoners—in the 1960s and 1970s through practices of informal segregation and in one prison for men considered to be at risk from their peers (Priestley 1980), and from the 1980s in separate wings for prisoners deemed vulnerable; these prisoners were known as "Vulnerable Prisoners," or VPs, and the wings as "Vulnerable Prisoners' Units," or VPUs.[32] In 1990, riots swept through the prison estate and prisoners targeted VPUs. One man, who had been remanded in custody after being charged with a sex offense, was killed in HMP Manchester (more commonly known as Strangeways). In response, and following pressure from a number of third sector and government organizations, the Prison Service decided to rationalize the accommodation of men imprisoned for sex offenses, and to hold them in increasingly specialized prisons. In 2003, HMP Stafford became one of these specialized institutions, operating as a "split-site," with half of the prison accommodating "mainstream" prisoners and half of it holding VPs. In 2014, the year before I conducted fieldwork, the prison "rerolled" to become one of six prisons in the country to only hold men convicted of sex offenses.[33]

Stafford was a medium-sized public sector category C (medium security) closed prison located in the center of a small market town in the West Midlands.[34] According to the Prison Service, it had the capacity to hold 741 prisoners, and throughout the fieldwork period it accommodated approximately this number of men. The prison had first opened in 1793, but most of the site was built in the Victorian period. The buildings were large, dark, and secure, but they were also clean and well maintained. Most of the wings consisted of long corridors three or four stories high, with small cells coming off the central walkways in which two men normally slept, and there was very little room for green space inside the prison's imposing brick walls. Stafford's history was reflected in its traditional prison officer culture: officers were highly loyal to their staff group, had a "them and us" orientation toward prisoners, and were suspicious of management.[35] Almost all were White, the vast majority were male, and many had spent careers of up to three decades in Stafford. Stafford had a historically strong branch of the Prison Officers' Association (the biggest and most influential trade union for prison officers), although in the time preceding the fieldwork period, the branch had faced organizational problems and its influence had weakened.

Many, but by no means all, officers in Stafford were resistant to change. Generally, though, they felt that the reroll had been a good idea: Victorian prisons like Stafford were at risk of closure, and officers felt that giving Stafford a specialist focus would help it to stay open. Similarly, like all public sector prisons, the prison had recently been affected by efficiency savings, benchmarking, and new working arrangements for staff, which had resulted in reductions in staff numbers and staff morale across the prison estate (Independent Monitoring Board 2012, 2014).[36] In other establishments, these cuts had contributed to higher levels of prisoner violence and reduced staff feelings of safety (HM Chief Inspector of Prisons 2015). In Stafford, however, officers felt that their prisoners were highly compliant (prisoners convicted of sex offenses are commonly considered to be more compliant than "mainstream" prisoners are), and thus that they could adapt to the new staffing arrangements without this impacting too much on the safety of the prison. Unlike many prisons at the time, Stafford was still able to run a consistent and clear regime: prisoners were generally unlocked at the correct time, almost all were in work or education, and association (the period when prisoners were allowed out of their cells to socialize with each other) was held most days.

Part of Stafford's safety and stability was linked to its traditional culture and the working practices of staff. In the past, Stafford had a reputation as a "Cat C [Category C] dumping ground," in the words of a former manager—it was a prison which had received a disproportionately high number of men considered to be difficult or confrontational. As a result, the prison had prioritized order, and had sought to enforce it through the implementation of clear, consistent, and somewhat controlling regimes and processes. Many of these ways of working had been carried forward following the reroll. Officers refused to unlock wings for association periods without the correct number of staff. Across the male prison estate (with some exceptions), one uniformed officer is supposed to be available for each thirty unlocked prisoners. In most prisons, if there are not enough officers for the entire wing to be unlocked—for instance, if officers are unwell or are outside the prison staffing a prisoner in hospital ("on a bedwatch")—staff sometimes unlock the wing anyway, or sometimes compromise by unlocking part of the wing. In Stafford, if there were not enough staff, everyone on the wing would remain locked in their cells. On residential wings, prisoners were unlikely to be unlocked if only one officer was on the wing, even if the numbers adhered to the ratio. Officers strictly unlocked landings in pairs and made sure that several officers were available at the servery when meals were distributed, in case of confrontations. Periods of movement, exercise, and the end of association periods were announced by staff loudly shouting in the middle of wings, and officers summoned individual prisoners by yelling their surnames from the ground floor. In the decade immediately preceding the reroll, it had been important to keep the two halves of the prison totally separate from each other, to ensure that the VPs were kept safe from "mainstream" prisoners. It thus had unusually restricted internal movement for its security level, and a larger number of gates and fences than would be expected in a category C prison. In the words of one officer, who prior to joining Stafford had worked in an open prison for women, Stafford was a "proper prison."

The management team was less fixated on ensuring safety, and instead aimed to develop a new rehabilitative vision for the rerolled prison. The new Governor (the official in charge of the prison) said that he had high aspirations for Stafford and stressed the importance of loosening the regime to ensure it was "appropriate for the prisoner profile." He had a progressive agenda, used the language of morality and decency, and repeatedly stressed the importance of officers referring to prisoners by their first names rather than their surnames, despite significant opposition from staff. However, he was aware that many of his proposed changes—such as greater provision of treatment programs and "through the gate" employment opportunities, as well as the reintroduction of "release on temporary license" for people convicted of sex offenses—were dependent on external funding and policies.[37] A particular concern for Stafford at the time of the fieldwork was that it received no funding for resettlement. Policy stated that prisoners were supposed to be released from resettlement prisons near to their local area, and that in these prisons they would receive help setting up housing and employment. However, at the time of the fieldwork, there were not enough spaces for people convicted of sex offenses in resettlement prisons, which meant that many prisoners were released from Stafford without having been given help to secure housing. In the years since the fieldwork was completed, reports by the Chief Inspector of Prisons have suggested that the prison has largely succeeded in adapting to its new population, and that, prior to the COVID-19 pandemic, had significantly improved its resettlement provision (HM Chief Inspector of Prisons 2016, 2020).

As a category C prison, Stafford's population was serving a diverse range of sentences. At the time of the fieldwork, 131 (around 18 percent) were serving determinate sentences of under three years;[38] 429 (57 percent) of four to ten years; 123 (16 percent) of ten or more years; and 64 (9 percent) were serving indeterminate sentences of life, or Imprisonment for Public Protection (IPP).[39] Stafford's population was most striking for its age, which was much higher than in most "mainstream" prisons, in part due to the then growing tendency to prosecute people for historic sex offenses. The mean (and median) age of those it accommodated was forty-six; 169 (23 percent) of those it held were aged sixty or over, and its oldest inhabitant was ninety-two. The older population contributed to Stafford's safety and calmness, but it also increased the frequency of health problems and disabilities among the prison's population. Throughout the fieldwork period, managers discussed the possibility of turning the Care and Separation Unit (colloquially known as Segregation) into a palliative care unit. Around 250 prisoners (a third of the population) stated that they had a disability, and around 80 (approximately 11 percent) stated that they had more than one. I met dozens of prisoners who used walking sticks, walkers, or wheelchairs, and others who were unable to leave their cells because of their health conditions. Systems had been put in place to make things easier for them, for instance, by assigning prisoners to bring them their meals or push them to work, and minor alterations had been made to the buildings to make them more wheelchair accessible. Nevertheless, the Victorian buildings had not been built with older men in mind, and many struggled with the loud noises, the cold, and the distances they were required to walk between buildings.

The ethnic background of prisoners in Stafford mirrored that of the population of England and Wales, and there was no significant overrepresentation of any ethnic group. The majority of men held in Stafford (621, or 83 percent) identified as White British, 46 (6 percent) identified as Asian or Asian British, 40 (5 percent) identified as Black or Black British, and 40 (5 percent) identified with other ethnic backgrounds.[40] Twenty-seven prisoners were foreign nationals. Stafford had an unusually active and open gay community; 17 prisoners had registered as bisexual, and 18 as homosexual (a combined total of around 5 percent of the prison's population), while 47 had not disclosed their sexuality.[41] There were monthly meetings of a gay, bisexual, and transgender (GBT) support group, which was normally attended by approximately 40 prisoners, and had been set up by a charismatic Supervising Officer.[42] I was told that the prison accommodated 1 trans woman, but I never knowingly met her.

I started my fieldwork in May 2015 and spent five months interviewing prisoners and prison officers and engaging in what anthropologist Clifford Geertz (1998) called "deep hanging out." I spent at least four days a week in the prison and was often there over weekends. I stayed in a bed and breakfast locally, and normally arrived at the prison at 9 a.m. and stayed until most prisoners were locked up at 6:15 p.m. (sometimes, but not often, leaving at lunchtime to write up notes in a nearby coffee shop). I then sometimes stayed for an hour or two to chat to officers or to privileged prisoners who were allowed to stay unlocked until 7 p.m. I was given keys, which meant that I was able to move freely through the prison and could avoid being either a burden on the prison staff or too closely monitored by them. Given that the prison had so recently been run as a split site, I chose to focus primarily on two wings, which had had different purposes prior to the reroll. One held just over 100 prisoners and was on the old "mainstream" side, and one held over 150 and was on the old VP side.

Over the course of the fieldwork, I conducted forty-two long semistructured interviews with prisoners and twelve shorter interviews with prison staff. Most prisoner interview participants were selected randomly, but I selected some participants purposively, after talking to them and finding their stories interesting or their analyses insightful. Interviews with prisoners had a mean length of four hours and were mostly conducted over several sessions in a private room and recorded on a digital recorder. Participants' ages ranged from twenty-four to eighty-eight, with a mean age of forty-three, and seven prisoners (17 percent) were aged sixty or over, meaning that the sample was slightly younger than the prison's population. The sample was 76 percent White British ($n = 32$), 12 percent Black or Black British ($n = 5$), 2 percent Asian or Asian British ($n = 1$), and 10 percent other ($n = 5$), meaning that I oversampled Black men and undersampled Asian men. Prison officers were selected opportunistically, although I ensured that I spoke to officers of different ages, genders, and levels of experience. These interviews had a mean length of an hour and a quarter, and were mostly conducted in staff offices, although one was conducted—at the officer's suggestion—in a nearby pub. All of the prisoners I interviewed have been assigned pseudonyms, but I have not assigned pseudonyms to prison officers or to prisoners I spoke to but did not interview.

In addition, I spent a lot of unstructured time in the prison. I filled twenty-six notebooks with detailed conversations and observations and recorded an audio diary every evening. I visited workshops, attended the chapel and education classes, joined in with the choir, and went to the Senior Support Group, a sort of day center for elderly prisoners. I also spoke to managers, administrators, and psychologists, and attended meetings of the Prisoner Council, the Equalities Action Group, and the GBT support group. More importantly, I spent a lot of time on wings, chatting to prisoners during association periods and having cups of tea in the office with members of staff—a necessary task as interviews with staff were often difficult to complete due to the requirements of their job. I also helped prisoners pack teabags and sachets of sugar into plastic bags to be distributed across the establishment, learned more than I ever expected to about industrial floor cleaning, lost several games of pool, and got told off by prison officers for eating my sandwiches in public places ("No eating on the landing!"). I was often given soup for lunch by prisoners who worked on the servery—a kind gesture, but against the rules—and once had to hide myself and my soup in the staff office when the Governor unexpectedly came onto the wing for an inspection, to the amusement of staff and prisoners.[43] After the fieldwork period ended, I returned to the prison for a few special events, and cried at a viewing of the film *Pride* which was held in the chapel for LGBT History Month.

Prisoners and officers were initially bemused by my presence, and although they were polite and helpful throughout, my position in the field was almost totally structured by the interaction between my gender and my participants' master status as "sex offenders." I turned twenty-five during the fieldwork, and am White, middle class, relatively short, and slim. I have always looked young for my age, and in the words of a senior female academic I once met, I "look like everybody's daughter." Superficially, my gender and gender presentation made the fieldwork much easier. Officers and prisoners were often chivalrous. They brought me cups of tea and coffee, helped me find people I wanted to interview, and apologized if they swore in front of me. Overall, though, my femininity became a burden which encumbered my attempts to conduct an appreciative ethnography. Staff were clearly worried about my safety and limited where I was allowed to go on wings. I was never allowed in cells, and on one wing I was only allowed on the higher landings if I was accompanied by a member of staff. Prisoners feared that they might be judged based on their behavior with me. This was not unreasonable: officers noticed who I spoke to, and often described people I thought of as key informants as "pests" or "wing Casanovas." Other prisoners initially worried that I might judge or even report them based on what they said in the interview and were careful when I tried to move the conversation into sensitive areas such as sexuality or compliance. One said that he was worried because he could not trust his own judgment of what was and was not appropriate to say to a woman. I was inextricably embedded in the disciplinary net which encompassed the prison:

> No disrespect, but you're a young female. This is a sex offenders' prison. So, seeing you on the wing, standing down there by the phones. You've got staff that sit there, it's almost like the staff are sitting there, "Let's see who's pretending to talk to her, and who keeps walking past." You know what I mean, don't you?
> *Yeah, I know exactly what you mean.*
> It would make people, maybe some people who probably want to have a conversation with you, like, "I'm not going to go over to her, because look at the staff down there. They're watching, and maybe she's thinking, 'Oh, I've seen him walk past a couple of times, does he want to speak to me or is he just being a bit dodgy about it?'" (Nigel)

> I can come out of this room now [after our interview], and all night tonight, [it'll be] "Oh, three hours on a date with Alice!"
> *I'm sorry. [laughs]*
> That's what happens, Alice! It's like before dinner, I was in my scruffy work clothes and I thought to myself, "I'm seeing Alice, I'm having this meeting, and after that I'm not going back to work. Do you know what, I'm going to treat myself, I'm going to have a shower and put my shirt and jeans on." And before you know it you've got, "Oh, you're scrubbing yourself up for Alice!" And it's like, no, I'm doing it because I'm not going back to work, and I'd probably have my shower this afternoon and if I have one now, then I've got all of my association to play pool and make my phone calls and whatever, rather than spend half an hour of it in the shower. (Harry)

In order to counter the distance which existed by default between me and my research participants, I tried to encourage prisoners to trust me as much as possible. I partly did this strategically, but also because many prisoners spoke movingly about the pain and discomfort of being considered a sexual risk, and I did not want to add to this pain. I joined in with jokes, accepted most of their compliments, made time to hear their side of the story, and said kind things about them if I thought they needed it. I also answered reasonable questions about my life outside (the city I lived in, my broad interests and hobbies, whether I had siblings), although I avoided giving unnecessary details (my date of birth or where in the city I lived).

Some relationships became too close. My discomfort with challenging small inappropriate acts—comments about being a "good-looking girl" (Harry), for instance—meant that relationships could be pushed up to the boundaries of acceptability. At several points during the research, I became uneasily aware that if conversations were overheard by staff, they could be considered improper, my access might be restricted, and the person I was talking to might be condemned as a manipulator. At the back of my mind, I occasionally worried that I *was* being manipulated without realizing it, and I had a few uncomfortable experiences during the fieldwork period. One man deliberately monopolized my attention when I went onto his wing, telling me, "I like to play games with you." Recognizing the strangeness of my role in the prison, he commented on how I was seen by other prisoners and how I held myself on the wing, and he came up to me after I had spoken to younger men and asked if I ever wondered how attractive men ended up in prisons like Stafford. One day, he deliberately sprayed his inhaler in my face in front of an officer to see how she would react (she ignored it). Another prisoner divulged that a man who had recently been released from the establishment had told his friends that he would follow me home from the prison so he could find out where I lived. Another man, who had a history of sexually assaulting female members of staff and of publicly masturbating within the prison, stood a few meters from me one lunchtime and kept asking me to step closer to him, until other prisoners intervened. During a conversation on the wing, one man repeatedly brushed my leg with his hand, and then followed me round until I spoke to him and said I hoped I had not given the wrong impression and that I was in the prison as a professional. I was often conscious of being watched while I was on the wing, sometimes by individuals, and sometimes by groups of men who I could see talking to each other about me.

These interactions were individually manageable but cumulatively unsettling. When officers became aware of them, they mostly reacted with concern, although a few implied that I had provoked attention with a friendly female demeanor. One male officer, intending to be kind, warned me, "There's a risk that they become a bit too familiar. You sit up there and you're chatting, and they think, 'Oh, Alice and I have got a bit of a rapport, maybe I should try something.'" I became intensely self-conscious and engaged in extreme levels of physical self-regulation. After an incident when I was told off by a female member of staff for taking my jumper off and exposing my elbows on a hot day, I developed my own prison uniform—jeans and a long-sleeved top—which I wore whatever the weather, something prisoners sometimes remarked on: "It's so hot out there and you're wearing a jumper. I know you're in a sex offenders' prison but come on!" (Shezad). Despite only needing to wear glasses for distance, I wore them all the time I was in Stafford, worrying that people would read something into any decision to take them off. I spent a lot of time regretting my age, gender, and size, and thought that my research would be easier if I were somehow less feminine, although in the years since I have realized that womanhood is not easily excised. I kept remembering other times I have experienced sexual harassment, and in the years since I have been reminded of my experiences in the prison whenever sexual harassment and sexual violence are discussed.

While I remained frustrated by the limits these dynamics imposed, I learned to use them as an intellectual resource. Prisoners often used me as an example in conversations about gender dynamics in the prison, opening avenues of conversation which might otherwise feel abstract or taboo. I was also able to see how these interactions worked in practice: who prisoners and staff told me to be careful around; how people reacted when they heard other people tell me to be careful around them; and who could tease, talk to, and touch me without being disciplined. I occasionally draw on these interactions in what follows, but they informed all my reflections and analysis, making this book a deeply, if quietly, personal one.

CONCLUSION: A CAUTIONARY NOTE

The academic conversation about imprisonment has normally taken place in three distinct realms: one normative, which discusses the functions an idealized institution could fulfil; one theoretical, which soars above the prison and comments on its relationship to political, economic, and racial injustices; and one empirical, which is deeply rooted within the prison and accounts for the daily realities it produces. Work conducted in the first realm has focused too much on what imprisonment ought to say, work conducted in the second has defaulted to criticism without paying attention to what real prisons say, and work conducted in the third has paid too little attention to what the prison says at all. Unless these realms are brought closer together, there is a real risk that sociologists of imprisonment will be able to provide detailed descriptive accounts which fail to address the deep questions about justice which come into play when we discuss punishment. Meanwhile, normative and critical theorists will produce work that takes place on a higher plane than the messy realities of lived experience, and which therefore criticizes systems which do not exist and suggests alternatives which will never work.

This chapter and its predecessor have mostly been in the first two realms, and those which follow are mostly in the third, but the book as a whole brings the three together, using normative theory to critique current practice and using empirical descriptions to advance normative theorizing and feminist advocacy. It aims to build a bridge between conversations about the experience of imprisonment and discussions about the just response to sexual violence, thereby broadening the theoretical repertoire on which prison sociologists can draw and simultaneously deepening the empirical knowledge of penal theorists, abolitionists, and reformers. The book is deeply embedded within Stafford and its primary goal is to accurately describe the moral conversation which that prison produced, but throughout it lifts its gaze to reflect on what this description tells us about how we should do punishment differently. Like any good ethnographer, though, I urge a note of caution before these findings are too widely generalized. In some ways, Stafford was like all prisons: it was an institution in which one group of people were held against their will because they had been found guilty of acts deemed to be illegal. In many ways, though, it was different—both because it was a prison which held people convicted of an especially shaming category of crimes, and because of its own history, culture, and architecture. Throughout the book, I try to disentangle which elements of the moral conversation were caused by the structure of imprisonment, which were imported by Stafford's population, and which were caused by institutional variations in the way Stafford imprisoned people. To this end the next chapter describes three factors which shaped what Stafford morally communicated, none of which are structurally integral to imprisonment but also none of which were specific to Stafford: the labyrinthine legal process which led people to be imprisoned there, the stain applied to them by their conviction, and the psychologically demanding rehabilitative regime which tried to discipline them. However, the only real way to understand what all prisons say to the people they hold is to conduct more research in more prisons. This book, then, should be seen as a starting point, and not as a conclusion.

Distorting Institutions

Structuring the Moral Dialogue

As social scientists, we inevitably imagine our subjects before we enter the field, and these projections are sometimes confirmed, sometimes replaced, and sometimes distorted by the real people we find lurking behind them (C. Russell 1999). The reading I completed before starting fieldwork in Stafford led me to expect to meet many people who either falsely maintained innocence for their convictions or who told stories about their offenses which were incomplete or misrepresentative. Estimates vary, but existing research suggests that around a third of men convicted of sex offenses insist that they were wrongly convicted (Hood et al. 2002; Kennedy and Grubin 1992), and these claims are more common among men convicted of sex offenses than they are for those convicted of most other crimes (R. Mann 2016). Forensic psychologists have found that people convicted of sex offenses excuse, minimize, and neutralize their offending, and they describe these as "cognitive distortions," twisted thought patterns which they think enable (re)offending.[1] Similarly, feminist researchers have shown that people who rape are particularly likely to have inaccurate and stereotyped views about rape and rape victims (Johnson and Beech 2017). These findings have led many people conducting research with men convicted of sex offenses to imagine a duplicitous and misogynistic subject, and to conduct their research accordingly. Methodological texts caution interviewers against contaminating their research findings with their subject's views, overwriting the victim's version of events, or engaging in "passive collusion" (Digard 2010, 215) by accidentally reinforcing or confirming their subject's cognitively and morally distorted thoughts. Instead, even qualitative scholars encourage new researchers to cultivate a distance from their objects of study.[2]

Even before starting fieldwork, I was uncomfortable with the epistemological scaffolding which underlay these recommendations. Like many criminologists,

I have an instinctive desire to probe official narratives (Becker 1967), and my research orientation is appreciative (Matza 1969). I have always sought to describe the world as it looks to my research participants, and narrative criminology (Fleetwood et al. 2019) has encouraged me to understand the stories people tell as constitutive of that world, and not as something which blocks us from understanding it. I was therefore uncomfortable with assuming that any distance between the prisoners' stories of their offense and that officially validated by their conviction was a product of the prisoners' dishonesty or psychological and moral faults. I also questioned whether it was appropriate to prejudge research strategies based on their feared effects on research participants' worldviews, as I had reservations about evaluating empirical research through a therapeutic or disciplinary framework. Finally, I had read research challenging the straightforward assumption that denial and offense neutralizations are dangerous. Some researchers argue that false claims of innocence can serve useful functions for people by helping them maintain relationships with friends and family (Lord and Willmot 2004) and stay safe in prisons in which identification as a "sex offender" could lead to violence (Vaughn and Sapp 1989). Claims of innocence, neutralizations, and excuses can also help people stave off feelings of shame and stigmatization which might otherwise overwhelm them and even hinder their prospects for desistance (Blagden et al. 2011; Maruna and Mann 2006).[3]

Nevertheless, when I started fieldwork, I was still nervous of either being duped by participants, writing over their victims, or reinforcing misogyny. Many of these swirling worries centered on how I would respond to the claims of innocence I expected to hear, and I decided to pursue a strategy of professional impartiality. I hoped to avoid forming a view about people's guilt or moral responsibility, and certainly never to give it away. I planned to ask questions neutrally—"As someone who says they're not guilty, why do you do the things the prison wants you to do?"—and to speak in ways which would neither risk me supporting distorted thinking nor disrespecting the story of the victim. In practice, it was difficult to maintain this objectivity while also developing the relationships on which good interviewing and ethnography depend. I felt that sounding suspicious created distance between me and my research participants, and on the rare occasions that I was directly asked if I believed in someone's guilt, my attempts to wriggle out of answering were justifiably criticized for sounding "robotic." I also began to realize that most prisoners cared more about what other people thought than they did about what I thought, and that many would read something into my response almost irrespective of what I said. I started to align my questions with what prisoners said about their situation, asking things like, "As an innocent man, why do you do the things the prison wants you to do?" Although I continued to avoid articulating a view about people's guilt, I worried less about performing perfect impartiality when prisoners told their stories.

In so doing, I hoped to encourage prisoners to tell me as much as they wanted about what they had done and what they had been convicted of, and I decided to use the way they told these stories as data (Sandberg 2010). I knew that whether interview participants were consciously telling the truth or not, there was undoubtedly a gap between these stories and what, if anything, they had done. This is always the case with stories—the richness and complexity of experience can never be perfectly remembered or represented in language, and the demands of narratives and the expectations of real and imagined audiences further twist the stories we tell—and is particularly the case in stories about extreme, traumatizing, and taboo experiences. But I became interested in how the penal context deepened these gaps. Whereas existing analyses of the narratives of people convicted of sex offenses have tended to explain them psychologically and individually, I wanted to understand how they had been distorted—taken away from what was historically true—by the institution. I tried to look for patterns in people's stories to see where the penal context might be shaping them. Did prisoners describe moments where their stories had shifted, or where they had told different stories to different audiences, or felt that someone was trying to shape how they talked about their convictions? Were they setting their stories against official narratives or stereotypes, and how did they use their stories to counter these alternative truths? How did they interpret each other's stories, and what made them more likely to trust each other? What did these tensions say about how their stories had been shaped by their imprisonment?

By asking these questions, I identified three institutional mechanisms which distorted prisoners' stories: the legal system, the "sex offender" stain, and the rehabilitative regime. All prisoners in Stafford had been admitted there after passing through a legal system which imposed denunciatory convictions on them, but which operated in such a byzantine way that its outputs were difficult to believe and easy to challenge. These convictions exposed them to the staining "sex offender" label, which threatened their social identity so thoroughly that it encouraged prisoners to resist it while simultaneously enabling this resistance through its own extreme characterological implications. They were then subjected to a rehabilitative regime which rewarded them for telling their stories in an institutionally approved way, but which as a result allowed these stories to be interpreted as the shallow product of incentivization. Taken together, these factors had three distorting effects on the moral dialogue which existed in the prison. They encouraged prisoners to tell stories that were not true, whether by falsely claiming innocence to avoid being found guilty in court and to evade stain in prison and afterward, or by falsely claiming guilt to progress through the system as smoothly as possible. They also facilitated the telling of untruths by allowing prisoners to tell different stories to different audiences and to explain this by saying they were being pragmatic. Finally, these distortions were so thick that they sowed confusion and mistrust, eroding the ability of others in the prison to confidently trust either the stories they were told by prisoners or those implied by their convictions.

I was never able to determine precisely how these institutional distortions altered individual people's narratives, and I had moments of frustration, both personal and intellectual, about whether I was being told the truth. I didn't want to feel lied to or like I was on the "wrong side," and I still feel that knowing the "true story" of prisoners' offenses would have allowed a deeper understanding of the prison's morally communicative effects. One of this book's central goals is to explain how imprisonment in Stafford shaped how people thought about what they had done, and doing this would undoubtedly have been easier if I knew whether individual people were lying, misremembering, or being as honest as they could be. But the difficulty of the intellectual task says something about the gap between the ideal of moral communication and how it happens in practice. Normative penal theorists talk about moral communication as though there is, or should be, a straightforward relationship between the offense that someone has committed and their punishment. Imprisonment should be imposed in response to a criminal act which has certainly been committed and should be taken by the person who committed it, by the victim, and by the rest of the community as a sign that it was wrong and that it mattered. However, the message which imprisonment in Stafford expressed was so deeply distorted that it was hard to decipher what it meant, or even to make clear judgments about what people in the prison had done. As this chapter will argue, this lack of clarity simultaneously deepened prisoners' shame and offered them the opportunity to escape it. The resulting moral dialogue was simultaneously condemnatory and confusing, and left prisoners, prison officers, and researchers unsure of where they stood.

THE LEGAL FRAMEWORK

It's not just the prison, it's the whole judicial system. (Shezad)

The legal system is the mechanism by which people are determined to be guilty of a sex offense and sentenced to imprisonment, and it was thus the main process by which people were selected for admission into Stafford. Although there was significant variation in how the men in Stafford talked about their experiences of the legal system, the overall picture which they painted was of an arbitrary and prejudiced collection of organizations, all of which were driven by their own internal logics rather than by an attempt to discover truth or promote ethical behavior. The system was experienced as an unpredictable and uncontrollable juggernaut, one which ate up the intimate details of people's lives and spat them out as verdicts of guilty and not guilty. This picture was painted in the most bitterly painstaking detail by those who had pleaded not guilty and who still steadfastly maintained that they were innocent, but it was gestured at, albeit with greater levels of resignation or understanding by those who said that they were guilty and deserved to be punished. Prisoners described the police as overly credulous to victims and as preoccupied by chasing convictions; the CPS as vindictive; the trial as chaotic, competitive, and alienating; the lawyers, including their own, as biased, lazy, and mercenary; and the judges as driven by their hatred of "sex offenders." They felt that none of the main players were there to find out or to describe the "truth," and that the trial deliberately sought to strip away context and history.[4] They maintained that the official account which this process produced, and which was encapsulated in the guilty or not guilty verdicts, failed to represent what had really happened—or at least what they told me had happened.[5]

Feminist studies of the legal response to sexual violence have similarly argued that these processes are uninterested in the pursuit of truth, although for different reasons to those articulated by prisoners in Stafford. These studies have convincingly argued that rape myths (Burt 1980)—such as the belief that people cannot be raped by current or former partners, that rape requires physical resistance, that false accusations are common, or that those who commit rape are identifiably different from those who do not—shape policing and prosecutorial practice all the way through the system (Hohl and Stanko 2015; Y. Russell 2016). These studies have shown that participants in adversarial court systems like those in England and Wales rely on and repeat these myths, with the effect that rapes which meet certain characteristics are more likely to result in a conviction (Adler 1987; E. Daly 2022; Lees 1993; Temkin, Gray, and Barrett 2018). What is not discussed within this literature, though, is whether the authoritative repetition of these myths by lawyers and judges affects the way people convicted of sexual violence think about and make sense of their crimes. It was certainly the case that many prisoners in Stafford repeated false views about the nature of sexual violence, views which may have been validated by their experiences of the legal system. The shadow of the legal system had other effects on the moral conversation which took place inside the prison. It promoted binary understandings of guilt and innocence, extended the meaning of criminal labels beyond prisoners' familiarity, and produced verdicts which had such a seemingly arbitrary relationship to what had happened that they generated a widespread sense of injustice.[6] In so doing, the legal system focused prisoners' attentions on how they had been blamed, rather than on what they had done, shaming them in a way which fostered self-preoccupation and stasis rather than reflection and transformation. It is also possible that, in some cases, it facilitated miscarriages of justice, and that some prisoners had been unjustly convicted.

The charging process was a major object of confusion and critique. Charging someone with a criminal offense is an act of denunciation—it applies a discrediting label to an alleged act—and in a few rare cases, the light which this process had cast on prisoners' past behavior had prompted them to think differently about what they had done. More often, though, prisoners resented the crudeness of criminal charges. Even when they acknowledged that they had done wrong, charging them necessarily entailed cutting and twisting a complex real-life event so that it fit into simplified legal categories. Prisoners often insisted that their charges were not specific enough to be meaningful and that they implied that offenses were more serious than they were. This criticism was particularly common among those convicted of rape, who often had a limited understanding of what rape is and who relied on and reproduced myths when they discussed their offending. John, for example, recounted arguing with his cellmate about his cellmate's offense:

> [He says,] "It was sex. Because we'd had sex before, it doesn't matter." "Of course it matters," I said, "You raped her!" "Nah, never!" He can't get rape into his head.
> *So it's almost like he doesn't understand what it is.*
> He doesn't. "I've had sex with a woman." I've said, "You raped her!" "She never said no." "It don't matter, there's two of you raped her!" Two grown men. It gets me mad.

Older men were particularly likely to repeat these myths. They had often been convicted of offenses committed decades earlier, and resented being criminally convicted of behavior which they said was normal when they engaged in it.

Ahmed's story exemplifies both the potential and the danger of charging people with capaciously defined crimes. He was the only prisoner I interviewed who had started his sentence believing that he was innocent and who had decided, over time, that he was guilty—legally, at least. He was convicted of the rape and false imprisonment of a number of sex workers, and said that he had done so while under the influence of drugs to punish them for stealing from him. In his trial, he had pleaded not guilty, insisting that he had believed that he was innocent as he "didn't understand that a prostitute could say no." At the same time, he indicated that he had felt ambivalent about his responsibility, but was reluctant to admit to having committed a shaming offense in front of his family:

> *Did you expect to be found guilty?*
> I had a feeling. I was, like, in two minds, I was saying, "Guilty, not guilty." I was telling the barrister, "I think I'm gonna get guilty." She says, "Why do you think that? Did you do it?" Because I had a distorted view, my views were, like, distorted, I was like, "No, no." I should have been more brave. And I was thinking about my family as well. My mum was there, my sisters were there all through the trial, and . . . I was thinking, if I say, "Guilty," how are they going to see me?

Over the course of his sentence, and following his completion of treatment programs, he had come to understand that what he had done was accurately defined as rape. He now said that he regretted not having "spoken the truth" in his trial by trying to "accept it and explain it":

> [In the trial] I said I was involved but I didn't do it as they say, you see what I mean? But now I would want to say, "Yes, that may have happened, but I believed, yes, this is what my beliefs was at this time, this is how I was seeing things, this is how I was feeling at that time as well, because of the pain, because of what they were doing to me." You see what I mean?

On the one hand, it's possible to argue that Ahmed's story offers an example of a successful denunciation. Over the course of his sentence, his understanding of his prior behavior began to align with legal and feminist conceptions of sexual violence as he came to realize that he had committed rape and that it was wrong.

For Ahmed, punishment did provide a moral education by forcing him to think differently about his behavior. On the other hand, this changed interpretation was largely technical. His focus was still on his own experiences, and the moral education did not appear to have generated deep feelings of guilt about what he had done. It also only happened once psychological treatment provided him with a different framework for understanding it than had been available in the trial, when his main goal had been to argue against the CPS story. At that stage, the denunciatory power of his charges had been so strong that it distracted him from thinking about his responsibility and failed to make him recognize the wrongness of the act.

In many cases, prisoners' failure to recognize that their behavior fell into the discrediting category encapsulated in the criminal charge had discouraged them from pleading guilty during their trial and continued to push them to insist on their legal and moral innocence during their sentence. Even those who had pleaded guilty insisted throughout their sentence that there was a gulf between what they had done and what their charges implied they had done. In charging people with specific crimes, the state had spoken in a language which was technical yet discrediting, and which some men in Stafford struggled to connect to their experience or to what they saw as the "real world meaning" (William) of these terms. In interviews I asked men what they were convicted of, and they often replied in words whose breeziness belied the severity of the crime, and which in many cases indicated that they struggled to remember precisely what they had been charged with. When I asked Jake, who had just recounted his offense with dismay and self-disgust, what he was convicted of, he replied, "Rape and . . . what was the other one? Oh, indecent assault." At worst, the technocratic language used in charges meant that prisoners struggled to understand what they had been charged with. Greg, for instance, a young man who appeared to have learning difficulties, said that he had pleaded guilty to sixteen internet-related charges, even though he didn't know what they all meant.

Many men said they had initially faced more, fewer, or different charges than those which they eventually faced in court. This instability and insecurity lent a game-like quality to the adversarial legal process. Ian said that he was in his early twenties when he was interviewed by the police and accused of having sexually assaulted a child when he was a teenager. He said that he was later accused of raping the same child and on the day of his trial his lawyer persuaded him to plead guilty to sexual assault so that he was not tried for rape.[7] Similarly, Tony said that when he was first interviewed by the police, he was accused of sexual assault, and had told the police that he could not have sexually assaulted his victim as they had consensual sex a few days later. After three days in a cell, the police interviewed him again and said that the sex was rape. When we spoke, Tony told me that he had decided to plead guilty to the sexual assault charge to get the rape charge and another sexual assault charge "thrown away," and he used a card game metaphor to describe himself as having "played a hand." In both cases, the main players in the legal process were pursuing goals other than the truth: the CPS wanted to get a conviction, and Tony and Ian wanted to spend as little time as possible in prison. In the end, both Tony and Ian pleaded guilty to charges which reflected neither the allegations made by the victims nor what they themselves said had happened, and it is highly unlikely that the official story which emerged from this compromise came close to whatever the truth was.

The policy of reducing the sentences of those who pleaded guilty early was also likely to distort the official story. There may be pragmatic reasons to encourage guilty pleas—to save money, to facilitate efficiency, and to save victims from having to testify (Nobles and Schiff 2019)—but it distracted the main players from the pursuit of veracity. Of the forty-two prisoners interviewed, twenty-eight had pleaded guilty to some or all of the charges against them, but nine of these (a quarter of all those who pleaded guilty) said that they were motivated primarily by getting a shorter sentence and didn't really believe that they were guilty. Some said they had changed their plea on the day of the trial and described themselves as having been pushed to do so by their lawyers. Frank, for instance, was convicted of raping a fifteen-year-old girl. He claimed that he did not know her age but admitted that it was wrong to have sex with her—"She was younger than what I thought she was, but this is the person that was pouring me Jack Daniels and rum and cokes"—but he contested the charge of rape, saying that she was a willing participant.[8] Nevertheless, he said that he pleaded guilty to get a shorter sentence:

> Right on the day of my trial, half an hour before I was up, I changed my plea from not guilty to guilty. The reason I did that was because they were threatening me to two or three years longer if I got found guilty. [. . .] So I call it self-preservation. I'll take the lesser sentence now. If I'm going to get a sentence, I may as well take the least sentence. So I changed my plea from not guilty to guilty because . . . I'm not saying what happened didn't happen, but what I'm saying is it didn't happen the way it's come out.

It is impossible to tell whether men like Frank authentically believed in their innocence. Many prisoners in Stafford were cynical when their peers claimed to have pleaded guilty for instrumental reasons and suggested that they were lying to make themselves feel good. James said that he admonished people who said they had pleaded guilty strategically, telling them, "You do not go guilty just because a barrister tells you to—it's your life!" Whether people believed in their innocence or not, the introduction of incentives into a process which is supposed to enable the production and discovery of truth damaged the credibility of its outputs by either encouraging people to plead guilty falsely or by providing them with a way to challenge their own professed guilt later.

People who had pleaded not guilty and been taken to trial also felt that the process had produced corrupted stories, and prisoners (and some staff) maintained that the alleged poverty of evidentiary standards during the trial meant that wrongful convictions were likely. It was extremely common for prisoners to say that they or their peers had been convicted based on little or no evidence or solely on "hearsay" evidence, by which they meant an account by a victim which was not supported by third-party corroborations, CCTV, or physical evidence. In part, these claims resulted from their (reasonable) failure to understand the complex rules concerning the admissibility of different forms of evidence, and in particular from a misunderstanding of what hearsay is.[9] However, many critiques of the admissibility of different forms of evidence demonstrated mistrust in the accounts of women and repeated rape myths which are sometimes used in court (Temkin, Gray, and Barrett 2018). It was common for prisoners—and sometimes prison officers—to say that it was easy for women to "cry rape," and many men said in interviews that they had been convicted because their victim had lied. Many of their more specific critiques of evidentiary standards directly targeted feminist reforms which had aimed to make convictions more likely. Several prisoners on different wings stated that it was only possible for men to be convicted on hearsay because Section 23 of the Criminal Justice Act had been removed, which "opened the door for anyone to say anything happened in 1921," in the words of a man I met on the wing. Sometimes they specifically named the 1993 Criminal Justice Act, and sometimes the 2003 act of the same name, but it is likely that they were referring to Section 32 of the 1994 Criminal Justice and Public Order Act, which removed the requirement that judges warn juries against convicting when there is no corroborating evidence, making it easier for men to be convicted when the only witness is the complainant (McGlynn 2010).

A specific critique of the legal system was made by the small number of men who said that they could not remember the events surrounding their offense. Zac said that when he was twenty-one, he had left a party drunk and had woken up in a police cell, where he was told he had tried to sexually attack someone while he was on his way home. He said that he had never contested his guilt but that he still could not remember what had happened. He described himself as deeply confused and alienated by the legal process: the CPS had been unsure what to charge him with, initially selecting sexual assault and then charging him with attempted rape, and he had eventually pleaded guilty on the advice of his lawyer. The process felt careless and left him with a lot of unanswered questions:

I never went in front of them and said, "I'm innocent, I'm innocent," I just told them the truth from my side. But I guess with the legal aid solicitors, all they wanted, to be fair, was to make a quick buck, the police just wanted to make a quick arrest. I wouldn't reprimand anyone, especially the police, because everyone had to do their job, but a lot of things didn't get looked at on my side, to be fair, the case was never looked at properly. [. . .] I was willing to accept it, whatever the case, you know. Look, at the end of the day, it doesn't matter for me, I have to . . . how can I say? I have to accept whatever the situation is but it's kind of hard sometimes, working with it, because you never know. That's how it felt, to be fair, they never told me the whole truth, they never said the whole truth to me.

Zac's situation, while not quite unique, was extreme. In most cases, the core of prisoners' criticisms was that the legal system promoted stories which contradicted what they insisted was the truth. Zac's criticism was that he still didn't know the truth.

Given the picture they painted of the legal system, it is unsurprising that men in Stafford expressed strong doubts about the fairness of the convictions it produced. It is perhaps more surprising that even those who said that they were wrongly convicted struggled to shake off the traces of their faith in the legal bureaucracy. These traces were most visible in prisoners' moral attitudes toward their peers, and they were often profoundly confused about how to think about the people they lived among. Shezad said that he didn't realize how flawed the system was until he was found guilty of sexually assaulting his wife's sister, who was a child. However, despite his overarching cynicism about the accuracy of the legal process, a small amount of trust in the system remained, and exposed him to a morally confusing situation:

> When I was outside, I always believed, you know, the justice system is fantastic in this country and the police, whenever they catch somebody, they know what they're doing, and a conviction, [that means] of course he has done it, that's why he was convicted. I was one of those people and I regret that, now I regret it, I feel sad because I've judged so many people in my life, when I've seen somebody in the media and all that. Because I went through it, it's like jumping in the water to find out how deep it is, and it's deep, very deep. So now, in that respect, I don't trust the system. I know [. . .] there are flaws in employment laws and employability and all that, even. You don't expect that to be in the justice system, especially the criminal justice system and police system. You expect them to be absolute, so when you go through that conviction, it brings doubts in your head. You don't trust what you hear. You don't trust the system on its own, and then in prison, there are other people that have done it, so you're confused in that side as well. How they might have done it, they might not have done it. Before, if he's a criminal, the general understanding is as well, "Oh, he's a criminal, he went to the prison, of course he's a criminal, what are you talking about? He's done it!" Now there's a chance he might not. That's the difference. I need to make a decision. It's completely changed things.

Shezad was here describing a deep feeling of confusion about what criminal convictions mean. Gone was his earlier clarity and belief that they represented an absolute and perfect marker of immorality, but he also struggled to believe that convictions meant nothing. Unable to trust in the capacity of the legal system to convict people correctly, but also unable to ignore what the conviction and sentence said about the people they lived among, Shezad and many other prisoners were left puzzled by the moral status of their peers and felt compelled to make their own decisions. Their lack of faith in the ability of the legal system to produce truth, together with their inability to completely discount the verdicts which it generated, would influence their social relationships with other prisoners as well as their orientations toward their own sentence.

THE "SEX OFFENDER" STAIN

Having heard what half of the prisoners, some of the prisoners are saying, when they are wandering about, I don't want [my family] to mix with those, be party to that at all. It's horrible, disgusting. It seems to seep under your skin more while you are in here and you just become . . . You know when you get muddy and you just can't seem to get rid of the stain on you? It's like that, it seeps into you and it gets worse the longer you are in here. It's just quite horrible. So I never want to expose them to that. *Okay. With the things you hear them say, what sort of things do you mean?* General comments related to . . . There were comments in the workshop when I worked there. When I first started, you had to wrap the plug around the tailboard and that was it and then the boards were being thrown back. "You can't have it as tight as that, you need it as tight as a five-year-old." And that's not the comments you should be saying in here. It's horrible. But they kept repeating the same comments over and over again and laughing and joking about it and it's not funny. It's probably why most of them are in here in the first place, with comments like that. (Louis)

Shame was difficult to avoid in Stafford. While rarely discussed by name, its effects were present every time someone insisted that they were not a proper "sex offender," every time they angrily ranted about the judgmentalism of staff, every time they whisperingly discussed disturbing rumors about their peers, and every time they nervously tried to imagine a postprison future. The men in Stafford varied in a great many ways—they had different histories, families, and demographic characteristics, they were convicted of different offenses, they were serving different sentences, and they approached these sentences in different ways—but they were united by the social identity they had been assigned and by the fact that they were forced to live with others who had been assigned it. Following their convictions, they had all become "sex offenders," and they shared the stain which came with this unwanted label.

The meaning of a sex offense conviction has been frequently discussed by scholars of punishment, and it is usually metaphorically described as a stigma (K. Hudson 2005; Ricciardelli and Moir 2013; Tewksbury 2012). Stigmas were most influentially conceptualized by Erving Goffman, ([1963] 1990), who described them as an undesirable piece of information which interferes in people's social identity and comes to dominate their personal relationships. This description certainly applied to the experiences of men in Stafford. Their conviction for a sex offense had become the principal factor governing their identity in prison, and they feared that it would continue to shape their lives for years after their release. However, a more illustrative metaphor to describe the experience of being assigned the "sex offender" social identity is a stain.[10] A stain is something which seeps into your whole being, which sets you apart, and which pollutes you. Like stigmata, stains are indelible and communicative. They are impossible to escape, and they say something about who you are. But unlike stigmas, stains are inherently physical and disgusting. They seep and spread, oozing through and past the boundaries of the body and attaching themselves to anyone or anything that touches them, accumulating in layers on people who have already been marked. As the quotation which opens this section highlights, stains contaminate, and this means that people are judged, and may judge themselves, by the company they keep. This oozing quality means that stains always speak imprecisely, and this imprecision is central to their communicative failings. Whereas penal theorists argue that criminal labels are supposed "to make moral sense of the social world" (Wilson 2007, 162) by meaningfully categorizing behavior—for example, by stating clearly that all nonconsensual sex is rape, and that rape is wrong—stains blur the distinctions between different types of behavior and different types of people. People in Stafford may have been convicted of different offenses, but the moral differences between their convictions and the acts which led to them were hard to view through the polluting miasma of the "sex offender" stain.

Focusing on the bodily components of stain draws attention to its tendency to produce disgust, a visceral emotion which speaks to our fear of contamination and our desire to draw moral markers (Nussbaum 2004). When asked how they felt about being assigned the "sex offender" label, a great many men used deeply physical language which indicated disgust and pollution. Jake said that the term was a "bottom-of-the-pit word" and Noah, who was serving a sentence for a nonsexual offense, said that he felt "dirty" whenever he heard Stafford described as a "sex offender" prison. Tommy, who was in a similar position, said, "I've always looked down on sex offenders and thought 'Dirty so-and-so.' I don't know. Now I'm with them. It's mad." Phil described it as "an obscene, vile word": "It makes me feel sick that I'm labeled like that, it really does make me feel ill." When asked why they had such a visceral response, prisoners often directly referred to the generalizing nature of the label. Rather than referring specifically to what they had done, or at least what they had been criminally convicted of doing, the term gestured toward a range of other acts and interests. In particular, prisoners complained that to be labeled a "sex offender" indicated that they had a sexual interest in children and were a "pedophile." Such a sexual interest was seen to be deeply unacceptable, and to move people outside of the category of humanity:

> Do you think being described as a sex offender is different to being described as a criminal? It has different connotations, or different effects?
> I think it's stronger. It's stronger. It's more . . . more disgusting.
> Do you think people see it as more disgusting, or it is more disgusting?
> It is more disgusting and people should see it as more disgusting. Because it comes in various categories, and some are quite horrendous, see what I mean? But you all put it under the same umbrella. (Ahmed)

Similarly, I asked Phil why he felt the term was so obscene and vile, and he replied, "Just the connotations, what it means, messing with kids, raping women, whatever it is. Sex offender covers such a broad subject. A burglar goes in a house and steals property. A sex offender could be almost . . . it's massive. It's just such a vile crime."

The oozing quality of stains means that they can affix themselves to environments as well as to people, and these stained environments can further dirty those who interact with them. This polluting feedback loop was at work in Stafford. Almost everyone who was imprisoned there was convicted of a sex offense, and so being there was taken to mean something about your conviction. In the eyes of the public, as Steven put it, "if you're a Stafford inmate then you're a pedophile, by definition." The prison certainly had a bad reputation in the town it stood in the center of. Members of the public occasionally shouted abuse at family members queueing to visit their loved ones, at officers leaving work, or even just at the men they imagined behind the prison's imposing walls. Prisoners were very aware of the low regard in which the establishment was held, and on several occasions (wrongly) insisted that abusive phrases like "pedo palace" and "monster mansion" were spray painted on the exterior walls. The prevalence of these myths indicated the strength of prisoners' anxiety about their status. Several people told me that they were worried that they might face physical or verbal abuse as they walked to the train station on the day they were released. Other men feared that they might be harassed if they were transferred to other prisons and people there found out that they had been in Stafford (through reading the address on old letters, for instance, or by letting something slip).[11]

Being labeled as a "sex offender" is powerfully expressive and semantically imprecise. Sexual morality in the Global North is in flux. Attitudes to and practices of sex have undergone huge changes over the past two centuries, particularly since the 1960s, but lingering ideas of impurity and sin are still associated with sex. Sexual autonomy is increasingly valued, with the result that many previously deviant acts—notably sex outside marriage and same-sex encounters—have moved into the mainstream while others have been criminalized. Whereas once only a narrow range of acts which broke well-established patriarchal rules were recognized as sexual violence (and even then were seen primarily as a crime of property), the growing attention paid to the subjective experience of sexual relationships and the extent to which they meet ideals of consent means that growing numbers of acts now fall into that category (Boutellier 2019). Despite the fluidity of the rules governing sexual practices, many people still believe how we have sex is indicative of our sexuality, and that sexuality is fixed and determines our identity. This belief, which developed in the eighteenth and nineteenth centuries, led to the establishment of new sexual categories like the heterosexual and the homosexual (Foucault 1998), but also the pedophile, the rapist, and the sex offender.[12] Once one has been placed in these categories, one is assumed to be inherently devious and permanently dangerous (McAlinden 2007a), despite evidence suggesting that only 20 percent of people convicted of sex offenses are reconvicted of sex offenses in the following twenty years (Lussier and Healey 2009), and despite the fact that people can be placed in these categories for very different acts.[13]

Being stained as a "sex offender" may not have sent a very clear message about what prisoners had done, but it had a clear and material effect on their lives and those of their families. The hyperpresence of their stained identities, and the fact that their convictions haunted the wings with such persistence, resulted from the decision of prison authorities in England and Wales to hold men convicted of sex offenses separately from other prisoners—whether in separate prisons like Stafford, or in VPUs within "mainstream" prisons. This decision reinforced the widespread belief among those who live and work in prisons that "sex offenders" are an essentialized category of person (de Vel-Palumbo, Howarth, and Brewer 2019) which is not only distinct from the "law-abiding majority" but also from other people convicted of breaking the law.[14] It also made prisoners deeply conscious of, and profoundly vulnerable to, the stains of the men they lived among, a subject which shall be discussed in more detail in chapter 7.

Social pressure and state policies also meant that prisoners' stain seeped onto their families and friends.[15] Many prisoners said that their families had experienced some of the social effects of being stained, suffering "dirty looks" (Kieran) or cruel comments from people in their communities. Others more abstractly considered themselves to be a corrupting influence on their families. Shezad said that he hated visits from his brother and sister, as he feared that seeing him depressed them:

> I know I like to see them and all that, see them happy, and especially my sister was very upset and all that, but how do I see myself now? If I'm even released, I'm still tagged as a very horrible individual and I'm just bringing them down rather than anything else. To me, they're doing this, they could be with their kids, they could be having fun, what's the point in coming to see me? I'm in here, I'm not going anywhere.

More concretely, Shezad was highly conscious that contact with his family exposed them to the tentacles of state regulation. Like other men who were convicted of offenses against children or who were deemed to pose a risk to children, he had been forbidden to have contact with his young daughter when he was imprisoned until the risks had been assessed by the prison, children's services, and probation. He said that facing these assessments had been too much for his wife and had contributed to their decision to divorce, a decision which he accepted as he said it would allow his daughter to have a life free from his corrupting reputation: "For her to have a normal life, I have to sacrifice being a father." Other men were less willing to end their relationships. Phil had been waiting for thirteen months to be assessed for contact with his young son. In the meantime, he was not even allowed to speak to him on the phone: "But when me and the wife are speaking on the phone, I can often hear him in the background saying, 'I love you Daddy, I miss you Daddy,' and the wife often turns around and says, 'Daddy loves you too' but I'm not allowed to say it because that's contact."

Prisoners feared that their stain would mark their future as well as their present, and here their stain was once more shaped by the interaction between legal

and social processes.[16] David Garland argues that the punishment of people convicted of sex offenses, particularly child sex offenses, relies on "a criminology of
the other" (2001, 136), which he describes as "a politicised discourse of the collective unconscious" which "trades in images, archetypes, and anxieties" (135) of
a deviant pedophile who threatens the most innocent and vulnerable among us.
What is so frightening about the pedophile is his invisibility—his ability to hide
in plain sight—and so once his actions have revealed his inherent deviousness,
the state must render this deviousness visible through criminalization, stigmatization, and registration. This instinct lies at the core of modern thinking about risk:
if we can only gather and systematize enough knowledge about a problem, then
maybe it won't hurt us. When risk thinking meets a moral framework which views
those who commit sexual violence as monstrous objects of disgust, it results in a
"punitive panopticism" (Wacquant 2009, 225) which shames people as it super-
vises them. The result is the growth of a state regulatory apparatus which in England and Wales includes mass imprisonment, tight and restrictive license conditions, and placement on the Sex Offenders' Register, all strategies which work to
emphasize and reify the moral difference between people convicted of sex offenses
and the rest of society. In so doing, the state enhances its own legitimacy by claiming the ability to soothe the fears it has helped to create.[17]

Prisoners in Stafford feared that they would be marked by their offenses forever: they would be permanently googleable, and therefore no one would ever
give them a job or start a romantic relationship with them. They were also highly
conscious that they would be restricted by tight license conditions, the breach of
which could lead to recall to custody; these conditions would be determined by
their restrictions and assessed level of risk, and may well include bans on contact
with children, the requirement to disclose convictions to new romantic partners,
or an inability to access the internet. They also knew that they would be required
to sign the Sex Offender's Register soon after their release, in some cases for life.[18]
Although they rarely knew the details of the restrictions to which they would be
subjected, rumors about likely restrictions were widespread, and prisoners pan-
icked about what they might mean for their futures and for their social identities.
Two areas of particular concern were the Register, which, while not publicly available in England and Wales, was considered deeply stigmatizing, and the impact of
the conviction on new romantic relationships. Michael, an elderly man serving a
sentence which he strongly contested, admitted that he didn't know "very much
about the practical elements" of being released on license, but he was "very both-
ered" by it and by the Register: "It's the same stigma that's attached to you forever
and a day." George, on the other hand, was optimistic about many areas of his
future, but not about his romantic prospects:

> If I ever do meet somebody, and you know you have an instant click with somebody
> or something, if they've got children, I know I can't do that, because obviously being
> convicted of a sex offense, you've got social services getting involved [. . .], and I

don't want to put that on someone I've just met! So if I click with you and then I find out you've got two children, I've got to then leave it and walk away! So for the rest of my life, I'm gonna be wary of who I meet. So what type of life can I have?

Prisoners rarely thought that it was wrong, in principle, for the state to involve itself in the intimate details of people's lives if doing so would help keep potential victims safe. They did not object to the punitive panopticon in principle. What they resented was the state intervening in *their* lives, because while other people might pose a risk, they rarely believed that *they* did. George put this clearly: "I understand that you've got security and that of the public and all that, but you've got to remember that people do change and are trying to start their lives again, but they always have the perception that you're doing something wrong, constantly." Future restrictions were painful because of what they symbolized about who you were, and about the future you would be able to build, and prisoners in Stafford believed that the state would work in conjunction with processes of social exclusion to subject them to a permanent stain.

That said, while the stain of prisoners' convictions was projected into the future, it rarely sank beneath the skin. Prisoners talked at length about how the label had affected their relationships in prison and might continue to affect them after their release, but very few had absorbed the term or identified with the category (see also Tewksbury 2012), and the force of their expressions of disgust indicated their unwillingness to be a "sex offender." This unwillingness resulted from three qualities of the staining label: its arbitrariness, its generalizing nature, and its disproportionality. First, prisoners were not labeled "sex offenders" as a direct and immediate result of their own actions, but because a complex and, they argued, unreliable legal process had produced a particular type of conviction. This process provided enough distance between their actions (if they were guilty) and the conviction for the "sex offender" identity to be similarly placed at a distance. The few who accepted the "sex offender" identity only did so because they saw it as a legal artefact. Harry admitted to being a "sex offender," but only in the most technical sense:

How do you feel about being described as a sex offender?
I'm a sex offender.
You accept it?
Yeah. It's what I am.
Does it bother you?
No. It depends how you're looking at that word "sex offender." Some people look at it as "sex offender" is "nonce" [person convicted of offenses against children]. If you ask someone, "What does a 'sex offender' mean to you?" "He's a nonce." But if you ask someone in this prison, they'll just say, "I committed an offense under the Sexual Offences Act." So I am a sex offender, same as a burglar, same as a murderer.

Many men repeatedly insisted that they did not deserve the label as they were not guilty, or because, despite being in Stafford, they had not been convicted of a sex offense (these claims were often misleading, as shall be discussed in chapter 4).

As the metaphor implies, the label was simply something that had been applied to them externally and which did not speak to who they knew themselves truly to be.

Second, many prisoners sought to escape the expansive implications of the "sex offender" label by distinguishing themselves from others bearing the same stain. In some cases, prisoners did this based on their appearances. Tony said that it was painful to be placed in the same category as people he described as "noncey-looking": "You see someone who's really weird to look at and you just think, 'On paper I'm the same as that' and you just think, 'Fuck.' You know, 'In the eyes of the world that could be me and I could be that, and we're interchangeable.'" Nevertheless, he was conscious that, as a young, well-groomed, and confident person who did not resemble a stereotypical "sex offender," he had been treated differently throughout his sentence. He told one story about walking with another prisoner past a group of men when Stafford had still held "mainstream" prisoners, and avoiding the abuse which had been directed at his companion:

> There was me and just one old guy who looked the part, the cartoon super nonce, and the wing we walked past was mains then, and as we walked past . . . I had quite a nice gray coat on, and he had a shitty red T-shirt, and we both walked past a gang of mains and as we got about five meters from them, all the mains shouted, "You in the red T-shirt! You fucking nonce!" like that, and I remember laughing, thinking, "Am I alright? Am I okay? I'm clearly going to the same wing he is, am I not? This coat must be alright then. I must have done my hair alright today." But I was okay because I could have easily been someone you'd have been having a beer with.

In other cases, prisoners' attempts to distinguish themselves from the mass of "sex offenders" were more directly based on the differences between offenses. There was a clear moral hierarchy in the prison, and prisoners (and staff) thought that offenses which were committed against children were worse than those committed against adults, and those committed against strangers were worse than those committed against girlfriends or wives. As Vince outlined, prisoners drew on these distinctions to highlight that they themselves were not really a "sex offender," or at least that other people were worse:

> People have different levels of what a sex offender is and whether it's to make them feel better or less worse about what they've done, but there's like a scale, a sliding scale, and obviously people who offend against children, that's, like, the bottom. That's the worst. Whereas somebody who has just, like, raped his wife, that ain't too bad.

Similarly, Ian suggested that the breadth of the "sex offender" category increased its staining power as it carried connotations of monstrosity. But the generalizing nature of the label was also the source of its denunciatory weakness:

> People do paint us all with the same brush. We're all said that we're all monsters, people think that because we're sex offenders, we're all balaclava'd up with a knife in a bush, that's what they think that we are, which is far from the case. It's never like

that. It's really wrong of people to think that. I had a different perspective before I came to prison. I thought, sex offenders and pedophiles, I had a really bad thing with them, you don't want to associate yourself with them, but since I've come here and I've looked around and like, fair enough, there are some people here who should be here, but [there are] some people that shouldn't be here, and you think, they've been given the short straw.

Shouldn't be here because of what they've done, or because of the type of person they are?

Shouldn't be here because the system's done them wrong. Certain prisoners that shouldn't be here because the system is just . . . Basically because somebody did a crime, or did so many crimes, [that person being] Jimmy Savile, that now everybody gets consequences for it.[19] For any little tiny bit of whatever they'd send them to prison. Even people that haven't done it are getting falsely accused and they've been sent to prison for it.

Rather than focusing prisoners' attention on what they had done, or making them realize through comparison that their offenses were as bad as those committed by other people, the breadth of the label instead pushed prisoners to focus on what they had not done and therefore who they were not.

Third, and as the quotation from Ian indicates, prisoners often thought that the scale of the punishment and the connotations of the stain were disproportionate to the severity of the offense. It is a central tenet of communicative and retributive justifications of punishment that the sanction should balance the crime in order to stop punished people from being distracted from their guilt by their suffering. Prisoners in Stafford, however, felt that the staining label added an additional quantum of punishment, and it pushed them to experience themselves as victims of the state (Tewksbury 2012). They were highly conscious of the effect that their stained identities would have on their futures, and as Frank described, they considered this unending punishment to be excessive:

It's like relationships and everything. As far as I'm concerned, I made a mistake. One mistake. If it had been repetitive and always happened or whatever, I could understand the severity of what they're trying to do. But no. It's like I've said before, you've got different types of people in here and they all require different needs. Some people haven't got a chance, as in they can't look after themselves, they've not got anything about them as such, and you've got other people that—like myself, if you like—made the mistake, and if I could change it all, but I can't, so I've got to live with it. But I don't see that you have to be penalized for the rest of your life for that one mistake.

Similarly, Keith thought that the staining label was unjust:

I did sex offend and I've never denied it and I fully accept responsibility and all that comes with it, but I'm no longer a sex offender. But I am in the eyes of society and I always will be. So I think "sex offender" is a bit unfair but there's not much you can do about it really.

Taken together, it is clear that the stain which affixed itself to Stafford and to its prisoners may have drawn attention to the nature of prisoners' convictions, but this attention did not necessarily contribute to, and arguably hindered, meaningful reflections about the offense. Imprisonment in Stafford was simply too staining, and prisoners did anything they could to escape.

THE REHABILITATIVE REGIME

> When I got in here, with probation, I said, "Look, I'm innocent, I am innocent," and she said, "I go by what the courts say," and I've had to accept that. (Phil)[20]

The trial system combined with the stain of the "sex offender" label to promote a binary and oppositional way of thinking about offense stories—either you were guilty or you were innocent, either your victim was lying or you were a bad person—but a few prisoners said that there was more room for nuanced and complex stories of responsibility and moral identity once they entered the prison. Ahmed's story of moral education illustrated this, as did Zac's insistence that his probation officer helped him make sense of his conviction: "She looked out for me and tried to make sense of both sides." These experiences gesture toward the possibility of more destaining spaces existing in prisons, in ways which mirror the recommendations of some moral communication theorists. Antony Duff (2001), a penal theorist who holds out hope for punishment's morally communicative capacities, has proposed that it is in relationships with staff members like probation officers that the moral message can be refined. Certainly, people in prison have the opportunity to develop relationships with staff members which allow more information to be shared than is possible in the context of a trial, potentially enabling them to tell stories about themselves and their pasts which are both more satisfying and (perhaps) more reflective of the truth than those which led to their imprisonment. The closeness of these relationships could—again in theory—allow prison officers, psychologists, program facilitators, and probation officers to communicate more effectively and productively with prisoners than CPS lawyers or judges were able to, perhaps persuading them to think differently about their offending, or enabling them to discuss what they had done or process feelings of shame and guilt. The practice in Stafford was far from this ideal, however. These relationships were formed in a context which had already been distorted by the legal system and stained by the "sex offender" label. The moral division of labor described in chapter 2 meant that prison officers did not consider discussions about the offense to be their responsibility, and the specialist staff who did discuss offending with prisoners did so in a way which was driven by its own disfiguring rehabilitative logics. As a result, how prisoners thought and talked about their offenses became a direct target of penal power, twisting their reflections into a site of either compliance, resistance, or friction (Rubin 2015).

Modern penality is often described as managerialist and bureaucratic rather than moralistic or reformative, as preoccupied by meeting targets and delivering services rather than by responding to moral wrongs or curing psychological and social ills. Malcolm Feeley and Jonathan Simon (1992) argued that the Global North has seen the emergence of a morally neutral "new penology" in which the justice system no longer seeks to punish or cure bad or broken individuals, and instead focuses on managing actuarially defined "dangerous" categories of people.[21] The discourse of danger was certainly powerful in Stafford, and risk judgments had a large influence on life there. In theory, the allocation of rehabilitative treatment and prisoners' living conditions in prison and postrelease were determined by the outputs of structured risk assessments, all of which were nominally based on scientific knowledge.[22] Prisoners' conditions in prison, and in some cases their chances of release, were linked to whether they were seen to be working to reduce this level of risk.[23] As a result, they were strongly incentivized to engage in what Jason Warr has called "narrative labour": to share the prison's interpretation of them as dangerous and fit into the mold of change it provided them by casting "themselves as the penitent" (2020, 36), and thus lower their risk level.

In theory, the rehabilitative regime in Stafford, like in other English and Welsh prisons, was oriented to manage future dangerousness rather than to redress past wrongdoing.[24] In practice, the two are hard to disentangle. First, prisoners' convictions have been found to be statistically correlated to their future reoffending, and convictions were therefore one of the inputs into risk assessments. Second, and more importantly to our purposes, the stories which prisoners told about their offenses, and the extent to which they accepted guilt, shaped the way risk was assessed and treatment was distributed. This practice was propelled by the belief that taking full responsibility for past offending would help prevent future occurrences. Despite the lack of evidence that excuses or denial cause criminal or sexually deviant behavior, much offender treatment in the past thirty years has sought to correct the "cognitive distortions" which these excuses and justifications allegedly represent and to persuade prisoners to come out of "denial" and to accept their guilt (Maruna and Copes 2005; Maruna and Mann 2006). Much of the work which took place in the Sex Offender Treatment Programme (SOTP), the main offending-behavior program available in Stafford at the time of the fieldwork, centered on identifying and correcting such distortions. These programs took place in groups of about ten or twelve prisoners. For the first half of the course, participants took it in turn to discuss their offending, while others in the group corrected any excuses or justifications. In the second half, prisoners drew up a list of their potential triggers and risk factors and developed relapse prevention plans to stop them from slipping into their old ways. Given the centrality of the offense to the content of the program, only people who accepted at least some guilt for their offense were able to participate in the SOTP.

The rehabilitative regime in Stafford thus sought to educate prisoners not just that they had done wrong, but that they were fully and autonomously responsible for their offenses. Their main tool was material incentivization.[25] Some of this incentivization worked through the Incentives and Earned Privileges (IEP) scheme. The IEP scheme is intended to promote good behavior by assigning each prisoner a status—basic, standard, or enhanced—depending on their levels of compliance. Having a higher status should result in improved material conditions, such as the capacity to earn more money or to arrange more social visits. In 2014, controversial changes to the IEP scheme limited the discretion granted to different prisons, and among other things, meant that only people who were meeting the demands of their sentence plans and giving something back to the prison (by serving as a mentor or a wing representative, for instance) could achieve the highest status. People who maintained that they were innocent, and who were thus unable to complete treatment programs and meet the terms of their sentence plans, were no longer able to access the associated material rewards. However, the IEP scheme was not the only form of inducement available. If prisoners were considered not to be addressing their offending behavior, they might be unable to get the "highest trust" jobs in the prison, and I interviewed two men who had lost their jobs because of maintaining innocence.[26] Completing the required treatment programs and thereby reducing your risk level was also widely believed to be necessary for prisoners on indeterminate sentences (at least 9 percent of Stafford's population)[27] to be granted parole, and to keep postrelease license conditions as loose as possible.[28] Prisoners therefore faced a strong incentive to participate in treatment and to say that they were guilty, irrespective of whether they believed it.[29]

It is common for prisons to try to shape how people behave, but by seeking to regulate how prisoners talked about their offenses, Stafford strove to expand its zone of influence. Some men, like Tony, ceded the territory to the prison. Having pleaded guilty for pragmatic reasons during his trial, he said that his hardheadedness continued to drive him in the prison, and he told members of prison staff that he admitted guilt so as not to risk losing his enhanced status or his highly trusted job:

> It was a hard decision and it's really hard on a day-to-day basis, "Yes I'm guilty, no I'm not maintaining innocence." I don't need you to believe me, I don't need anyone to believe me, because I know what's happened. But no, I'm not officially maintaining innocence.
> *But you kind of are, you're not in the technical way but you are kind of internally, morally?*
> To friends, to family, yeah. To you, because this can't affect the outcomes. But if I were to admit that I was maintaining innocence in here, my status would change dramatically.

Others more actively resisted the prison's attempts to interpret and intervene in their public statements about their convictions. James steadfastly maintained that he was innocent even though his relationship with his probation officer had become extremely hostile as a result:

> I've got a probation manager who's a bit of a—pardon my language—but dickhead. I do not like the bloke. He's above himself [. . .]. He thinks he knows better than everybody else, he thinks he knows about the facts of life and in fact he knows bugger all. I just don't like working with him. He says I'm "in denial." Hang on a minute, I'm far from in denial, mate! I'm innocent! I know I am because nothing on my body, not one part of my body, touched that lass and I told him that and he doesn't like it because I won't conform to what he wants.

This battle between prisoners and prison staff was sometimes complicated by the legacy of the trial and the official narrative which it had produced.[30] Vince had pleaded guilty to robbing and raping an acquaintance while he was drunk. In his sentencing hearing, the CPS lawyer had said that he had planned the offense and deliberately got drunk to help him build up courage, and the risk assessments which had been written by his probation officer all repeated this interpretation. Vince said that he disagreed with this version of the story but had been reluctant to challenge this narrative in court, where the victim was present.[31] He insisted in our interview that the attack had been an extremely poor decision that he had made impulsively, and said that he had frequent arguments with his probation officer as a result:

> It's like, pseudo psychology. Do people do that? Like, "Oh, I need to get brave now to go rape." It's absolute bullshit. And that is the stuff they're coming up with and how can you argue with them sort of arguments when they don't make sense? And what you're saying is, "It was spur of the moment, didn't really listen to what, you know, my victim, I was thinking of my own needs, [. . .] didn't have any inhibitions because of the drink, sort of thing." I dunno, maybe it's catch-22. Whatever you do, you always come out wrong because either you're minimizing it, "This just happened," or . . . It's like they're just waiting for you to fuck up. Every time you speak, it's like they're waiting for you to say the wrong word. And she puts in the wrong stuff, she never puts in like, "Fair play, he really recognizes, like, what he's done." She never puts none of that in there.

Men like Vince and James critiqued the ability and right of their probation officers, and by extension the prison, to claim interpretive power over their stories. Both men mocked the psychological knowledge which their probation officers claimed and insisted that truth was on their side. Even Tony only allowed penal power to shape what he said to officials about his offense, and it didn't stop him from asserting his innocence to his friends and family (and to me). In all these cases, the prison was only able to mold what people said publicly, and its system of incentivization struggled to operate on the private sphere.

The fact that offense discussions were at the core of the prison's rehabilitative strategy discouraged many men in Stafford from participating in the limited amount of treatment that was available. Less than a quarter of the men I interviewed had participated in either a SOTP or a Thinking Skills Programme (a treatment program which was not specific to sexual offenses, and which was available to people who maintained innocence). Ethnographic research of treatment courses for sexual offending has argued that, by asking people to repeatedly tell their offense narratives and by pushing them to develop "relapse prevention" plans, such courses construct men convicted of sex offenses into "sex offenders," people defined by and autonomously responsible for their crimes who must constantly work to stop themselves from slipping into their old transgressive ways (Fox 1999; K. Hudson 2005; Lacombe 2008; Waldram 2012). But irrespective of the content of the courses, prisoners in Stafford said that even participating in them was stigmatizing. It was only possible to take part if you admitted guilt, and prisoners described treatment programs as only necessary if there was something wrong with you. James continued to resist his probation officer's attempt to persuade him to consider taking part in the SOTP: "If I had to do that program, that would mean that I would be admitting to something that I haven't done, and I see that as a fruitless exercise anyway, when I don't think like a person that is a sex offender." Tony was relieved that he had been assessed as posing too low a risk of reoffending for him to be suitable for courses: "I didn't feel I need any treatment. I don't feel I need anyone to help me to think."

This was not the only reason Tony didn't want to participate in the SOTP. Like many other men, he said he simply did not want to spend extended periods of time discussing offenses with other prisoners.[32] To do so would potentially be extremely upsetting and could make social life on the wing harder as he would have to face people knowing what they had done. Worse, he feared that he might somehow be corrupted through this knowledge, and this belief had been reinforced by what he had been told by a programs worker:

> In reality, I didn't want to do them. I've got no will to sit in a room with people who aren't friends listening to things that have happened to them throughout their lives and things that they've done potentially to children. I don't want to hear about it in a direct sense. I don't want to face that person all the time. I don't wanna know! Not for me to judge, but I don't want to sit there and listen to that, and the programs [worker] came to see me when they told me I was too low risk, and they told me, "If you did it, not that you can, but if you did, it would potentially just fuck you up."
>
> *Did they say that?*
>
> That is a quote. That is an exact quote. Not I've changed it a bit, that is exactly what they said. "Potentially sitting in a room with those people could just fuck you up." Great. I don't believe I need any help with anything. I'd rather be left alone to be fair. I would have done it if I had to.

By centering much of its rehabilitative work around the offense, Stafford, like other prisons in England and Wales, not only incentivized conscious dishonesty and ensured people who steadfastly maintained innocence were unable to participate in treatment courses, it also heightened the discomfort which prisoners already felt about living among people convicted of sex offenses. The environment was already stained, and programs both added and drew attention to this stain.

There is, however, a coda to this story. A couple of years after I completed fieldwork in Stafford, a large-scale evaluation of the SOTP was published which found that not only did it fail to reduce reoffending, but that those who completed the SOTP were slightly more likely to reoffend than those who did not (Mews, Di Bella, and Purver 2017).[33] The report suggested several possible reasons for this increase, including that discussing offenses in a group may, counterproductively, make offenses seem "normal" or even allow treatment participants to share information about offending (how to access websites displaying illegal images, for instance). These possible explanations—none of which have been empirically tested and which are therefore merely hypotheses—nevertheless echoed many of the critiques made by prisoners in Stafford and indicated that part of the problem with the program design was that offenses and offense narratives were so central to it. As a result of the publication of this report, the SOTP was replaced by new treatment programs which do not require prisoners to discuss their offenses and which people who maintain that they are innocent can attend. The effect which these changes will have on the rehabilitative regime remains to be seen.

CONCLUSION: DISTRACTIONS AND DISTORTIONS

Early advocates of the penitentiary hoped that isolation would reform prisoners by leaving them with nothing to do but talk to God and delve into their consciences. Modern prisons, however, provide numerous means of and motives for distraction. Prisoners in Stafford had been funneled through a seemingly arbitrary legal system, stained by their resulting social identity, and now faced multiple obstacles which had been placed by the bureaucratizing rehabilitative regime. They had been subjected to a form of moral communication which produced a deeply painful and damaging form of shame, and which fashioned stories which were difficult to read. This lack of clarity created difficulties for prison staff and prisoners who were forced to interact with people whose stories and histories confused them and about whom they struggled to make judgments.

Facing a permanent threat to their position in the moral community, provided with the alibi of an unjust legal system, and offered rehabilitative opportunities which encouraged them to follow certain narrative scripts, it is unsurprising that many men in Stafford avoided attending to their consciences. While many faced their feelings of guilt and sought to transform themselves, others sought relief in denial and excuse-making, and some may have been justified in their insistence that they were not guilty. In fact, so confusing was the environment that it was impossible—for prisoners, prison officers, and researchers—to disentangle who was telling the truth about their innocence and who was denying as a way of rejecting shame. Like a smudged manuscript, the institution was stained in a way which made it difficult to decipher. Nevertheless, in the following two chapters, I will delineate how these different men made sense of their convictions and did their time in the tangled web of motivations and opportunities provided by the prison. The next chapter focuses on what the prison communicated to those who, on the whole, thought they were guilty, and the subsequent one focuses on those who more straightforwardly insisted that they were innocent.

4

Managing Guilt

Living as a "Sex Offender" in Prison

Being imprisoned for a sex offense is akin to being asked the questions "Who are you, and how are you going to live your life now?" Two years after completing fieldwork in Stafford, and while carrying out research for another project in another English category C prison for men convicted of sex offenses, I met and interviewed Emmett, a man who had answered these questions early in his sentence.[1] He had been arrested seven years earlier, just days after his youngest daughter had been born, and had been charged with two sexual offenses. He said that while he was held in prison awaiting his trial, he had decided to kill himself rather than "be remembered as being a sex offender":

> At that point, I can't even begin to describe to you, Alice, I hated myself. I detested myself. I truly, truly hated myself. And because of that I didn't want to be . . . I'm going to be honest with you, death was probably easier, because I didn't want to be here anymore. I wanted it gone. I wanted the hatred and self-loathing I had for myself, and the guilt and shame I felt for what I'd done, and put people through, and people that I loved through, now, I wanted it to stop. I wanted it to end. And I didn't see a way out.

Emmett was not alone when he contemplated dying by suicide. Home Office analysis of England and Wales data indicates that people arrested for sex offenses are twelve times more likely to kill themselves than people arrested for other crimes (Lindon and Roe 2017), and a recent meta-analysis and systematic review of international studies shows that people in prison for sex offenses are also at an elevated risk of suicide relative to other prisoners (Zhong et al. 2021).

Emmett said that he stopped eating for four weeks to weaken his body and increase the chances that a suicide attempt would be successful. Fearing what he might do, his family came to visit him:

We had a chat, and basically they read me the riot act [reprimanded me] and told me how selfish I was being. And going through some home truths really, that the children had a right to know and, you know, in ten years' time, the children had a right to be able to ask me why [I'd committed the offenses]. And even if they turned away from me, I've got to give them that opportunity. And also for everyone else, as well. For my family, and I guess for some of the victims. Because I felt that [my death was] what the victims and their families would want. But then people were saying, "Well actually, no, it may not be what they want."

After a night of reflection, he decided to stay alive and dedicate his life to making amends. His first step was to confess to all the crimes he had committed. He was initially arrested for two offenses against two victims and had been told by his lawyer that he was facing a two-year determinate sentence. He now confessed to dozens of other offenses against dozens of other victims, many of which had not been reported to the police, and was eventually given a life sentence with a minimum tariff of eleven years.[2] His attempts to cleanse himself ran into some difficulties, however. One victim, when interviewed by the police prior to the trial, accused him of an act for which he claimed innocence. In the end, Emmett pleaded not guilty to that charge, maintaining that "you can't tell a truth halfway," but he feared that continuing to maintain innocence on this charge would cause him problems when he applied for parole.

The next step was the pursuit of self-understanding and change, which he said he achieved through "a lot of self-reflection, honesty sessions with myself, my partner at the time, with my sister, with my mother, with my father and my brother, and exploring things, exploring why, why did things go wrong for me." He also participated wholeheartedly in treatment programs, believing that he deserved to be subjected to them. When I asked him if he was troubled by the fact that participating in such courses implied that he had a problematic sexuality, he was taken aback:

Who, me? Oh, you're joking, aren't you? What, with what I'm here for?
Yeah, but—
And what my past is?
Yeah, but—
No! Are you crazy?

Nevertheless, he described such programs as a secondary resource, providing him with an "affirmation" that he had changed and giving him psychological language with which he could describe himself and his thoughts.

By seeing his sentence as a chance to make amends, Emmett found a way of coping with his imprisonment which also helped him live with his guilt and his stained identity. I asked him during the interview if, seven years into his sentence, he still hated himself:

No. No I don't. I haven't for a little while. I don't like what I did. I hate what I did, and I hate the pain I've caused. But I guess to a degree I've compartmentalized it. I still have blips, do you know what I mean? I still have blips, because you know, you look at where you are, I look at the fact that I was proud of my work. I was a proud father. [pause] But, I look at where I am now, and I think, I feel happy I've done everything I can to put that part of my life behind me. I feel I've done everything I can to make good on the bad that I've done and make amends. I often check with my Offender Supervisor, or probation, and say, "Look, is there anything more I can do?"[3] I can't change, I can't erase the past, and I would love to. I would happily give my life now if I could erase that past, happily. I'd do anything to erase that past. But I can't. And so I've got to accept it, accept that I don't like it, accept that I don't like my actions, I don't like what happened there, but I've done all I can to try and understand it, and prevent it happening again in future, and try to live my life well now, and I hope, when I get released, I have the opportunity to be a good person, and again, try and make amends for things that I feel I've done.

He imagined his sentence just as many moral communication theorists would: as a penitential ritual (Duff 2001) which would help him process the guilt he rightly felt, and thereby become a better person. In the concrete form which it actually took, however, this ritual was more complex than he imagined it being, and his story thus offers one illustration of what happens when an ideal of punishment comes into contact with sociological reality. First, his ritual failed to live up to its purifying promise because of differing accounts of precisely what he had done. Second, the prison didn't recognize the penance he had engaged in. Despite his attempts to align his journey of personal change with that prescribed by the prison, the prison prioritized its own institutional functioning over acknowledging the ways he was changing. As just one illustration, our interview was interrupted by Emmett's Offender Supervisor arriving to tell him that his pretariff parole hearing—a hearing which might enable him to be moved to open conditions for the last few years of his sentence—had been postponed for administrative reasons, to which he responded with equanimity.

Being arrested, convicted, and imprisoned for a sex offense imposes an inevitable break in people's identities and often shatters their personal relationships (Kotova 2016). It exposes them to a staining label, which through both shame and legal restrictions changes their social and civic identity. Faced with this reality, many people consider suicide. When people survive, they have two options. The first is to reject the "sex offender" identity and resist some of its social implications by claiming innocence. The second is to find a way of living as a "sex offender" within the conditions imposed by imprisonment. Prison sociology has a vibrant tradition of producing typologies describing how people adapt to these conditions.[4] This literature delineates the many ways in which prisoners can orient themselves to penal power—through withdrawal, rebellion, conformity, and innovation (Crewe 2009, 149–53). However, prison sociologists' lack of interest in imprisonment's morally communicative dimensions means that these typologies have rarely considered how prisoners' feelings of shame and guilt and their attitudes toward their convictions shape their orientations toward their sentences. In Stafford, however, there was a clear relationship between prisoners' orientations to penal power and what they thought about what they had been convicted of—or more simply, between how prisoners "did their time" and how they felt about what they were doing time for. Men who, like Emmett, felt extremely guilty about their offenses, treated their sentence as an opportunity for repentance and transformation, and often embraced the institution which they felt gave them this opportunity. Those who insisted that they had been wrongly convicted saw their sentence as fundamentally unjust, and either existed in a constant state of conflict with penal authorities or resigned themselves to their situation when they became too exhausted. And the many who existed somewhere in the middle—who acknowledged some level of legal guilt but did not experience the painful sentiments of moral guilt—regarded their sentence as an unfortunate reality which must be borne and tried to manage their imprisonment in a way which exposed them to as little pain as possible.

In this chapter and the next, I present a typology of prisoners' patterns of adaptation to their convictions and their sentences.[5] In this chapter, I will focus on the men who thought they were guilty—although there was significant variation in how guilty they felt, and what difference this made—and in the next, I will focus on those who maintained that they were innocent. Together, these chapters argue that how prisoners "did their time" demonstrates how they reacted to the moral condemnation which was implicit in their conviction, sentence, and imprisonment: some made the condemnation their own, some challenged it, and some managed it. All, however, rubbed up against the kinks of power as it existed in Stafford, and even those who felt the most profound regret, and who therefore welcomed their punishment with the most fervor, were sometimes thrown off course by the framing of the moral conversation.

Before we start, however, it is worth acknowledging that typologies are an imperfect tool. They are inherently blunt and imprecise, and often imply that there are fixed differences between forms of adaptation, or, worse, types of people. My goal in presenting one is not to elide difference, nor to suggest that this typology is the final story, or even that it would be found in the same form in different institutions.[6] Instead, I use it to demonstrate that there was a patterned relationship between how prisoners heard their condemnation and how they served their sentence, and to give a rough indication of what this pattern was in Stafford.

This typology emerged inductively from the data, and the groups are primarily distinguished by eight different factors: prisoners' orientation toward their sentence; the type of offense for which they were convicted; the way they thought about the legitimacy of their conviction; their attitude to their victim; the type of shame they expressed; their attitude to the condemnatory "sex offender" label; the extent of and the reasons for their compliance; and their general orientation

TABLE 1 Prisoners' adaptations to their convictions and imprisonment

	The repentant	The redeemed	Fatalists	Negotiators	"Mainstream" prisoners	The resigned	Activists
Orientation to sentence	Opportunity for change and amends	Opportunity for self-imposed change and amends	An experience to be endured	An experience to be managed	An experience to be managed	An injustice to be accepted	An injustice to be resisted
Type of conviction	Contact offenses against known children	Contact offenses	Noncontact offenses against children	Varied, often rape of adults	Nonsexual	Historic offenses, often against children	Rape of adults
Attitude to legitimacy of conviction	Totally deserved	Totally deserved	Technically guilty and morally undesirable	Technically guilty but morally irrelevant	Accepted guilt, but not for sex offenses	Totally undeserved	Totally undeserved
Attitude to victim	Mostly repentant	Mostly repentant	Seen as abstract	Indifferent	Absent	Angry	Angry
Type of shame/guilt	Guilt and self-disgust about offense	Guilt and self-disgust about offense	Lack of guilt, fear of abuse because of "sex offender" identity	Ashamed of "sex offender" identity	Ashamed of proximity to "sex offenders"	Ashamed of "sex offender" identity	Ashamed of "sex offender" identity
Attitude to "sex offender" label	Deserved but limiting	Deserved but limiting	Technically accurate	Inaccurate	Irrelevant, didn't apply	Unjust, to be ignored	Unjust, to be challenged
Extent of and reasons for compliance	Normatively motivated engagement	Prioritized personal moral instincts	Compliant due to fear and dull compulsion	Instrumental compliance, with negotiations	Instrumental compliance, with negotiations	Instinctively compliant but challenged rehabilitative regime	Instinctively resistant
Orientation to power	Performative regulation	Cynical, knowing	Submissive, perceive power as total	To be oriented within	To be oriented within	To be accepted, where possible with integrity	To be challenged

toward power in the prison. The description of each group opens with the story of one man, as a way of trying to emphasize the real humans whom I do not want to obscure with schematic descriptions. In the ensuing description of the type, I name every man who fell into that group, so that this classification can be carried forward and shape how readers respond to the rest of the book.[7] In most cases, it was easy to spot patterns in interview participants' strategies, but a few men were harder to place. Exceptions to the patterns have been discussed where appropriate, and at the end of each chapter I will discuss what can be learned from the men who showed signs of shifting between groups about the effects of penal power and the capacity of prisons to shape the behavior and attitudes of the men they hold.

THE REPENTANT

The repentant, who made up a sixth of the men I interviewed, corresponded to the ideal wrongdoers imagined by many moral communication theorists, and they described punishment working on them in a way which echoed this theoretical ideal of punishment.[8] They felt extreme guilt and shame for their offenses, and saw their sentences as both a deserved punishment and as an opportunity to transform themselves into the responsible citizens they felt themselves truly to be.[9] They had all pleaded guilty to their offenses, which tended to be serious and often penetrative contact offenses against single victims; these victims were often underage and known to them, and were in several cases their stepdaughters. Almost all *repentant prisoners* had sentences of at least ten years (at least five of which would be served in prison), and some were serving indeterminate sentences. For most *repentant prisoners*, their offenses had led to their first conviction, shattering a strongly held sense of themselves as a "good, kind, productive citizen" (Peter), a "perfectly normal person," "a really good stepfather," and a "really good husband" (Keith), and leading to serious impacts on their victims and on their families. They did not consider themselves to have persistent sexual interests in children or in violent sex, and they described their offending as growing out of personal unhappiness, poor self-management, and broken relationships, rather than out of faulty desire. They told stories which echoed the "redemption scripts" identified by Maruna (2001, 85–108): they were inherently good people who for complex reasons had done terrible things, but who were consciously and deliberately changing themselves for the better and unleashing their inner righteousness. In so doing, they allied themselves to the rehabilitative demands of the prison, redeeming themselves in ways which were generally compatible with, but not subordinate to, the demands of the institution. To them, imprisonment was a moral crusade, willingly undertaken and consciously embraced, rather than an unfortunate experience to be endured.

Jake was a classic example of this type. He was a White man in his late forties and described himself as "an OK guy that went off the rails." Despite being physically and sexually abused by his father when young, he said he had a "good upbringing." Following a short sentence for a property offense which he served as a teenager, he stabilized his life, got married, and had children. When his marriage broke down, he started to abuse his underage stepdaughter, although he said that at the time he had seen it as a relationship. When "the news got out," he handed himself into the police because he feared for his safety at the hands of his victim's family. He pleaded guilty to one charge of rape of a child aged under thirteen and four penetrative and two nonpenetrative counts of sexual assault against a child, and was given a fourteen-year sentence. At the time of the interview, he had been in prison for nearly six years, and felt that he had replaced the profound guilt and self-disgust he had felt at the beginning of his sentence with a self-reforming impulse:

> *How does your conviction make you feel about who you are?*
> That's a difficult one, because I don't feel as bad as I did when I first come in. Like originally it made me feel like I was scum. I'm the scum of the earth. Crawl back under your rock, leave society alone, sort of thing. It made me feel that I wasn't worthy of being a human being. Made me feel that I couldn't put the past behind me. I felt it was always going to haunt me, so I'd never move on. I felt like I didn't deserve to be around people, I deserved to be a loner. It just . . . I don't know. It just made me feel really bad that . . . I couldn't believe what I had done, and how far I'd took it, allowing it to happen. I felt that I was the instigator, she was the innocent party. [. . .] I didn't feel that I'd done a proper job as a father or stepdad. I'd let everybody down, basically, for my own stupid greed and it's horrible. I felt horrible. But now I don't feel as . . . I feel I've come on a long way, so it's like . . . I can't mend what I've done, I'll never be able to mend that, but I can mend myself to be a better person.

This change had occurred within the prison, and he considered the Rolling SOTP (R-SOTP), which he had completed in a previous prison, to be particularly significant in this process.[10] Nevertheless, he retained responsibility for the change, which he had achieved by making use of the resources provided by the prison:

> I feel I've come a long way in such a short space of time being in prison. So, I've embraced everything, put myself forward for this and that and the other. I've not let the prison come to me. I've gone to them, whether it's education or courses, things like that. [. . .] I just don't want to sit back and fall away into prison. I want to reach out and do things.

He felt that he had "moved on" from the shame he felt at the beginning of his sentence. He would regularly think about what he had already accomplished: "I've got my paperwork on myself [from my time on the R-SOTP], so I can just look back at that and think. It just reminds me of where I've been, what I've done, what I've got through, how much I've learned." The official paperwork both validated how far he had come and inspired him to continue the redemptive task he had set himself. He still occasionally thought about his offense, and he saw such thoughts as "a warning mechanism, so if I was to go wrong again, I'd have that in my head that, yeah, you don't have to go there, it's not right." Rather than pulling him back into the past, such thoughts encouraged him to fashion his future in a way which he thought was morally justifiable.

Repentant prisoners like Jake considered themselves to be responsible for their moral reconstruction; this correlated with the fact that their pain resulted not from the shame of criminalization but from the guilt associated with their actions. They often recounted long lists of victims—ranging from the actual victim herself to the victim's family, their own family, or even people who had read about the case in the paper—and were disgusted at themselves for the hurt they had caused. In interviews, they either referred to their victims by name or by their relationship with them ("my stepdaughter" or "my neighbor"), rather than by their abstract criminal justice label "the victim" (Ievins 2019). They also showed some acknowledgment of the potential effect which the abuse might have had on their victims' lives: William, for instance, said that he hoped that his stepdaughter was still able to become a teacher, which is what she had always wanted. In most cases, their feelings of guilt predated their formal enmeshment in the legal system, and many *repentant prisoners* described their arrest and conviction as an opportunity to rebalance the moral scales:

> Before I even got arrested, I did try and commit suicide. So that's how hard it got for me, you know, so, but to be honest with you now, I'm glad it wasn't successful because I can now see a light at the end of the tunnel. I know it's not nice in here and that but there's life after prison isn't there? [. . .] And that's where I've paid my debt so I won't feel so bad because I've paid for what I did, you know, and I'd always admitted from the word "Go" what I'd done. You know, I pleaded guilty to what I'd done and I think that's helped me to cope because I did tell the truth and I pleaded guilty, and I took the punishment on the chin. [. . .] I actually wanted to be punished. I needed to because if I didn't, I'd have killed myself by now. In fact, prison saved my life without any doubt. I'd have drunk myself to death or I'd have killed myself because of the guilt because I did feel bad about it. (Keith)

Repentant prisoners shared the widespread belief that the legal system was flawed and that its outputs were often inaccurate, but such was the magnitude of their remorse that many of them pleaded guilty to or accepted charges which they felt were technically unfair. In doing so they had many different motivations. William had hoped to protect both the victim and his daughter from having to testify, Louis could not believe the victim would lie and so that outweighed his own inability to remember the event, and Peter was reacting to members of his legal team who persuaded him that it might be unwise to accept some charges and challenge others. Despite his more pragmatic approach, he accepted the process:

> I've had time to grow as a person in here, so I can't really complain. I'll be as right as I could be by the time I get out. I've done what I can, yeah, so with me I think it's been fine. [. . .] I accept it because I'm guilty, so I've got no complaints. You get whatever you get.

Similarly, Keith accepted that he had had sexual activity with his underage stepdaughter but disagreed with, and had pleaded "not guilty" to, a charge of a penetrative sexual assault. Nevertheless, like other *repentant prisoners*, he was more preoccupied by the moral significance of what he had done than the injustice of what he had not done, describing himself as "guilty as charged. Well, not as charged, but guilty anyway."

Repentant prisoners experienced their sentence as deeply morally infused, and as their only opportunity to both honor their offense and to move on from their shame.[11] They were caught between past and future and were determined to change their lives while nevertheless feeling compelled to deliberately remember their offenses. In some cases, they engaged in ritualized processes of repentance which often mirrored those praised by early prison reformers and moral communication theorists (Tasioulas 2007):

> So you have to be on the ball, if you like, all the time, 24/7, and that's why I said to you, that's why I think every single day when I get up, the first thing I think is—I know this sounds daft—but I'm really happy because I'm glad I'm breathing, I'm alive. That's the first thing I think when I get up in the morning. The next thing I think is, coffee and a smoke. [interviewer laughs]. I'll not lie. But when I have that, I sit there sort of like I'm repenting, remorse, sort of getting the motions going and then I think through my day and what I'm going to be doing. I also think which is the best way to do it. And that way, that protects me from doing anything or saying anything I shouldn't. (William)

Similarly, Keith had "learned a lesson" about "how easy it is to become, for want of a better word, a bad person," and he required himself to be constantly "on guard" to prevent himself from sinning again. The moment at which *repentant prisoners* forgave themselves would be the moment they put themselves at risk of slipping back into their old ways. Louis put this simply: "I feel really bad for what I've done and I cannot take it back. I will make sure it haunts me for the rest of my life to make sure I never do it again."

At the same time, they were trying to build a better future and feared that remembering their offenses would trap them in the past. They were involved in an ongoing process of rebirth and self-reconstruction, one in which they felt simultaneously pulled backward by remembering what they had done and propelled forward by their campaign for change:

> *Do you think about it a lot?*
> A lot, yeah.
> *Do you think that's good, to think about it?*
> I don't think it's good, because it's overtaken my life, but I've got to think about it.
> Because it keeps me in check, you know what I mean? (John)

As such, while *repentant prisoners* believed their punishment was deserved, and that the "sex offender" label and the resultant restrictions were inevitable, they became frustrated when they felt that they had been blocked from moving on. They were certain that they would not reoffend, but this was ultimately because of them, rather than because of external restrictions. Peter, a popular but private man who was convicted of an offense against a child, said that his awareness of the restrictions which would be placed on him after his release dragged him back into the past:

> *How does your conviction make you feel about who you are? Or maybe how did it and how does it now?*
> Yeah, I mean, just terrible. Yeah. I wanted to be dead. [laughs] Which is just shame, you just feel shame. And especially now, when you've sorted yourself out, you look back and you just think, "What the hell?" Different person. But yeah, I mean I never felt good about myself anyway. It's one of them anyway. Not good. [laughs]
> *When you look back now, does it feel like . . . who was that?*
> It's a double-edged sword really. I feel proud of myself for how far I've come, but you're never gonna lose that, especially because they don't let you really. When you get out of jail you're watched so much, and being a VP, you put a little foot wrong and you're fucked, for want of a better word, they'll drag you back in, not that I'm ever gonna, but I mean . . .
> *But you can get recalled [returned to prison]?*
> I wish you could do your sentence and be allowed to get on!

Many *repentant prisoners* complained about being described as a "sex offender," as the term implied too strong a link between the offense and the identity, as though "that's all you're good for, that's all you can do" (Nigel). While some directly if politely challenged uses of the term, others tried to embody this challenge:

> If it's a badge I've got to wear, I've got to wear it. There's nothing I can do about it. I can't, the only thing I can do is try to show people by my actions, by the way I talk, the way I treat people, I can show them I'm a little bit more than what they think, than the stereotypical sex offender. [. . .] I can only say, "Well look, yeah, alright, I did make a mistake but that's not what I'm all about, yeah? This is the real me. That was a bad time for me, it should never have happened. This is the real me." And you know, I am quite capable of walking past a fifteen-, sixteen-year-old girl without jumping on them, you know. (Keith)

Overall, *repentant prisoners* were highly conscious of their stained identities, but they believed that their authentic, reformed selves were still visible through the murk.

These men insisted that their repentance was authentic and internally motivated and sought to manifest it in their compliant and engaged behavior within the prison. They often pushed to undertake treatment courses and were in regular contact with their Offender Supervisors and Offender Managers (see chapter 3, note 20). They sought trusted and responsible positions within the jail, which they saw as a way of "repaying" (William) their moral debt, as an opportunity to "make use" (Luke) of their time, and as a symptom of their inherent goodness: "I tend to try and do the right thing, it's just in my nature to want to help people" (Peter). Difficult experiences within the prison were reconstructed as opportunities to improve as people: one *repentant prisoner*, for instance, described his challenging relationship with his cellmate as "just another opportunity to show self-control in here." Their decision to obey the rules of the prison was normatively motivated, a consequence of their recognition of the legitimacy of their imprisonment and thus the legitimacy of the rules, although their compliance also had a fatalistic edge:[12]

> *Why do you do the things the prison wants you to do?*
> Because it's the prison rules. It's the system, it's the way it is. That's what it's all about, being in prison. You broke the law, you have to abide by the rules. And if you don't, then you're down the block [in Segregation]. You get bad reports. You can get extra days for it [. . .]. I believe in following the rules. You just do what you've got to do in the best way you can, and in the only way you can. The rules are important for when you're released as well. So, it's no good coming to prison, not learning anything, breaking the rules while you're in prison, to come out and do it again. (Jake)

The desire to conform within prison was an opportunity both to practice and to perform prisoners' newfound conformist identities, and they thought that punitive reactions to rule infractions were in the service of a greater good. While *repentant prisoners* maintained that they were agents of change—"only you can change you" (John)—they saw compliance with authority as a sign of virtue, and thus they wanted to demonstrate it:

> I do whatever the prison tells me to do for the simple reason, I'm here to show them that I'm a respectful, genuine human being. I've got no problems with rules, I've got no problems with doing what I'm told to do, and the vast majority of the time I understand why these things have to be done, because they don't want chaos. [. . .] Other than that, I just do as I'm told to do, it's all part of the regime . . . Well I don't like that word "punishment," that's not the right word. I'd rather use "correction." Accept rules and regulations. Because I'll be first to admit I've always lived my life pushing up to the boundary. Unfortunately, I've overstepped the mark once in my life and that's why I'm here now. (William)

Repentant prisoners insisted that their obedience was genuine, but they nevertheless hoped that it would be rewarded by the system and reflected in risk assessments and license restrictions. While many prisoners insisted that their participation in treatment had been genuinely transformative, others were a bit more pragmatically motivated. Louis was desperate to do the SOTP "to prove that I am not going to be a risk to my kids," in the hope that he might be allowed some form of contact with them. Peter, similarly, hoped that compliance within the prison might minimize the chance of being recalled when on license: "If you go out and you've done all you can and proved you're a good person and you made a mistake, then they will let you get on a little more." Jake agreed:

I'm quite content with myself. I'm happy with what I'm doing, which is a good thing because when I'm released it shows probation that I'm a changed person. I'm not that horrible person I used to be before. And everyone's . . . Nobody's perfect, but I feel I've redeemed myself, in a way.

Compliance was thus performative without being narrowly instrumental. It was morally motivated, but a marker of its righteousness was its endorsement by official agencies. *Repentant prisoners* sought to align themselves with mainstream moral values, and thus the intention of this deliberate compliance was not to fake goodness to achieve a desired result, but to have one's goodness rubber-stamped and reinforced by the institution.[13]

Their belief in the inherent goodness of the system, and the moral value of adhering to it, led to frustration if their efforts to change themselves were not recognized. This was more than the censorious criticism of an institution for failing to live up to its stated values (Mathiesen 1965) and could represent a deviation between prisoners' processes of repentance and the forms of rehabilitation enabled by the system. Prisoners were on a journey of change, but they were also held in stasis within an institution whose orientation was toward risk management, and on a sentence which was justified by what they had done in the past. Peter indicated the frustration he felt when trying to show Offender Supervisors and Offender Managers that he had changed: "You've got to prove yourself beyond doubt and that feels weird because I'm never gonna cause a problem. I'm not naturally a nasty person but they think you are." In its most extreme forms—when institutional power worked against prisoners' efforts at repentance—this could lead to a process of detachment and separation from the institution.

The Redeemed

The redeemed were a small subsection of *the repentant* who had similar attitudes toward their moral responsibility but who related differently to the institution. They accepted their guilt, had worked hard to change, and saw their imprisonment as a moral journey, but unlike *repentant prisoners*, they had become frustrated by the system because they perceived it to be blocking their progress.[14] The two men who were the clearest examples of *redeemed prisoners*—Nigel and John—were significantly over tariff on life sentences, even though they felt they had addressed their offending behavior. They claimed that the prison had not met its side of the bargain, but they nevertheless persisted in their own moral campaign and maintained that its disentanglement from institutional demands had rendered it more honest.

A few years previously, Nigel had been in a category D (open) prison and had been expecting release. A Black man in his early forties, he had spent more than half his life in prison on this and other sentences. Suddenly, and with very little warning, he and many other life-sentenced prisoners had been returned to the closed estate. A few serious offenses had been committed by men who had been "released on temporary license" from open prisons, and as a result all prisoners on life sentences in open prisons were returned to the closed estate to be reassessed, as were all men convicted of sex offenses.[15] Two years later, he was still in a closed prison, and his route to either a different institution or to release was unclear, and it was several years before men convicted of sex offenses were able to return to open prisons. He reacted to this situation with exasperation, and complained that his experience had broken the rules of retributive justice:

> You know, if I'd done something wrong then you can kind of accept it, right? So to be moved back because somebody else has gone and committed crime . . . I still can't get my head around it and I still can't get my read around that. That's going to be two years now. I just don't get it.

His frustration grew in Stafford, where he felt that his sentence was purposeless and complained that he had been "left here to rot."[16] Since arriving in the prison, he had been approached by psychologists three times to be assessed for programs he had already completed. He felt that prison officers were unwilling to recognize or adapt to the pain of his situation, instead accusing him of having a "bad attitude" and giving him "daft little nickings [adjudications][17] and really daft little IEPs and warnings."[18] He found this particularly challenging as these punitive reactions were often responses to behavior which had been encouraged on SOTP courses and which he saw as an indispensable aspect of his reformed character:

> I feel like Stafford don't really want you to be yourself. If you're yourself, and yourself happens to be someone that's got a bit of personality, and someone who's quite willing to challenge certain things, if you're like that naturally, it won't work out. So you can't be yourself then. You have to kind of not be like that. And I don't like hiding who I am, because I've learned—these are things that I've learned in prison from doing certain courses—you have to show who you really are. If you have to pretend to be something else, then aren't you learning to manipulate the system then? That's not right!

Nigel expressed a common assessment of cognitive behavioral courses—that the conduct they encouraged felt irrelevant within the prison environment (Laursen and Laws 2017)—but his critique went deeper than that. He no longer believed that the processes of self-change that he felt morally required to pursue were compatible with the requirements of the prison system. Instead, he accused the prison of promoting manipulative behavior which was typical of his offending past.

Having lost faith in the value and likelihood of endorsement by the organization, Nigel's focus had shifted inward. He no longer sought validation from outside and instead tried to follow his own moral compass:

> *Why do you do the things the prison wants you to do?*
> Why do I do it? I try not to do it! [laughs] I try to do things for me now, not for the prison.

He was critical of staff, whom he censured for breaking principles of justice through their "heavy" (King and McDermott 1995) use of power and whom he frequently described as "robots." He had repeated verbal arguments with them, and during the fieldwork period was placed on a "basic" regime as an act of discipline and was also physically restrained—both unusual occurrences in an ordered establishment like Stafford. He insisted, however, that his antagonism to the institution was a sign of his reluctance to twist his morals for personal advancement, and of his insistence on pursuing what was right rather than what benefited him: "I'm not willing to back down, because I'm not, I'm not willing to kind of like change all my moral thinking just because this is a different prison. I'm not willing to do that. If that means I might get a little bit of trouble I can accept that, that doesn't really affect me."

For prisoners to follow the path of redemption, then, they were required to see their moral journeys as unconstrained by the demands imposed on them by the institution. This sometimes placed them in conflict with the prison authorities, but they insisted that having broken these bonds allowed them to behave with greater honesty. Nigel said that he had once thought of himself as, and performed being, totally transformed. He now contested this simplistic narrative of repentance, penance, and change, insisting that he was still morally complex:

> In the last few years I've reverted back to being . . . rather than showing everyone, "Oh, I've changed so much, look at my courses that that I've done, look at my record, I'm so brilliant, no nickings for ten years, fifteen years, I'm so fantastic," it's almost like now I've reverted back to . . . you know what, I'm not gonna do that no more. I'm not gonna pretend to be Mr. Nice Guy. I'm just going to show the real me, yeah. I mean I kick off every now and again—it's not even kicking off, it's just me being me, I don't see that as kicking off. They [the officers] do obviously go, "Yeah, look at him kicking off." I'm not kicking off, I might shout about because I'm angry and frustrated not because like I'm kicking off, it's not kicking off. So I'd rather just like . . . I'd rather staff look at me and think, "You know, sometimes he's a bit wild." At least they've got the right opinion of me rather than, "Oh he's so fantastic, you know Nigel, he's such a fantastic guy, oh he's so helpful and he's so safe to be around, we really trust him." I'd rather them think, "Not too sure about him." And that's the truth, that's the real me, ain't it.

FATALISTS

Fatalists, who made up about an eighth of the interview sample, admitted that they were guilty of their offenses, which tended to be noncontact, internet-based offenses against children.[19] They did not appear morally troubled by them, however, and were instead preoccupied and in some cases overwhelmed by the consequences of their convictions. Despite receiving quite short sentences, they found imprisonment hard, were haunted by concerns about their safety within and beyond Stafford, and were worried about their ability to find housing and employment on release. Any shame they experienced resulted from their convictions and their imprisonment rather than from what they had done. Within prison, they were vulnerable and relatively powerless in their relationships with prisoners and with staff. This powerlessness was reflected in their relationships with themselves: many *fatalists* alluded to experiencing inappropriate sexual urges, which they relied on external constraints to control. Nevertheless, unlike *repentant prisoners*, they did not see their sentence as an opportunity for personal transformation; their focus was on "getting through prison" (Greg), which for them was a largely negative experience to be endured.

Derek, a White man, had had a difficult childhood, spending much of it in foster care. When he turned eighteen, he had moved away from home and worked in the army and then in the service industry. He was now in his late forties and had limited contact with his family. He alluded to a persistent sexual interest in teenage girls, and this was his third conviction for a sex offense, and the first to result in a custodial sentence. He had been participating in a community-based SOTP when he was charged for his current offenses. At the time of the interview he had served eight months of the year he would spend in prison as part of his two-year sentence for breaching his Sexual Offenses Prevention Order and downloading sexual images of children.[20] He had pleaded guilty to his offenses, and considered himself "very lucky" to have received the sentence he had: his probation officer had wanted him to receive longer, but she was on holiday when he was sentenced and was therefore unable to produce a pre-sentence report.[21] He knew that his offense was wrong, but he found it counterproductive to dwell on this, and instead focused on getting through his time in prison:

> I do feel guilty, but I try not to let it ruin my life. I've just got to get on with what I'm doing.
> *And why and how have you done that, tried not to let it ruin your life?*
> I don't want to, because if I go out and it's ruined my life, I'm just going to sit and get depressed and probably do something stupid and then end up back in here. How I've managed to do that is just come out of myself, get on with life, play pool, go to work, or carpentry, education, whatever. Just get on with life.

Rather than being overwhelmed by remorse, his desire not to reoffend was based on his desire not to come back into prison. To him, his sentence had a deterrent effect, instead of a moral meaning: "The whole experience has taught me that I'm not going to be coming back here, so what I've done in the past, I'm not going to do again."

He was a low-status prisoner who was occasionally derided, to his face and behind his back, about his offense, but he had never experienced physical violence. He had few resources to counter these insults, and instead managed them by insisting he did not let them "bother" him: "Some people on here, they call you 'pedo,' and I just go 'whatever' and just ignore them." His approach to his sentence was to let it affect him as little as possible: "I just want to get on, do my last four months, get out, and then forget about this place, [put it] as far back into my mind as I possibly can." In addition to disregarding insults, he made comparable attempts to overlook his sexual attraction to young girls:

> I definitely don't want to come back, so I'm not going to be doing . . . So I've got to try and steer myself, because if I see a good-looking girl on the outside . . . Because I was told [. . .] if something stirs my fantasies, to tell my probation officer. I told her there was one evening I went for pizza. There was this young girl in the shop, dressed in a . . . when I saw her from the back, the skirt was so far up, you could almost see her backside. So I ordered my pizza, and I had to get out of the pizza shop. I said, "I'll come back in five minutes for my pizza." So I just got out of the situation. That's part of the stuff I learned on the [SOTP] courses I was doing. If you find yourself in a particular situation, get yourself out of it. [. . .] Distract yourself. So if I feel tempted to go on the computer and download stuff, distract yourself. Go out, play PlayStation, whatever.

His approach to his own behavior was managerial rather than transformative. He wanted to use institutional mechanisms to reduce his risk—to others, but more importantly to himself. He had a bureaucratic conception of self-change, the aim of which was neither to make amends nor to reform his identity, but to block out an aspect of his sexuality to make sure that he did not come back to prison.

Other *fatalists* shared this morally neutral model of self-management, and reflected it in the ways in which they talked about their offenses, which they spoke of more as legal violations than sins. They acknowledged that what they had done was wrong, but they demonstrated very few signs of guilt. Many did not have identifiable victims as their offenses were image-based and their victims had rarely been found by the police. Those who did have identifiable victims rarely named them or spoke in any detail about the effect which the offense might have had on them, perhaps because they rarely knew or had even ever met them. *Fatalists* had mostly pleaded guilty, primarily for instrumental reasons, and they tended to see their punishment as comprehensible but excessive, indicating that the condemnation which they heard in their convictions and sentences did not adhere to how they saw themselves and their offending. Samuel, for instance, felt that his sentence did not reflect how uncharacteristic his crime was: "It was my first offense, never been in trouble with the law before. It was just an error of judgment, a mistake, so I think it was unfair what I got for it." Others tried to excuse their offending, insisting that their underage victims had consented. Greg had numerous charges relating to downloading images of children, but he insisted he had not understood this was wrong until he was arrested:

> I thought they were enjoying it, the ones in the images, because they were smiling and that. I know now that obviously they were being abused but back then I didn't

think anything different. [. . .] I was on bail for seventeen months and I had all that time to think about it and I never went near anything while I was on bail. I had basically three years without it. I understand that they were victims and people. People shouldn't be putting that sort of stuff on there anyway.

Like many *fatalists*, Greg neutralized his offending as "just a stupid mistake" and insisted that it was not part of who he was: "I'm not a criminal, I'm just someone that has messed up."

Some *fatalists* had prior convictions for sex offenses, but for all whom I interviewed, this was their first prison sentence. Their preoccupation before their sentencing had often been the fear of imprisonment, and they were particularly worried about their safety given their offense categories: "Being gay and also through grooming someone and they're a boy and also having pictures, I was absolutely terrified. I was scared of being stabbed, abused, raped, I was absolutely petrified" (Samuel). Many had considered or attempted suicide while they were waiting to be sentenced, although these feelings had lessened once they entered the prison and started to feel safer:

> I could have gone over the edge. When I was on bail, I was thinking suicidal thoughts and that. Luckily, touch wood, I didn't do anything about those suicidal thoughts. I just carried on. It's not happened in prison. Just waiting seventeen months for it [imprisonment], it was hell, it was. And I was in the newspaper before I went so I had to put my hood up when I was taking the dog for a walk. People were looking at me like, "Oh there's him." And when helicopters used to go past, I used to think they were spying on me. I was paranoid and everything. [. . .] When I came to prison, that weight off my shoulders was struck off, and so there's less to carry now. (Greg)

Fatalists had a low status in Stafford and were often discussed behind their backs and ridiculed as "creepy," and other prisoners made comments about them when they interacted with me: "Look how many nods he does when he goes past Alice! You can tell he's a creep." As long as they were careful about who they interacted with, however, this dislike rarely led to more direct bullying, and no *fatalists* reported having experienced violence in Stafford. Nevertheless, they feared that if their convictions became known, they might "get a lot of abuse" (Samuel). They tended to have a few friends, who were often other *fatalists*, and often remained in their cells during association periods with the small number of people they trusted.

Fatalists tended to tolerate the "sex offender" label as technically accurate and denuded of emotion—"My offense was sexually related so I'm a sex offender" (Oliver)—although they felt it gave an unfair impression of their offending to those outside the prison: "It just puts you in a category with bad offenders, which are the people you see on the news" (Barry). Within the prison, they saw their label as an equalizing and neutral description of their category of offending, and they insisted that other prisoners made the same ethical judgments: "People accept it, you're all the same, we're all in the same prison" (Barry). Derek put it simply: "We don't look at ourselves as 'sex offenders.' We've just done something that we shouldn't have, and we're all just men. We're just in here getting on with doing our time, and that's it." Their attention was focused on risks to their safety, and as long as they were protected, they were unconcerned by the more existential and emotional effects of shame.

In their interactions with powerholders, they were compliant and submissive. They struggled to identify instances where they had ever disagreed with or challenged a member of staff. Their compliance sometimes had instrumental motives, in particular the desire to get good reports and thereby ameliorate their license conditions, but it more often indicated the belief that their subordination was so inevitable that it was impossible to imagine alternatives:[22]

> *Why do you do the things the prison wants you to do?*
> Because they're the rules and I abide by the rules. You go to work when they shout that route [movement to work] is on, you go down, everybody's there for the route when they call route, you just go down there.
> *But why? You could just not? Why bother obeying the rules?*
> Well, I like to, I like obeying the rules because if you obey the rules, you get a good report! Not only that, that's the way I am, I always obey the rules, because the rules are there, set, and you've got to abide by them. You know, you can't say, "No, I'm not going to work now, I'll go at half past one," you can't do it! (Barry)

It was as though *fatalists* failed to realize they had the capacity to resist, to challenge power, or even to negotiate with staff. They accepted power as inevitable, which resulted from their understanding of themselves as rule-bound people and was symptomatic of their vulnerability. They had rarely experienced direct coercion in prison, and even getting into an argument or being asked to walk to work faster would disturb *fatalists*, who went out of their way to go "under the radar" (Oliver) and avoid "hassle" (Derek). Barry acknowledged that staff sometimes shouted at him unnecessarily, but he felt there was no point in opposing them: "I just blank it, he's an officer and he can do what he likes anyway." Their vision of power was top-down and authoritarian, and *fatalists* found it easier "to accept that we're their cattle" (Greg).

This compliance extended to their attitude toward their offending behavior, both within the prison and outside. Their goal was to ensure that they did not return to prison, and their locus of control was external. They therefore allowed institutional power to intervene in all aspects of their lives, as long as this served the greater good of preventing them from being imprisoned again. Oliver had asked his Offender Supervisor for advice on who to be friends with in the prison, and hoped that taking part in the Healthy Sex Programme would help him manage his urges: "I still have thoughts and it still needs to be controlled."[23] Similarly, Barry felt that having taken part in the Thinking Skills Programme would help

him "enjoy the normal things in life instead of those things that are not appropriate." He realized that he would never be "cured" of his problematic sexual interests,
but what mattered was better management: "It's gonna be there but it's controlling
it and putting it in the back of your mind, instead of it being in the front with
everything else in the back."

Unlike *repentant prisoners, fatalists* did not willingly engage in a righ-
teous process of self-change. Their priority was getting through their sentence
unscathed, and their anxieties about the external world—whether bullying from
other prisoners, authoritarian behavior from staff, or the fear of being imprisoned
again—concerned them more than the internal drive toward self-renewal. They
therefore submitted to all forms of institutional power, in the hope that this might
protect them from other prisoners and from themselves. They made use of institutional discourses about control and monitoring, but this use of officially sanctioned language did not indicate that they had bought into the aims of the prison.
They were docile and malleable and rarely challenged institutional means, but they
hoped to serve their own ends—not coming back to prison again—and they were
much less focused on a more broadly construed idea of rehabilitation, repentance,
or redemption.

NEGOTIATORS

Negotiators were the most numerous group, making up a third of the sample.
Almost all of them had been to prison before, and they said their previous sentences were not for sex offenses. They were also highly likely to have served part of
their current sentence on "mainstream" wings and to be familiar with and express
elements of "mainstream" prison culture.[24] They had an ambiguous attitude to
their guilt, generally admitting that they had done something technically illegal
but neither morally troubling nor indicative of a problematic sexuality, and they
thought their sentences were unfair and focused on making them as tolerable as
possible. The offenses they had been convicted of varied, although they were rarely
committed against prepubescent children.[25] However, they made sense of their
convictions in similar ways: they did not see themselves as proper "sex offenders,"
they contested the official versions of their offense narratives, and they did not
see Stafford as a suitable prison for them. They were not very worried about their
safety, and they retained a strong sense of agency and a belief that "prison is what
you make it" (Darren). They frequently used metaphors about "playing the game":
in games, the rules are set by someone else, and regardless of whether you agree
with them, you win by playing within them and turning them to your advantage.[26]
While they contested official narratives of their convictions and found much of
life in Stafford to be illegitimate, they performed some degree of submission to
both, hoping that in doing so they could make the situation "livable" (Ahmed) and
retain the elements of their identity that mattered most to them.

Mark, a White man in his early thirties, said that he had been "mischievous" when he was younger, selling drugs and breaking into cars from the age of twelve. He received his first prison sentence when he was fifteen—he said that the judge gave it to him because of his "attitude" after he showed up to his sentencing hearing wearing shorts, leather gloves, and a hat—and he had served five sentences by the time he was twenty-one. After a relatively long period outside prison, in which he fathered three children and started a stable and loving relationship, he entered a period of extreme stress:

> Then one day I was out drinking and started sniffing [cocaine] again, to the point where I woke up the next day and I had police banging on my door. I was arrested on suspicion of rape. Next thing you know, my bird [girlfriend] was in bits, she had our baby in her arms at the time, and when I got took to the police station I was interviewed and that, and then I think the next day I got charged. I was smelling myself, see because when you've had sex you've got that smell on you, and I was smelling myself. I couldn't smell anything.

When I interviewed him, he repeatedly stated that his memory of the evening was cloudy. At one point, he implied that he was innocent, and said that his girlfriend had been told that the victim was untrustworthy because she had accused several other men of rape and was "under the Mental Health Act." At other times, though, he indicated that he believed that he might have done it, although he did not believe that the conviction said anything about his character:

> When I got sentenced, I was coming to terms with the fact could I have actually done it while I've been drunk and whatever's happened in my head has heightened it? So in that sense I do feel somewhat . . . like some empathy and sympathy towards the victim, because I know in my head that if I was sober none of this would have happened.

He was deeply frustrated at the injustice of being called a "sex offender"—or, worse, a "nonce" or a "pedo"—and said that he found it painful when people yelled abuse at the prison from the streets outside. Despite having been extremely sociable on his previous sentences, he now spent much of his time either alone in his cell or with a small number of trusted associates, as he feared hearing other prisoners talking about their offenses. He hated being away from his family and had a detailed plan of how he would tell his daughter, who was only a toddler, about his conviction. He worried that he would struggle to find work after he was released, and that he might face violence and unfair accusations:

> On this sentence alone, I found it hard the first six months of my sentence, because it's a long time away from my daughter, and that's the only reason why I'm finding this sentence a lot harder than I have any other sentence previously, because I've never been convicted of anything like this before in my life. It's not me. I don't see myself as one of these on here. Now I've only got fifteen months left. The only thing I'm worried about is when I get out, because now that I'm labeled as a "sex offender," who's to say that when I get out whoever sees me is going to go and make false accusations again?

He said that he treated the conviction and sentence as a "wake-up call that I need to change" and had completed drug and alcohol awareness courses while in prison. His motivation for change was less fervent than it was for *repentant prisoners*, however, and he saw his sentence as something to be got through as quickly as possible, rather than a deserved punishment or an opportunity for transformation: "I think just crack on with it, keep your head down. The longer you can keep your head down for, the more time's going to fly, and you keep yourself busy." His family was the most important thing to him, and while he was in prison, his main priorities were, first, maintaining his enhanced status and thus his eligibility for family visits, and, second, ensuring that he did not place any "hurdles" in his path, such as restrictive license conditions, which might block him from living with his family after he was released.[27] As a result, he was significantly more compliant than he had been on previous sentences, and he was even willing to participate in the SOTP, although he was not looking forward to it: "I know I'm going to find it difficult to do, because what I don't agree with, with them courses, is that . . . Alright, I've committed a sex offense—if I have, I have—I can't really go in there saying, 'Oh yes, I did this and I did that' when there were drugs and alcohol involved."

Like Mark, *negotiators* tended to acknowledge technical guilt, but they displayed few signs of distress at what they had done and they rarely, if ever, mentioned their victims. Instead, they spent much more time in the interview complaining about their categorization as "sex offenders." They tried to dilute the legitimacy of this categorization with a diverse range of tactics. Some had pleaded guilty to offenses which they insisted were not sexually motivated. Harry was convicted of inciting prostitution for financial gain ("pimping"). He accepted being labeled as a "sex offender" as technically accurate but misrepresentative—"I've fallen through the sex offender net"—and he insisted he did not feel remorseful or guilty about what he had done, instead experiencing shame due to how he would be seen:

> I'm ashamed that I've come to prison. I'm ashamed that my daughter's gonna know that I've come to prison. I'm ashamed that my daughter's friends in the future might learn that I've come to prison. I'm ashamed when I see my missus bring her mum and dad on a visit and they've got to look at their daughter's partner that's supposed to be protecting them, I'm ashamed there, but the crime itself, I'm not ashamed of that because what happened, happened. There was no victims, no force, no nothing like that, so I've got nothing to be ashamed of there. It was purely out of naivety. I'm ashamed that I let myself fall into that, but I haven't got nothing else to be ashamed for. I hope that doesn't make me sound like a bad person.

More often, *negotiators* insisted that the encounters which had led to their convictions were complex and "murky," in the words of one man, and that the legal language which had been used on their charge sheets did not reflect the intricacies of the situations which they described. Some, like Frank, pleaded guilty to offenses like rape which they felt distorted the facts of what had happened or implied that the offense was worse than it was. Others, like Mark and Zac, said that they were simply unable to remember the events surrounding their crime. Frequently, *negotiators* said that they had pleaded guilty in order to make their sentence as short as possible, treating the trial system as a game to be played rather than an impartial search for truth.

While all *negotiators* questioned the legitimacy of their imprisonment, they rarely appealed their conviction or their sentence, and were unlikely to think of themselves as straightforwardly maintaining innocence. One reason why *negotiators* rarely appealed was that they thought the best way of dealing with their sentence was just to "crack on" (Harry), to cope with the situation rather than try to change it. But in most cases, there was nothing absolutist in their rejection of their convictions or their labels. The ambiguity of Steven's situation was typical:

> I did something that subsequently I think looking back was illegal, not right. It was thirty years ago, twenty-nine years ago. I didn't do what I was accused of but I certainly did something. I told the programs people exactly what I did do. I told everybody that stood up for me what I did. I'm not innocent, I just didn't do what I was accused of.

Their attitudes lacked the purity of those who straightforwardly maintained their innocence, and they saw themselves as the victims of complexity rather than injustice.

Much of the frustration felt by *negotiators* centered on the fact that they did not feel that Stafford was a suitable prison for them, and that it reinforced the stain of their convictions: "When you are here, the fact that you are a convicted sex offender is constantly highlighted because of the fact that it's a sex offenders' prison, which in turn makes life a little bit harder [. . .]. There's no getting away from it" (Darren). Their sensitivity meant that they often insisted that the label influenced the regime even when it didn't. Vince, for example, reported feeling annoyed whenever he heard staff shouting about not leaving female staff alone on the landing, or insisting on "shooting the bolts" on cell doors so that prisoners could not shut them—both relatively standard practices in men's prisons:

> I can understand they've got to be professional and it's all about risk assessments and there's protocols and obviously they go through all the training and that, but treating everyone with the same glove, sometimes it can grate a little bit because not everyone's in for the same offense, not everyone's got devious intentions. Some of them, just like me, just want an easy ride and to get on with it.

This ongoing sense of stigmatization was heightened by *negotiators'* awareness that Stafford's other prisoners were convicted of sex offenses, and *negotiators* were highly attuned to this stain. Like Mark, many *negotiators* were discriminating in their choice of friends, refusing to let other men into their cells unless they knew they were not convicted of child sex offenses.

Negotiators were broadly compliant, and this compliance was generally instrumentally motivated. They followed their sentence plans without enthusiasm and avoided disagreeing with staff unless they thought it was sufficiently important. Their focus was on making their life in prison as easy as possible, and so their strong tendency was to conform: "If you are going to consistently play up and not abide to the petty rules, then they are just going to downgrade you on the IEP system or take away privileges. The prison is run on incentive. The better behaved you are, the more you are going to get" (Darren). Their intention was neither to be symbolically obedient nor defiantly resistant, but instead to get by as well as possible within the parameters set by the institution: "You've got to live, haven't you, whether you're incarcerated or whatever, you've got to live your life" (Paul). *Negotiators* tended to depersonalize power, seeing it as simply "the system" or the way things were. Officers were seen as conduits for, rather than sources of, authority, which in fact resided in the rules: "It ain't a winning or a losing game, it's just protocol, and you've just got to follow it" (Harry). This compliance extended to their reluctant willingness to engage in treatment if it was placed on their sentence plans. They insisted that they did not need to be treated—as Harry said, "I don't cause any offense with my sex"—but they were loath to resist and face the consequences.

However, there were limits to what *negotiators* were willing to do and getting by within the prison entailed maintaining some feelings of pride and autonomy. They became frustrated when they perceived officers using their power unnecessarily heavily, and verbally challenged those who spoke to them disrespectfully. Many *negotiators* walked deliberately slowly to their cells at the end of association periods as a small-scale act of resistance; others refused to call officers "boss" (a common nickname for officers in England and Wales) or made jokes which undermined officers' professionalism:

> If you were to go in my cell now and look on my wall next to my door, I've just drew a poster of a monkey scratching its head and a load of words next to it going, "Who knows what's next? Bang up?[28] Association? Route? Work? Education?" and the monkey's just like that [scratches his head] with a lightbulb above his head. And for me, that's my sort of comical sort of, I know that the staff come in my cell while I'm at work to do their checks and I know that will be the last thing they see when they walk out, but rather than me directly going up to a staff member and saying, "You don't know your arse from your elbow, you couldn't get pissed in a brewery," for me, I just stuck a little poster there and if they were to question it, I'd say, "That's for me." (Harry)

Other *negotiators* wanted to avoid the mechanics of coercion becoming too visible, and so deliberately locked their own doors or walked to their cells before they were told to: "I'm well aware what the system is, the system is 6:15 bang up. I don't need a person to tell me that, I already know that. So I would rather just do the thing and not have to hear it" (Tony). In its most extreme form, this insistence on retaining a sense of agency resulted in some *negotiators* maintaining that they were not compliant and that everything they did was for their own benefit:

> I don't really do the things the prison wants me to do, to be honest with you, you know. I go to work and that because I wanna get out of my pad [cell], but if I don't want to go to work, I come back and I don't go. Courses I've got to do, I've asked to do them, I've not been told to do that, I've asked to do them. [. . .] But prison officers who say, "You've got to do this, and you've got to go there," I tell them, "Stick it up your . . ." If I don't want to do something, I won't do it. (Tommy)

While they were willing to play by the rules of the prison, they hoped to do so with "dignity" (Frank). Just as they reluctantly accepted their conviction as an unfair fact of life, they saw the prison as the unavoidable reality within which they existed and to which they were forced to adapt. *Negotiators* took for granted that both their stigmatization and the prison were fundamentally illegitimate, but they actively resisted neither, instead preferring to work within both to create a livable space for themselves. Ahmed summarized this approach: "It's not a pleasant place. Yeah. I don't like it. Don't like it at all. But it's just . . . You go through it, innit. [. . .] A good analogy: I'm the stream, I'm just flowing through, I come to a lot of turns and I'm just going through." *Negotiators* felt unable to challenge their overall situation—either the way Stafford functioned or their convictions and stigmatization. Nevertheless, they sought out ways to exercise their agency, and like a stream, they found a channel in the immovable rock through which they could move more freely.

"Mainstream" Prisoners

Of the forty-two prisoners interviewed, four said that they had not been convicted of a sex offense and were instead held in Stafford because they needed protection from other prisoners because of either debts or feuds or because they had been convicted of nonsexual violent offenses against children. When I looked at these men's files at the end of the fieldwork period, however, it became clear that two of them had previously served a sentence for a sex offense. One *"mainstream" prisoner* asked me not to look at his file, but a google search suggested that he had also served an earlier sentence for a sex offense.[29] These prisoners, and others I spoke to informally, form a subsection of *negotiators*. Their attitudes toward power and their strategies for adapting to their sentence were similar, but whereas most *negotiators* sought to undermine the "sex offender" label by showing how it had been misleadingly applied to them, *"mainstream" prisoners* rejected it outright and projected an image of themselves as "normal" (Noah) prisoners adrift in a sea of "sex offenders."

Tommy was a representative example of a *"mainstream" prisoner*. He was a Traveler in his thirties,[30] and a dedicated husband and father who estimated that he had been to prison at least ten times before and was currently serving an indeterminate sentence for violent but nonsexual offenses. He claimed that he was in Stafford because he was entangled in a feud with prisoners he knew from outside and so he was treated as a VP. When he arrived at Stafford, he had publicly announced that he was not a "sex offender" and had shown his paperwork to other prisoners. He was thus able to protect himself from stigmatization within Stafford, but he was concerned that he would face judgment or even violence in future prisons: "Every prisoner in the country knows what prison this is, you know what I mean, and now I've got that stigma stuck with me for the rest of my sentence." He had also decided not to tell his family where he was being held, as he felt that they would be "disgusted if they knew I was on VPs" and "if they knew what people I'm around." He presented himself as totally different from most of the people he lived with, but this was as much to do with what they were like as prisoners as it was to do with their offenses. He subscribed to the popular view in Stafford that there was a fundamental difference between "sex offenders" and "criminals":

> *To what extent do you feel like you can be yourself in here?*
> Not a lot, to be honest with you. I've gone into my shell a bit, you know. I'm trying to have a laugh with people and that, [but] because it's a VP prison, I don't know, they come across offended or maybe intimidated. [I'm] just trying to have a laugh and then they're running off putting apps [applications] in behind your back and that.[31] You know, you're put on the TAB 2 for bullies [monitored as a bully] and you know, I've never been a bully in my life.[32] But that's just the mentality of the VPs in the prison, you know what I mean? And in a normal prison, a normal situation, you can have a laugh.

Tommy was accustomed to a particular style of behavior in prison—boisterous, playful, and relatively loud—but he found it difficult to behave in that way in Stafford and felt that prisoners there were likely to inform or "grass" on prisoners to staff. He thought that most prisoners came from a different, more middle-class background than he did: "They're not my kind of people, if you know what I mean." He had found a small group of friends, mostly other *"mainstream"* prisoners or those with prior prison experience, with whom he tended to socialize, and he spent a lot of time on his own, which he reluctantly admitted helped him to stay out of trouble. Nevertheless, he said that he hoped to be transferred out of Stafford to a "mainstream" prison where he would feel more at home.

"Mainstream" prisoners insisted that they were fundamentally different from those who had committed offenses against children, and they expressed frustration when they felt they were unfairly stigmatized as "sex offenders":

> *When you're in here, how do you feel when people use the term "sex offender" and fit you within that bracket?*
> I think that's one of the things that does my head in, because I'm on that side [of the prison] and obviously the road's there, and you hear people shouting up, "Fucking

nonce, fucking pedo!" and all the rest of it. In some ways it's degrading because I'm getting tarred with the same brush as everyone else. (Owen)

Similarly, Edward was initially reluctant to be interviewed, and only relented when I persuaded him that I wasn't just interested in "sex offenders." These identity claims were possible because "*mainstream*" *prisoners*' paperwork showed an offense which was not sexual in nature, and they had normally displayed this paperwork to their peers as soon as they arrived in Stafford. They loudly and frequently proclaimed that they and other "*mainstream*" *prisoners* were not "sex offenders," often telling me so as soon as we started talking or materializing as soon as they saw me talking to another "*mainstream*" *prisoner*.

"*Mainstream*" *prisoners* claimed that they were sometimes treated differently by officers, that they were given more "leeway" (Noah), and that female officers were more comfortable around them. However, they had mixed feelings about this differential treatment. They "wouldn't like to think they see me as a sex offender" (Tommy), but they also questioned the justice of being treated differently in the prison, claiming that all prisoners merited their punishment: "You break the law, you break the law" (Owen).[33] "*Mainstream*" *prisoners* were thus in a complex position. They saw themselves as simultaneously members of and apart from the wider community of prisoners. They presented themselves as fundamentally different due to their current offenses and they worried that by demonstrating sympathy for "sex offenders," they might be placed in that category. Nevertheless, they were also incarcerated in the same institution and most of them, presumably, knew that they had served similar sentences in the past. While they constructed their identities in ways which relied on and reinforced moral distinctions—between "criminals" and "sex offenders," "normal" and "abnormal"—they felt that the state was morally obliged to treat them all the same.

CONCLUSION: THE MEANING OF GUILT

Theories of punishment are written in libraries and university offices, but punishment is lived in places like Stafford, and it is lived by people whose diversity of attitudes, reflections, and orientations cannot be adequately represented in a typological description. Nevertheless, this chapter has attempted to sketch how prisoners who accepted their legal guilt allowed this knowledge to shape how they undertook their sentence. *Repentant prisoners* felt profound and piercing remorse, and as a result threw themselves into their sentences and grasped them as an opportunity to atone and change. When the prison did not meet them halfway, or was perceived as holding them back, they disengaged from it, forming a sub-type which I have termed *the redeemed*. *Fatalists* felt differently about their guilt: they acknowledged that what they had done was both illegal and wrong, but this knowledge did not grieve them in the same way. They did not experience their sentences as morally meaningful, but they did hope that the power of the state would protect them from abuse from other prisoners and from their own sexual urges. *Negotiators*, finally, tended to accept that they had broken the law, but they rarely felt that what they had done was wrong, or seemed troubled by it. They frequently complained that they had been unjustly stained and expended significant effort on rescuing their reputations and managing their sentences so that their time inside was as tolerable as possible.

These descriptions add depth and nuance to our understanding of adaptation to imprisonment, showing how deeply prisoners' consciousness of their staining convictions had permeated their experience, and indicating that their orientations to power within the institution were entangled with their own processes of moral reflection. They also complicate and develop idealized understandings of punishment as a tool of moral communication or moral education. Penal theorists have suggested that punishment could send two justifiable messages to people convicted of crimes: "What you have done is wrong" and "You should feel guilty about what you have done." The stories depicted in this typology suggest that imprisonment in Stafford did not send either message, and neither provided prisoners with new moral knowledge nor deepened their remorse. The men who felt the wrongness of their crimes most deeply—*repentant* and *redeemed prisoners*—said that they felt guilty about, and aware of the injustice of, their offenses long before being imprisoned, whereas those whose attitude to their convictions was more equivocal—*negotiators* and *fatalists*—rarely described a meaningful change of attitude during their imprisonment.

Furthermore, differing experiences of punishment did not seem to be the factor which caused prisoners to think or feel differently about their offenses. A much more plausible explanation lay in the nature of the crimes committed and in the histories of the men. *Repentant* and *redeemed prisoners* were normally convicted of abusing people they knew. The harms which they had caused were therefore very visible to them, and in most cases had led to the traumatic breakdown of their families.[34] Furthermore, their offenses and their convictions had interrupted lives which they had previously seen as normal and respectable, and thus both what they had done, and how they had been condemned, had deeply challenged how they saw themselves. It is consistent with research on shaming (Harris 2001) that the shame they experienced as a result was largely constructive, pushing them to make amends and change their behavior.[35] *Negotiators* and *fatalists*, on the other hand, had often been convicted of offenses before this one, with the effect that this particular conviction did not sever their sense of self in the same way. They were less likely to know their victims, and in the case of *fatalists*, to even be able to identify them, and thus the harm was less visible to them. Finally, they often found scripts for excuse-making. *Fatalists* had normally committed internet-based offenses which did not involve direct contact with their victims. Similarly, the offenses committed by *negotiators*—the rape of partners or sex workers, or sexual contact with people under the age of consent—may well be viewed with more leniency by the wider public, seen as tasteless and unpleasant but not necessarily beyond the pale.[36] They were shamed for behavior which they did not necessarily consider to be totally wrong and so they rejected their shame through excuses rather than absorbing it as guilt.

In most cases, imprisonment seemed to be unable to change the minds of those it most directly operated on, but not in all. Two men whom I classed as *negotiators*—Ahmed, whom I introduced in chapter 3, and Vince—seemed to be undergoing a process of moral change, and Vince may have been joining the group of *repentant prisoners*. Vince had pleaded guilty to raping an acquaintance while drunk and been given an indeterminate sentence, and there were many similarities between his situation and Ahmed's. He had previous convictions for violence and his offense had involved violence in addition to that which is inherent to rape. He had also focused on his own situation during the trial, and when his sentence had started, his primary focus had been on maintaining contact with his family and ensuring that he progressed as effectively as possible through his sentence plan. Unlike Ahmed, he seemed to be growing in remorse. He said that he had always accepted that he was legally and morally guilty, but said that he only started to feel the wrongness of what he had done and his responsibility for it as his sentence progressed, and as workers from treatment programs came to speak to him:

> *How does your conviction make you feel about who you are?*
> Like I said, I think I said earlier, angry. Regret. But I have to own it. It's taking ownership. It's only over the last, you know, quite recently actually, I think because of the SOTP coming over to see me, I've started thinking about it a bit, like the impact I've had, the impact I had on the victim, I should say. Because a lot of it—I know people say—there's so many emotions that go on at the time of the sentencing and then trying to deal with the sentence after, a lot of it was dealing with the loss. A lot of it was self-centered as well—I'm just being honest—you're trying to adapt to it, the effect on your family, and all these sorts of things, and although I did think of the victim, like, "Fuck, it's a shame" sort of thing, it's only recently you start thinking, you start comparing it, because I've got little nieces growing up now, I've got my mum, my sister, and if something like that happened to them, my blood goes cold sort of thing. I suppose the realization's starting to seep through now, now I'm starting to settle into my sentence, it's like, now, this is what you've done. You've got all these different courses, you know, to jump through but ultimately it's down to your decisions. You do it again, it's black and white, it's a life sentence, you know, whatever sentence and that, and also there's another victim as well. So I suppose the actual offense, it's regret.

In most cases, imprisonment in Stafford did not teach prisoners something that they didn't already know. But what it could do—and what it seemed to be doing for Vince and for *repentant prisoners*—was provide them with the mental space to reflect on the effect of their actions on other people and on themselves. Legal philosopher John Tasioulas has described repentance as a "moral discipline" (2007,

489), which, in its ideal form, involves guilt, reflection and self-blame, confession and apology, reparation, and moral growth. *Repentant prisoners*, and Emmett, the man I described at the beginning of this chapter, engaged as fully as they could in these elements of repentance. For them, imprisonment served as "both a vehicle for, and a prompt to, repentance" (Tasioulas 2007, 496).

As a vehicle though, Stafford was ineffective at taking people to their destination.[37] It removed people from the harms they had caused and the people who could most effectively morally communicate with them, and it denounced them in an impersonal way which tended to produce destructive shame and encourage prisoners to focus on mitigating their stain. The staining label attached to them distracted *negotiators* and *fatalists* from thinking about what they had done, and they saw the rehabilitative regime as something to bargain with or something to use rather than something which might change them. Even *repentant prisoners* were often diverted from their path. They threw themselves into their imprisonment, seeing it as a ritual which would allow them to change and to be reconciled with the community. But the system in which they were held did not recognize the significance of this ritual and continued to see them as objects of risk, prompting them to become frustrated with how punishment was applied to them, and in some cases try to disentangle themselves from the prison. Even when people insisted that they deserved punishment, there were limits to the forms of punishment they were willing to accept. In the next chapter, we will move on to discuss those who insisted that they did not deserve punishment, as they maintained that they were innocent.

Maintaining Innocence

Contesting Guilt and Challenging Imprisonment

William, a White man in his early fifties, was serving a fifteen-year sentence for the sexual abuse and rape of his stepdaughter. At the time I interviewed him, he was a *repentant prisoner* and an evangelist for the SOTP who told me he often interrupted other men to tell them their behavior or conversations were sexually inappropriate. He had not always been so dedicated to self-transformation, however. During the eleven months he had spent on bail awaiting his trial he was, in his words, "in denial." Despite acknowledging to himself and to his family that he had committed his offense, he told the police and his lawyers that he was innocent:

> I knew I was lying. I knew. It was done for many reasons. One, so I could see the children, explain to the children. I told them everything. I didn't lie to them. I told my mother, my father. I tried to sort my finances as best I could. Tried to reason with my wife because obviously she's another victim.

During this period, he had considered suicide, describing himself as "ashamed, remorseful, disgusted," but, like Emmett, who was described in the previous chapter, he was saved by the intervention of a family member and decided to dedicate his life to making amends. At the moment his suicidal thoughts were strongest, his daughter arrived on his doorstep, and he realized the further harm he would do by dying:

> It were bizarre, as if she knew, we were that close, you see, and it just knocked me for six. I thought, what are you doing? You are leaving all your crap at your children's doorstep. You've got to stand up and man up and deal with it and put this really disgusting thing I've done and everything, chaos I've caused, I've got to be the one to go out there and put it right and the only way I can do that is by going to prison, correcting my pattern of thought, and getting myself up, mobile, and moving forward again.

When the case finally went to trial, he decided to plead guilty, even to charges which he contested. He was charged with the rape of a child under the age of thirteen, but despite insisting in the interview that he had only started to abuse his stepdaughter after she turned thirteen, he had pleaded guilty.[1] His reasons for doing so were twofold: first, to protect both his victim and his heavily pregnant daughter from testifying, and second, to receive a slightly shortened sentence. Within the prison, he insisted that he was still pleased he had made this decision, but he nevertheless repeatedly reminded me that he contested one of the charges.

Maintaining innocence is often described as though it is an absolute, something which exists in binary opposition to accepting guilt. But just as the previous chapter showed that there are different ways of acknowledging that one has committed a crime, William's story demonstrates that there are also different ways of insisting that one has not. While he was on bail, William knowingly deceived people about his crime, and research on others who have moved from "denial" to acceptance supports the idea that some people convicted of sex offenses consciously lie about their guilt in the hope that doing so might protect them from shame and keep them safe (Ware and Blagden 2020). Not all claims of innocence are this unequivocal, however. Even after William pleaded guilty, he still insisted that there was a gap between what he had been convicted of and what he had done, and certainly some psychologists would place his claims into the category of "offense denial."[2] By doing so, they would be operating on the assumption that the distance between his story and his conviction existed because his story was wrong and not because his conviction was, although it is possible that his claims of partial innocence were more accurate than his claims of complete innocence had been. Even if William was not telling the truth, however, he was not necessarily being deliberately deceptive. Since Freud, psychologists and psychoanalysts have argued that the inability to remember or accept certain truths might be a product of unconscious processes of denial, and it is possible that William's insistence that his offending had started later than his victim had said resulted from an inability to accept or even remember what he had done. Whatever the reason for his insistence that he was innocent of that one charge, it was clear that he accepted a significant amount of legal and moral responsibility, and he did not consider himself to be illegitimately imprisoned.

In the previous chapter, I presented the first half of a typology demonstrating that how prisoners in Stafford thought about their convictions and their offenses affected how they did their time. I argued that even when prisoners did not contest the most fundamental claim the prison made about them—that they were guilty of a sex offense—they still challenged the implication that they deserved to be stained as "sex offenders." Some prisoners—those I deemed *repentant* and *redeemed prisoners*—did so by trying to transform themselves so that they were more than "sex offenders"; others—*fatalists* and *negotiators*—claimed that the label was either inaccurate or merely technical. In this chapter I present the second half of this typology, and focus on people who categorically insisted that they were innocent. These men, who made up around a third of my interview sample, were steadfast in their insistence that they should not be in prison at all, let alone in a prison which communicated the stigmatizing moral message which Stafford did. The morally inflected nature of their imprisonment shaped the way they responded to penal power, just as it had for prisoners who maintained guilt. As I argue in this chapter, the fact that Stafford claimed authority over prisoners' moral identities pushed those who maintained innocence to challenge the way their sentence was carried out and to resist the realities of life in a prison in which they insisted they did not deserve to be.

Through this description, I hope to make clear that if we want to evaluate the legitimacy of imprisonment, we must also consider the legitimacy of convictions and sentencing. This seemingly straightforward point has often been neglected by prison sociologists, who have conducted most of their research with "mainstream" male prisoners, a group who are less likely to maintain innocence than most prisoners convicted of sex offenses are (R. Mann 2016). This empirical difference has allowed prison sociologists to claim that most prisoners consider the fact of their imprisonment to be legitimate, even if they question the legitimacy of their treatment inside prisons (Crewe 2009; Sparks, Bottoms, and Hay 1996; Sykes [1958] 2007).[3] These sociologists thus imply that prisoners' judgments about the justice of their situation rely on the same distinction between the allocation and delivery of punishment which the idea of morally communicative institutions calls into question. In Stafford, however, the two assessments of legitimacy were less obviously distinct, and prisoners who steadfastly maintained that they were innocent often challenged or questioned the way the prison used power over them.

Without knowing whether prisoners were really innocent, or really believed themselves to be innocent, the direction of this relationship is unclear. It is not possible to know whether being in prison unfairly led prisoners to think the way the prison worked was unfair, or vice versa. What is clear, though, is that the form these claims of innocence took was shaped by the context in which they were made. Imprisonment in Stafford was morally communicative—being there said something to prisoners about who they were and what they had done—and the prison's stain combined with its attempts to discipline prisoners' sexual identities to repeatedly focus prisoners' attention on why they were there. In so doing, the prison pushed them to insist on their innocence over and over again. Irrespective of the veracity of these claims, Stafford was not simply the site in which prisoners expressed their claims of innocence, it also helped to create them.

ACTIVISTS

Activists constituted just a tenth of the interview sample.[4] In almost all cases they had been convicted of the rape of an adult woman and steadfastly maintained their innocence, attributing their incarceration to false allegations and unjust systems.[5] They took pride in their refusal to submit to power, and were almost ideological in their rejection of the legitimacy of their conviction and of the prison.[6] They deliberately nurtured the anger which they felt at their situation, and got through their sentence by intentionally challenging penal power. None had active appeals, but they all said that they intended to appeal and spent a lot of time rereading their paperwork and thinking about the injustice they had been subjected to. Rather than bringing them to despair, these rituals, they said, helped them manage psychologically by giving them both hope and the energy to cope with their imprisonment (see also Wright, Crewe, and Hulley 2017). The frustration they felt about their convictions often blended into broader cynicism about the legal system, and they resisted the fact that they were in prison as well as the power of the prison in which they were held. They had prior personal and familial experience of criminalization and of the drugs trade, and most of the prisoners in this group were either Black or from other minority backgrounds, which may have contributed to the active mistrust which they placed in state actors. Irrespective, their preexisting familiarity with the legal system meant that they did not express any shame at their imprisonment, but they were nonetheless devastated by the fact that it was for a sex offense. Whereas their previous convictions had been consistent with how they saw themselves—as honorable criminals, as strong men, as rebels— being convicted of and imprisoned for a staining sex offense called into question their masculinity and their morality (Sim 1994; Thurston 1996).

Terry, a Black man in his early fifties, had spent much of his life involved in the drugs trade, and had served several prison sentences for offenses related to drugs and violence. When I initially approached him for an interview, he said no and offered no explanation. Months later, however, he said that his cellmate had vouched for my trustworthiness and he was willing to speak to me, although he insisted that the interview take place on a weekday: "The weekend's my time." He was currently serving an IPP sentence (see chapter 2, note 39) for raping his girlfriend, a charge which he unequivocally rejected, complaining that only ten of the twelve jurors had believed that he was guilty: "In this day and age, how can ten people think you're guilty and two don't?"[7] He had appealed his conviction toward the beginning of his sentence, and his appeal had been rejected by the Criminal Cases Review Commission as it did not have a legal basis.[8] Nevertheless, he insisted that the matter was not settled: "I still don't agree it was right, and until they can prove to me it was right, it wasn't right. End of story. I ain't gonna take their answers." He hoped to prove his innocence upon his release, and in the meantime, he deliberately kept his memory of the injustice alive, engaging in a practice of embitterment which mirrored *repentant prisoners'* ritualistic acts of contrition:

> I just laugh at it now. I read my deps [depositions, or trial paperwork] and the more I read it, the more discrepancies I see and the more I laugh at it.
> *How often do you read them?*
> I've read my deps so many times over the years, it's like I know them inside out.
> *Doesn't it drive you a bit crazy?*
> No, because it just shows me how corrupt the system is.

Terry reacted to the alleged illegitimacy of his situation with defiance. He had served significantly longer than the tariff of his IPP sentence, which he attributed to his ineligibility to do the SOTP as he was maintaining his innocence. He refused either to lie about his offense—"They can keep me as long as they want, I ain't gonna change"—or to "crack" under the pressure:

> If they took it [the SOTP] off my sentence plan, I'd go home tomorrow, but they won't. It's part of the system, playing their games. Trying to see when you're gonna crack or when you're gonna flip out. And if you can play the game, play the game. It's a game, at the end of the day! [. . .] Some guys can play, some guys can't. I've seen loads of IPPs mess up. [. . .] I've seen a lot of them make a right mess of their lives. I'm not going down that road.

Terry reconstituted surviving his sentence into an act of resistance. By claiming that the system wanted to break him, he invested his insistence on coping with political meaning. In his refusal to be beaten, Terry was demonstrating control over the situation and over himself:

> Jail is what you make it. You want to make it hard, spend your time down the block [in segregation], running around doing this, that, and the other, go for it. I don't plan on doing it that way. The easier I do my bird [sentence], the better it is for me, at the end of the day. I can sit back and kick back, put my DVD player on and watch what I want with nobody bothering me. It's up to you how you want to live. If you want to be an idiot, be an idiot. I'm not an idiot.

It is a common trope among prisoners that people are responsible for how they do their time, but Terry's approach was marked by its agentic language, desire for isolation, and contempt for other prisoners, all of which were typical among *activists*.

In almost all cases, *activists* claimed to have had consensual sex with their accusers, who were often ex-girlfriends. They spoke of their accusers with bitterness and contempt, saying that they would struggle to trust women in the future: "That's gonna be a task for me, because I'm always going to be thinking, 'Is this a setup? Is this a trick again?'" (Cain). This bitterness radiated outward, and *activists* maintained that both their accusers and the legal system were financially motivated, often making incorrect claims about compensation for victims or payment-by-results schemes for police officers or prosecutors.[9] Terry insisted that the woman he had been convicted of raping was paid a thousand pounds for each year he spent in prison, although this is not how compensation for victims of serious crime is calculated:[10]

> When I first went to prison, right, I spoke to the OMU [Offender Management Unit officer] there and she turned round and said to me, "Do you know for every year you got, she got a grand?" I said, "Behave yourself!" She said, "No, the law now, for every year you get, she gets a grand. So she done herself a good five grand there." She says, "The longer you stay in here, the more she'll get." I said, "Behave yourself." She said,

"It's the law." And I said, "Well best of luck to her." And I said, "If that's what it was all about, let her carry on."

Cain maintained that the police were financially rewarded when they secured convictions, and that sex offense convictions were among the cheapest to procure:

> If somebody gets battered severely, they have to pay money to look for the person. If somebody gets murdered, they have to pay for that, to get the person. A man comes in on a sex offense, no, you don't have to do nothing. You don't have to put out no money out there. Don't have to even get forensics. You don't even have to pay forensics. So, that's where the money is for them. And it's a big lie, yes.

They thereby presented their convictions as symptomatic of wider corruption and injustice, politicizing their own allegedly illegitimate positions within the system.[11]

Activists repeatedly challenged the legitimacy of their situation and of the legal system, but they were unable to change the basic fact of their imprisonment. Despite priding themselves on their masculinity and control, this was one area in which they were helpless: "I feel like I've let myself down, even though I haven't done nothing. There's nothing I can do to help myself out of the situation" (Cain). Faced with this specter of powerlessness, *activists* deliberately maintained a feeling of anger at their situation; as shame researchers have argued, unacknowledged or disintegrative shame can produce feelings of rage and anger as shamed people displace the threat to their sense of self and condemn those who have dishonored them (Ahmed 2001).[12] James recalled the advice he had given to a friend who had been struggling to adjust to his sentence:

> I says, "Listen, the way I get through my time is I keep myself angry." He's like, "You what?" I went, "It's true. I'm not a very angry person but the rage I've got inside of me, that's what keeps me going." I says, "The rage I've got against the bloody police and the courts and that for finding me guilty of something I didn't do." And he says, "Oh well, whatever works for you!" And I says, "Well that does work for me." But then you've got, on top of that, losing my kids and losing my ex-partner at the same time, and it's like all that's worked up into what?
> *And how does that rage help you keep going?*
> Well let's put it this way. I've got my fight back. I lost my fight, that's one thing I did lose. It wasn't when I came into prison, it was when I lost my ex and my kids, because I still had my fight. It was losing them, that was it. I lost everything. And then all of a sudden I found this, like, I just wanted to smash something up! And I thought, "I'm going to use that!" [. . .] It gives me the energy that I need.

Activists devoted significant time and energy to reading paperwork from their trial and considering their legal positions, even though none of them were currently appealing or had concrete plans to appeal. Focusing on this apparent injustice had become a clear coping strategy independent of its likelihood of concretely affecting their position.

Activists expressed no desire to maintain connections, or to reconcile, with those whom they perceived to be the law-abiding majority. Their politicized anger was consistent with their earlier involvement in the drugs trade and their histories of opposition to the state and to the legal system. They felt no shame at having broken the law, and in Braithwaite's (1989) terms, they were members of a deviant subculture which reinforced their belief that lawbreaking was not immoral. They did, however, feel profound shame at having been convicted of a sexual offense, a form of offending which was deeply stigmatized within the communities of which they were members:

> *Do you think you've changed the way you see yourself on this sentence? In Stafford?* Offense-wise, yeah. That's . . . never mind knocked me down a few steps, it's knocked me right down. See, my family's grew up around crime. Not no crime like this. So yeah, it's put a bit of a downer on me. Knocked my confidence a little bit, do you know what I mean? (Kieran)

Activists described their previous offending as consistent with their dominant and sexually normative masculine identities, but their current convictions challenged these identities and disqualified them from their lifestyles. Terry insisted that his current conviction was totally "out of character," and said that, on hearing of his conviction, his mother had said, "If they told me you'd shot and killed somebody or gone and robbed a bank or something, I could have believed that, but for you to do something like this, that isn't you." *Activists* described themselves as "pissed" (Terry) by their subjection to the staining "sex offender" label, which excluded them from both mainstream and prison society: "We're scum of all scum, ain't we, sex offenders. That's what we're looked at as" (Kieran). The displacement they felt because of their current situation was exacerbated by their earlier experiences of prison: *activists* had spent their previous sentences on "mainstream" wings, where they had witnessed and sometimes participated in the abuse of people convicted of sex offenses, and they now occupied a fallen position within the prisoner hierarchy. Some *activists* repeatedly and explicitly challenged implicit or explicit stigmatization from officers, Offender Managers, and other prisoners:

> If someone says to me I'm a sex offender, I say to them point blank, "Listen, I'm not a sex offender, I didn't do what I was accused of or found guilty of, and one day I will prove that." It's just depending on when, that's what it comes down to, it's when I will prove it. (James)

Higher status *activists*, on the other hand, responded by contemptuously ignoring the label: "You think what you want to think. As long as I know I ain't done it, do you know what I mean. Everyone's entitled to have a mind of their own" (Terry).

The cynicism which *activists* felt about the legal system was targeted at the courts, the police, and the prison. They considered the whole system to be corrupt, and they asserted their agency by refusing to submit to it. Like *negotiators*, they often used metaphors about "playing the game" to describe the way they behaved within the prison, but *activists* used these metaphors to describe a competition with the system rather than getting by within a system of arbitrary rules.[13] In some cases, their acts of opposition responded to the prison's rehabilitative demands: *activists* were steadfast in their refusal to do the SOTP, for instance, and James recounted volubly resisting when officers confiscated photographs of his children because of the risk he was assessed of posing to people under sixteen. *Activists* also challenged and resented the more day-to-day power which operated on the wing. Just as they coped with their convictions by denying them, they also responded to imprisonment with resistance, although this rarely took dramatic forms. Kieran wrote frequent complaint forms as a way of expressing his frustration with what he saw as a fundamentally unjust system. He knew that doing so aggravated members of staff, and so he was careful to remain technically within the rules:

> One of the managers come a few months ago and tried to label me as a prolific complainer. [He said,] "I'm checking up as to what the PSI [Prison Service Instruction] says about prolific complainers."[14] Now what he doesn't know is I've done the information digging for him. A prolific complainer can put one complaint in every day, so I put it to him, I said, "If you label me as a prolific complainer, I'll put one complaint in every day."[15] And I says, "And I'll make sure that one complaint contains ten complaints." I'll play him at his own game. It's the only way you can beat them, ain't it.

Terry similarly tried to resist staff power without making things harder for himself. He thought that staff were trying to break him, and he thus defiantly insisted on getting on with even the most difficult prison officers, reconstituting his compliance into a form of resistance: "I get on with them for the simple reason, when they do things, I let it go over my head. That gets to them more than it gets to me."

However, despite their history of opposition to the police and to the prison system, they believed that people who sexually offend should be harshly punished and tightly regulated. This was not to say that they assigned any legitimacy to their own position in the prison. They thought it was wrong that they were in Stafford, and wrong that, as innocent people, they were subjected to state punishment: "We haven't done nothing wrong, so why should we be made to do the same as people who have pleaded guilty, who have admitted their offense?" (Kieran). However, they dedicated lengthy portions of the interview to their disgust and hatred of people who sexually offend, and they stated that they approved of the Sex Offenders' Register and restrictive license conditions for people convicted of sex offenses:

> I don't blame them for what they're thinking. I don't blame them, these Registers. Don't blame the way they've got it so strict. I don't blame them. So, for people to like moan about it, what the fuck they expect? What they expect, man? What they expect? [...] It is pissing, it is frustrating, but you have to think to yourself. You have to sit there and sit and actually think, "Yo, what if somebody had done that to my sisters, like? He needs to be on a fucking watch. He needs to, innit. He needs to go on

a watch. He needs to go on all these fucking . . ." I don't care. Because I don't want this happening again, you get me? So, really, I can't blame them, but it's horrible being an innocent person and have to go through that, so I can understand why people are actually moaning about it. Because me personally, it's a hard thing for me. It's a hard thing. I reckon that it's going to ruin me. (Cain)

As far as *activists* were concerned, it was right to punish and discipline true "sex offenders," but it was wrong that they themselves were punished and disciplined. They resented having been drawn into a staining web, but they thought it was right that this web existed.

THE RESIGNED

Resigned prisoners, who represented almost a quarter of the sample, maintained their innocence, but differed from *activists* in that they tried to come to terms with their situation. They had been convicted of a range of crimes, most of which were contact offenses against children and related to events decades earlier. In almost all cases, they insisted that these charges resulted from false allegations and that they had never had any sexual contact with the people accusing them, and most *resigned prisoners* had pleaded not guilty during the trial. Their arrest and imprisonment had interrupted lives which they had seen as perfectly normal and law-abiding, and they said this was their first time in prison. *Resigned prisoners* were often in their forties or above, and prior to their arrest they had lived with their families and been in secure and meaningful employment. Following their convictions, most had retained the support and trust of their families, with whom they hoped to be reunited on release. In the meantime, their focus was on surviving their sentence, the impact of which they hoped to minimize: "It's a part of my life that I've got to get through to get to where I want to get to" (Ricky). They claimed integrity in their refusal to admit to something they said they did not do, and they did not comply with elements of their sentence plan which relied on an admission of guilt. In their day-to-day interactions, however, they attempted to acquiesce to their convictions and imprisonment, insisting that this made their situation easier to tolerate. They thus demonstrated what Schinkel (2014a, 72, emphasis in original) calls "*coping-acceptance*": they considered their situation to be unjust, but they tolerated it to make life easier. Nonetheless, some *resigned prisoners* found their situation easier to come to terms with than others. For all of them, coping-acceptance was a condition to be continually worked at rather than a state they had achieved, and the moralized nature of power, and the prison's attempts to regulate prisoners' offense narratives and sexualities, made it harder for them to submit completely.

Shezad's experience was typical of *resigned prisoners*. He was a Muslim who had been born in the Indian subcontinent, and he was in his early thirties. He had been proud of his family and his career in business before his imprisonment, but he was now serving a seven-year sentence for six nonpenetrative charges of sexual assault of a child, following what he insisted were the false accusations of his underage sister-in-law. He said his ex-wife believed that he was innocent, but the stress and disruption of his arrest and subsequent conviction had led to their divorce, and he had no contact with his daughter. I first met him when he approached me on the wing to complain (justifiably) about the wording of a demographic survey titled "The Social Experiences of Sex Offenders in Prison" which I had given out at the beginning of the project: "It says at the top 'sex offenders,' and some people in here, they're not 'in denial,' they're maintaining innocence." I apologized and we discussed the problems with the label, and after a series of conversations on the wing, he let me interview him. At this stage, he had only been in prison for a few months. He was struggling emotionally, and was highly conscious of the stigmatizing power of his conviction:

> I see myself as nobody. All my life, I've been somebody, I would say, but I can't see any point in that because I'm a criminal. It doesn't matter what I think of myself, but that's my title. Criminal XYZ. A criminal and a sex offender for life. "He's dangerous to that, he's dangerous to vulnerable people," because I am a sex offender. I know I am not. I know that. I've never been, but it doesn't matter.

He was in the early stage of his sentence, and was undergoing a process of self-mortification (Goffman 1961): his social identity had been destroyed by his conviction and his imprisonment, and his insistence that he was not guilty was not enough to resist the character which had been ascribed to him.

A few months later, however, as the shock of his incarceration wore off, he approached me on the wing to tell me how his attitude had changed as he adapted to his situation:

> At the start, you see things from the outside, as a free person now in prison. I had a good credit rating, good car insurance, you think about those things that matter. And you think about how your life was successful and all the things you've lost. And then you come to prison, criminal record, especially as a sex offender for life, you've lost everything. It's worse than being six feet under. And now, especially after talking to you, I stop thinking about what I had and what I have now. I'm in prison and I have to build my life now. It's a sort of acceptance, coming to terms with it. I have low moments when I think about what I've lost, especially my daughter, but not all the time.

This was acceptance borne out of the need to cope in the prison. Shezad had redirected his attention from what he had lost and toward how he needed to live. He remained extremely sensitive to misuses of power in the prison, and he never fully trusted me or my work, although he insisted it was nothing personal. I was a "professional" connected to an "institution," and I thus represented "the system," and there was an inherent inequality to our relationship. "You asked me all those questions, you know everything about me, but I don't know anything about you," he told me once. As the fieldwork period progressed, he became increasingly involved in the prison's social world, spending time in public areas during association periods, and he signed up for education courses within the prison. Although he never considered his situation to be legitimate, he recognized that it was real, and he tried to get by as well as possible.

This is what distinguished *resigned prisoners* from *activists*: *resigned prisoners* focused their energies on coping with the sentence rather than challenging their conviction. They were nevertheless steadfast in their maintenance of innocence. In interviews, they were consistent in their use of language—referring to the "accuser" and the "allegations" and never "the victim" or "the offense"—and they sometimes described the person whom they had been convicted of assaulting with contempt (Ievins 2019). They often expressed strong feelings of skepticism in the legal system and in women, and several *resigned prisoners* refused to let me record their interviews, fearing that I might not use the recordings in responsible ways.[16] Another did not let me interview him in private, saying that he feared that, as a woman, I might make a false accusation against him if there were no witnesses.

Some had chosen not to appeal their convictions, saying that to do so would be too expensive and difficult. Others had active appeals, but were aware that these were unlikely to succeed, and that they therefore needed to find meaning in other parts of their lives. Ricky asserted that "if there's an endgame, and it comes out guilty, I've still got my family, I've still got something to live for." Many *resigned prisoners* had dropped their appeals because they considered them to be hopeless. Victor reluctantly decided to stop pursuing his during my fieldwork period, as legal fees had got him and his wife thousands of pounds in debt: "You can try to fight and chase parked cars for the rest of your life or you can put it to bed." George had spent the first eighteen months of his sentence fighting his appeal, and he had found the experience profoundly stressful and upsetting:

> The first eighteen months of being inside, I was appealing and going through the appeal courts, and I had all my statements, and I was highlighting every night and writing, and it absolutely nearly killed me. [. . .] I went through that for a year and a half, trying to fight it, and I lost my appeal because I didn't have enough evidence. So it got to the point where I said either I carry on with this even though it's wrecking my head or I just draw a line.
> *And was it wrecking your head because you were just thinking about it all the time?*
> Yeah, it's just constantly in your head, thinking, "How can I prove my innocence?" and them saying no. [. . .] I'm past it now. It took me a year and a half to accept that it's not gonna work. There's no point in moping around and I've just got to get my head around it and that's what I've done. I've had to, otherwise you crack up and you just can't cope through what I was doing. I did four and a half, didn't I, and there was no way I could have done four and a half years being angry at the world.[17]

Despite no longer fighting his case, George had not given up hope that one day his innocence would be proven: "I know that one day those girls are gonna admit that

I didn't do it and it will all come out. Maybe it might be in thirty years' time, but I know that day will come." It was this targeting of the gaze away from the injustice of their current situation which united *resigned prisoners*:

> This is where you come if it becomes pear-shaped and you've just got to tough it out. Everybody has their own ways of doing that. My way is keep busy. Even when you're in your cell, write letters, read, drawings, whatever. You've got to accept the fact that this is it. And yes, sometimes you think it's a bad dream and you're going to wake up out of it, but I would have woken up before now, and you just hope that you can see it out and look after yourself so you've got some sort of life out there when you get back and get out. (Kevin)

It was in these small daily actions—keeping busy and mentally occupied—that *resigned prisoners* tried to accept their situation. It was not that they forgot the apparent injustice, nor that they never talked about it, it was simply that their coping strategies were centered on trying not to think about it.

Resigned prisoners were highly sensitive to the effects of the "sex offender" label, which they often described in physical terms. Phil said that being described as a sex offender "sickens me," and Ricky felt "disgusted" at being subjected to it. Much of their frustration derived from their sense that the label overwrote other aspects of their identity. Michael, a former academic, put this simply when I opened the interview by asking him to tell me a little bit about who he was and where he was from: "Who I am? Who I was is more like it really." Despite their dislike of it, *resigned prisoners* rarely challenged uses of the term, insisting that to do so would be counterproductive: "What do I do? Do I erupt and be violent? Where's that gonna get me? It's not gonna help me go home, is it. And that's my end goal" (George). Instead, they managed their stigma by appealing to their knowledge that they had not committed their offense, and fought to hold on to this knowledge in the face of the false judgments of wider society and the potential judgments of other prisoners in Stafford:

> *How does your conviction make you feel about who you are?*
> In a way it doesn't bother us because I know that I didn't do it. So in a way I just think I don't care. But then you've got to think . . . That's how I think about it to myself, but then what another person thinks about us, about my crime . . . They could be thinking, "Wow, you're a really bad person," but in a way I know I'm a good person because I know I didn't do it. They can't see my life, and I can't see theirs. It's a hard one, isn't it? In a way, I think they don't know what I've done, so in a way it's basically down to myself. Yeah, I don't feel bad about it, but I wouldn't like to be called it either. (Ian)

> I know it never happened, it's up to them to think what they want. In my mind, I know. (Martin)

Despite their submission to the fact of the sentence, *resigned prisoners* defiantly held on to their claims of innocence. They said that this knowledge was internal and could therefore survive independently of external ratification, allowing them to maintain a positive image of themselves despite the judgment they faced. It was as though they tried to split the person they knew themselves to be from the person described by the label. Phil tried to cope with the hurt he felt when described as a "sex offender" by thinking, "They're not calling me that, they're calling somebody else it."

When it came to obeying day-to-day rules, *resigned prisoners* were generally highly compliant. They distinguished between institutions which allocate punishment, like the courts, and those which deliver it, like prisons, and they tried to stop their belief that the former were illegitimate from infecting their engagement with the latter. When they challenged the legitimacy of the prison itself—Michael, for instance, described officers in Stafford as "contemptible"—this tended to result from the perceived overuse of power rather than a rejection of its actual usage. Their motivations for this compliance were partly pragmatic—"If you want to get on, that's the way to do it" (Gordon)—and partly normative. Prior to their arrest, *resigned prisoners* had seen themselves as law-abiding citizens, people who believed that order and authority benefited society, and to some extent these beliefs were carried over into the prison:

> *Why do you do the things the prison wants you to do?*
> It's what I've done all my life. You've got to get up and go to work in the morning, ain't you, you've got to stick to or almost stick to the speed limit, you've got to pay your car insurance, there's just things you've got to do in life and it's the same here. I mean obviously here there's the side where there is punishments for not doing as you're told and they're a lot swifter to come than they would be outside, but I think the main reason is that's what you do. Life is about obeying rules. You hear people say rules are there to be broken but really they're not. Rules are there for a reason and usually the reason is to help society run a little bit smoother, and it's just the same in here. (Phil)

Resigned prisoners complied because they believed that doing so said a lot about who they were: just as they had been good people outside, they were good prisoners in Stafford, with several of *the resigned* saying that they hoped that they exemplified the "model prisoner" (Kevin).[18]

But while they were compliant when it came to rules about daily life on the wings, they were consistent in their refusal to admit guilt and therefore often unable to follow their sentence plans. They generally had smooth if distant interactions with prison officers, but their relationships with Offender Supervisors and Offender Managers were more strained. It was as though they perceived two different and, ideally, distinct forms of power operating within the prison. The first, which they accepted as legitimate, regulated quotidian life, and concerned itself with work, mealtimes, daily behavior, and association. The second, to which they felt unable to submit, governed offending behavior, offense acceptance, and sexuality (Ievins 2022). These two forms of power often blended, particularly as prisoners' IEP statuses were linked to compliance with sentence plans, a source of real frustration for *resigned prisoners* who were often unable to achieve enhanced status as they couldn't participate in SOTP courses. Victor complained that he was unable to prove that he was no longer a risk as maintaining his innocence meant he could not comply with his sentence plan; this was particularly exasperating as he insisted that he had never been a risk in the first place:

> I understand the needs for what they do, linking privilege with addressing your of- fending behavior and whatever they take you as, I understand the need for all that, but what happens if you slip between the cracks? What happens if you are the ones who slip between the cracks?
> *And how does that make you feel, as one of the ones that slips between the cracks?*
> I just hope that I can prove them wrong. I think they treat you badly but I think that's understandable, but you just imagine that over time you're proving them . . . but how do you prove a negative? You just do what you do and get on with it and don't do what you're not supposed to be doing. Period. [. . .] When I look at the risk factors, there's nothing I can do except not be [laughs], except not offend.

Unlike prisoners who admitted their guilt, Victor felt that there was nothing posi- tive to be gained from his experience in the prison, and that he had nothing to work toward. He tried to adapt to the demands of the institution, but many of its imperatives, specifically those relating to offending behavior, clashed with his insistence on his innocence and blocked him from complying in the way that he wanted to.

The blending of the two forms of power made it difficult in practice for *resigned prisoners* to distinguish between the legitimacy of their convictions and the legiti- macy of the prison. As shown above, Phil considered that the day-to-day rules within Stafford helped everyone who lived and worked within it, but his insistence on his innocence had resulted in him having to fight to maintain his enhanced status and struggling to be assessed as suitable for his desired employment. None- theless, he was reluctant to admit to the offense:

> What stops me from just saying it, although it could make my life inside and outside prison a lot easier—I didn't do it. I didn't do it. And I cannot—I can't think of a word so I'll use "confess," I don't mean "confess"—I cannot confess to something I have not done. I mean, some of the lads have said to me, "Why are you doing this? You'll just make your life so much easier if you go, 'Yeah, I'm a dirty bastard, I did it.'" [. . .] But I can't. I just can't. I can't. I can't. I didn't do it and as much as they're gonna punish me for it, I can't say I did it because it never happened.

Phil claimed integrity in his refusal to lie, and it was implicit within this refusal that the institution that was asking him to was morally flawed. Phil said that, prior to his imprisonment, he had had faith in the legal system, but this had dissipated following his arrest and conviction:

> Before I had this experience, I tell you what, once I was in town, me and the wife, and a couple of lads started—I don't know what happened before—but they started

grabbing hold of this copper, throwing him on the floor, hitting him. Like a bloody idiot, I ran over to help him and managed to get one of them off and then the copper got up and got the other one, he arrested him and the other one got away. He thanked me and all that for it. And to be honest, if I saw that on the street now, I'd probably give the lads a hand! I've got no faith, I've got no confidence in the system. Now I can feel myself tightening up, I just think it's absolute crap, Alice, I honestly do. I don't think the system as a whole improves when you come to jail. I asked my probation officer, because she was going on about me maintaining my innocence, basically that I'm stupid [. . .], and I said, "Can you not even acknowledge that there is a percentage of people in prison that are innocent?" and she wouldn't even do that, she wouldn't even acknowledge that. That is their attitude: you're convicted, that's it. And it's bloody wrong. It's wrong. I'm no fan of this system. Always have been and now, like I say, I wouldn't go out and break the law but I've got no respect for it either. None.

Although Phil and other *resigned prisoners* said that they wanted to forget the injustice of their situation, the way power operated within the prison made this impossible. The prison did not disentangle its operations from issues of guilt and innocence, and this rendered day-to-day life in the prison a constant reminder of their criminal convictions and of the injustice which *resigned prisoners* claimed such convictions represented.

CONCLUSION: THE PERSISTENCE OF INNOCENCE

People who maintain that they are innocent are the fly in the ointment of moral communication theories of punishment. Such theories are written for ideal worlds in which laws align perfectly with norms, in which the innocent are never convicted, and in which the outcomes of trials echo historical reality. In the real world of Stafford, however, there were a great many flies. It is impossible to know if *activists* and *resigned prisoners* were truly wrongly convicted. It is also impossible to know if they genuinely believed they were wrongly convicted—if they had no memory of the offense or misunderstood the nature of sexual violence. It is also entirely feasible that they were consciously lying when they said they were innocent. Whichever is true, they consistently insisted that they were not guilty, and this insistence existed in the foreground of their daily experience and shaped their day-to-day orientations toward their sentences.

For prisoners in Stafford, the maintenance of innocence was not a condition or a belief, it was a lifestyle, one which required a deliberate rejection of a version of reality which was constantly reinforced by the prison and which was expressed in their relationships with various powerholders. Their claims of innocence had such determinative power because they were held in a morally communicative institution, one which told prisoners that they were a particular type of person. Such institutions feel different depending on whether the moral identity which they assign to the people they hold fits with the one people claim for themselves, and the two groups described in this chapter experienced their imprisonment as an affront to their sense of self but responded to this situation differently. *Activists* threw themselves into strenuous assertions of innocence. The anger which they felt energized them and contributed to their consciously articulated opposition to the prison and to the criminal justice state which it represented. For *resigned prisoners*, however, the fact that they held on to their claims of innocence was an unfortunate consequence of penal power. They tried to submit themselves to their situation and not to dwell on its apparent injustice, but the prison's regulation of the stories which they told about their offenses made such strategic forgetting impossible. *Resigned prisoners* tried to treat Stafford as an institution which delivered punishment and did not allocate it, but Stafford pushed them to engage with it as a morally communicative institution.

In theory, prisons are not supposed to treat people differently if they say that they are innocent. Prison officers in Stafford repeatedly insisted that they deliberately avoided looking into the circumstances of prisoners' convictions, fearing that if they believed in someone's innocence, they would treat them more leniently, or that they might treat those convicted of particularly serious crimes more harshly. They thought their responsibility was to deliver the punishment which had been allocated by a judge, and to leave questions of innocence and guilt in the past. As this chapter and the previous chapter have shown, however, this distinction is impossible to maintain. To put it simply, the experience of imprisonment is different depending on how you feel about what you have been convicted of. Prisoners carried their beliefs about their innocence and guilt into the prison, and their adaptations to their sentences were intimately connected to them. In some ways, this is unsurprising, even natural. People are interpretive creatures, and it makes sense that prisoners would feel differently about their imprisonment based on whether (and how) they accepted it as deserved. But as this chapter has shown, innocence was something which was maintained by Stafford as an institution, as well as by prisoners as individuals. The next chapter builds on this argument and describes the moralized nature of power in Stafford.

6

Moralizing Boundaries

Staff-Prisoner Relationships and the Communication of Difference

Edward, a "*mainstream*" *prisoner* who was serving a sentence for a violent assault, had been in Stafford since before it rerolled to become a specialist site. As someone who had been in the prison for so long, he had close relationships with prison officers. He told me that one day he had been having a cup of tea in the staff office with two of the most popular and professional officers on the wing when the conversation turned to the possibility of him being transferred to a different establishment. The officers suggested that doing so would be good for him as it would allow him to be around "normal people." Surprised, Edward asked them to explain what they meant:

> They just kept saying, "You are different to these." I'm like, "I know." I said, "Yes, but prisoners are prisoners. If I break the law, they break the law, you've just got to get on with it," and they were like, "Just trust me, they are wrong-uns."[1] That's what they said.

Edward's discomfort had two dimensions. He had developed some close friendships with other men in Stafford, describing them as "decent guys," and he thought they deserved better than being disparaged as "wrong-uns." He also didn't understand how these officers' judgmental backstage attitude could coexist with the friendly interactions he had seen them have with these specific men:

> What scared me the most was the fact how I've seen them with these guys, their body language and everything frightened me because I just thought, fucking hell, how the fuck can you be, like, that cold about it when I've seen you have cups of coffee with them? That, to me, is very confusing, very confusing.

When he asked the officers to explain the apparent contradiction, they gave a straightforward answer. The backstage judgment was authentic, and the professional courtesy was not:

> They kept saying, "Yes, but this is our job. When we come through here, we have to fucking work with these people if we like it or not because if I don't, I can't pay my mortgage." That's what one of them said. The other officer basically verified the same. That's what he said, he said, "When you come here you put on a mask, but you take it off as soon as you are through that gate because you don't want to think about any of these fuckers in here." That's what he said.

What had been invisible to Edward had been much more obvious to other men in Stafford. After the conversation had ended, he had gone to tell his best friend what he had heard, and his friend had laughed: "He sat me down and was like, 'That's the way it is in here.' He says, 'Because you try and get on with everyone, you don't see it.' But he says, 'We see it.' And that's when he said, 'The officers are a lot different with you than they are with people like me.'"

Officers in Stafford juggled two competing moral frameworks, both of which were evident in this story. The first was influenced by the punitive discourse about "sex offenders" which is prominent among members of the public and which was articulated by officers in backstage spaces like staff offices. This discourse imagines people convicted of sex offenses as permanently dangerous monsters, and suggests that it is necessary for public safety and public morality that they are condemned and isolated. Anyone who is too closely aligned with "sex offenders" is corrupted by association. According to this discourse, the offenses "sex offenders" have committed should shape the way everyone interacts with them. They have lost their claims to full humanity, and with them, their right to be treated the same as other prisoners and other citizens.[2] Prison officers in Stafford were influenced by this discourse. Despite claims to the contrary, officers did think about prisoners in Stafford as "sex offenders" and allowed their criminal convictions to play a role in their relationships with them. Officers described feeling psychologically, reputationally, and to some extent physically threatened by the population they worked with and by their staining convictions.[3] Many talked with distress about finding out what prisoners had been convicted of and about the frequent distaste and voyeurism, and occasional abuse, they had experienced when friends and family members found out where they worked. Their anxiety about working with people convicted of sex offenses was not narrowly targeted at issues related to sexuality. They also maintained that such prisoners behaved very differently from the "mainstream" prisoner group with whom they had been trained to work, and with whom most had worked prior to the reroll. Prisoners in Stafford were much older than a "mainstream" prison population would be, and much more compliant, but this threw officers off balance and combined with their concerns about the devious "sex offender" to make them deeply attuned to the real and imagined risks of manipulation and conditioning.

This condemnatory moral framework had to compete with officers' occupational morality. As the officers in the story made clear to Edward, most officers saw themselves as people doing a job, and while at work they tried to commit themselves to the norms of their profession. Prison officers' occupational morality asserts that while officers may have personal moral sentiments about the people they imprison, it is vital that these sentiments do not influence the way they do their job. They are to be understood as professionals working in a bureaucratic institution, whose job is to maintain security and order, provide care, and perhaps facilitate rehabilitation, but not to dispense or soften punishment. They are to behave impartially and use discretion fairly, and to avoid overt displays of emotion. This occupational morality was influenced by the growing rationalization of the prison in the nineteenth and twentieth centuries, and reflects the widespread squeamishness about punishment described by Elias ([1939] 1994) and Garland (1990). In our "civilized" society, we are uncomfortable with the uncontrollability and animality of the punitive impulse. We have therefore deliberately hidden it from view, punishing people behind prison walls, sanitizing our language, and upholding an ideal of professionalism among penal workers, "all of which tends to sublimate a rather distasteful activity and render it more tolerable to public and professional sensibilities" (Garland 1990, 235; see also Christie 1981).[4] The occupational morality created by these processes stresses that prison officers should focus on achieving the smooth running of the prison—policing the wings, responding to prisoners' queries, distributing food and clothes, and facilitating the regime—and should not see themselves as active participants in a morally communicative ritual. In a place like Stafford, this should lead them to quell any discomfort they feel about people convicted of sex offenses, or at least not to let it influence frontstage areas.

Edward's conversation in the wing office, and later with his friend, suggests that officers' attempts at frontstage impartiality had not successfully obscured their backstage judgment. The moment of explicitly verbalized moral judgment which Edward described was rare, as he was a *"mainstream" prisoner* who was trusted more than most prisoners were, but nevertheless most men in Stafford shared Edward's friend's insistence that officers morally condemned them: "we know what they think of us really," Jake summarized. In this chapter, I will describe how prisoners gained this knowledge, and how, despite officers' best efforts, their morally judgmental impulses pierced through their protective professional veils. It argues that officers in Stafford were torn between their competing moral frameworks, and were anxious about their dignity, their objectivity, and their authority. They were frightened that they might be judged for working too closely with these stained men, that their own moral instincts might lead them to behave unfairly, and that they might even be manipulated to use their power inappropriately. These risks threatened their sense of what it meant to be a prison officer, and as a result, they took refuge in an extremely distant form of professionalism (see also

Eriksson 2021). During periods of association, for instance, most officers came out of their wings to stand on the landings, willing to monitor prisoners and deal with any queries, but their physical presence on the prison landings was not matched by their willingness to engage.[5] With notable exceptions, officers rarely joined in with the games of pool and darts which prisoners played and nor did they engage in informal conversations. (Edward's experience of having a cup of tea in the office was unusual.) Avoiding informal conversations with prisoners meant that officers often knew very little about the details of prisoners' lives, making it harder for them to meet their needs or use their discretionary power wisely. Their fear of manipulation also discouraged them from softening their power in any way, encouraging them to police the wing more tightly than they would otherwise.[6] Prisoners, in turn, were highly aware that officers avoided and closely regulated them, and were sensitive to what this implied: that officers saw them as "sex offenders." Prison officers did not intend to be judgmental, then, but they put up moral and relational barriers to avoid doing so, and it was in the effects of these moral and relational barriers that prisoners perceived the judgment which so pained them. In officers' attempts to act as impartial automatons, they had become morally expressive agents, and what they expressed was condemnation.

ASPIRATIONS OF IMPARTIALITY

You've got to learn to have some sort of rapport with these sorts of people. (Officer)

Prison officer culture in Stafford was in many ways typical of English public-sector prison staff culture. Officers were proud of their uniforms and their roles, and distrustful of management. They said that they would do anything for their colleagues and the prison had historically had a strong union branch, although it had weakened in recent years. They showed very little sign of the brutality which had tarnished the Prison Service of the 1980s, but they certainly believed that they should be in charge and were somewhat heavy in their use of power (Crewe, Liebling, and Hulley 2014). They gave orders, summoned prisoners by yelling their surnames, and actively policed wings during association periods. They were less comfortable engaging in explicitly rehabilitative work or in talking to prisoners about their personal lives or their plans for the future. Many of these ways of working resulted from Stafford's particular history and had been carried forward after the reroll. The prison's previous function meant that it had tightly restricted internal movement to keep VPs and "mainstream" prisoners apart. They also were reflective of more widespread officer culture. Prison officers in England and Wales are socialized to prefer the security and order components of their role (Crawley 2004) and trained to have distant and distrustful relationships with prisoners (Arnold 2007). In the past couple of decades, rehabilitative and resettlement tasks have increasingly been taken away from prison officers and redistributed to staff members working off the wings (Crewe 2011b). Many of Stafford's more experienced officers were resentful of this deskilling: "All we are now is discipline tools, as officers. We are here to keep the peace now," one officer told me.

Despite their heavy and somewhat distant orientation toward prisoners, most officers in Stafford avoided making pejorative remarks to the men or making explicit judgments about their offenses. They tended to believe that a central part of their role was the capacity to overlook prisoners' offenses—"to switch off what they're in for"—as doing so made their work easier: "if you're worrying about a multiple murderer or a multiple rapist all the time, you can't do the job" (officer). Ignoring offenses was a strategy of self-protection which mirrored that followed by prisoners (see chapter 7): prisoners had been convicted of disturbing and upsetting offenses, and officers did not want to be contaminated by these thoughts. One female officer, for example, reported that she often woke up in the night thinking about what prisoners had told her:

> Some of the issues obviously can be mentally draining, because they stay in there [your mind]. If they have discussed some of the things that have happened to them and perhaps even why they do what they do, it stays there. You can't just make it all go away, because then if you care, you can't just switch that off and say, "Oh well, never mind, I'm at home now."

Another described the intrusive images which had followed her reading about the offenses of a man on her wing:

> He was a cleaner, and just before we started serving the evening meal I was reading through [the man's record], and then I had to shout him to get the [food] trolley. And I was looking at him as I was calling the numbers [saying what meals prisoners should be served], and just seeing him—he's there now, he's on that wing—I couldn't get it out of my head then. [. . .] That was very strange, because you could imagine it. The offense was obviously, it was sort of like against this little boy. He sort of like, he made, he made him go in the shower with him and made him wash him and obviously and all that. [. . .] I suppose it was graphic because when I saw him, I could just picture it and I was like, "That's really not a good thing!" So when you're dealing with the food or whatever, looking at the names and looking at the food and looking at him, you don't really want to be thinking about that!

Officers who were parents and those who had personal experience of sexual violence found thinking about offenses particularly upsetting: "At times I can't stand the place, I detest it. I think things have changed since I've become a dad" (officer). One staff member described struggling in her job after someone attempted to abduct her young son.

In most cases, officers protected themselves by avoiding talking about prisoners' offenses or looking them up on the prison's computer system. If finding out what prisoners were in for was unavoidable—for instance, if they had to do a risk assessment before escorting a prisoner to hospital, or if their role as an Offender

Supervisor required them to engage more deeply with prisoners—they tried not to dwell on the knowledge:

> It's just a moment of realization, "Oh, that's what he did," then you have to do your job. You just have to process it. If you thought about who they are and what they've done, you wouldn't be able to come in every day. (Officer)

> Sometimes you can read something that upsets you. Sometimes you can read something and say, "That's bad." But if you let that upset you, then you can't do your job properly. (Offender Supervisor)

Officers sometimes said that their professional requirement to act with impartiality made them uncomfortable by making them accustomed to the morally unacceptable. As one officer put it, "you almost get desensitized to the word 'rapist,' to the words 'child sex offenses.'" There is emotional and moral security in acknowledging the wrongness of crimes, but officers felt like they were in a moral and emotional limbo, aware that prisoners were stained but unwilling to pay too much attention to it.[7]

Officers believed that their role was to provide care and custody fairly and equally—to deal with the men as "prisoners" and thus to try not to think about them as "sex offenders." It was explicitly not their job, they thought, to be morally communicative, and they thought that if they were, they would be punitive:

> They've been convicted by a court of law and they're being punished, aren't they, so why should I make that worse? They've already been taken away from their families. They're serving their punishment, they shouldn't have to have any more. [. . .] You can perhaps look at the news and say, "Yeah, they deserve that," and I think the general public would do that, but in here, I'm not judgmental to them for what they've done. They're serving a sentence and, OK, I'm locking them up, but I'm paid to do that by the Prison Service, and that's what I'm here to do. (Officer)

> I don't think of them as a sex offender, I don't think, "Oh, I'm unlocking a sex offender today." If a door needs locking, it needs locking. If they need something doing, they need something doing. And you can't think of them as sex offenders, because if you thought of them as sex offenders, you would treat them different. (Officer)

Their professional ideal was impartiality and detachment, and they avoided learning about prisoners' convictions because they thought that this knowledge might lead them to treat prisoners harshly, distantly, or differently from each other: "I think it can affect the way you are with people. I've seen it affect the way people are with people, and I wouldn't want that to be the case" (officer). They recognized that what they thought about prisoners mattered to them, and they were reluctant to hurt them through explicit expressions of moral judgment. One officer, for instance, who said that he did struggle with prisoners' crimes, recalled how difficult he found it after a man on his wing had died by suicide, before reflecting, "That's another reason why it's important not to judge them.

What if one of these think, 'Mr. Bloggs is alright' and then one day I say, 'Fuck off nonce!' and then he hangs himself?"

Prison officers did not just fear that allowing their private moral sentiments to infiltrate their role as officers would push them toward punitiveness. They sometimes admitted in private that it was likely that not all prisoners were guilty, and they didn't want to let this knowledge affect their behavior. Like prisoners, they were particularly suspicious when the offense happened a long time ago or in cases where there was an adult victim, maintaining that it is easy for women to "cry rape" (Burt 1980). They also expressed some sympathy with those convicted of offenses against older children:

> My son is sixteen and I've seen some of the girls that he's friends with and I think to myself, "You look about twenty-one." And again, I'm not putting myself in that situation of saying, "Well, it's their own fault for dressing up," but I think to myself, "I can understand where the confusion may have happened." [. . .] So I've never yet met somebody who I've thought to myself, "Oh, he's genuinely innocent," but I have met lots of people where I think, if the shoe was on the other foot, it could have been me. (Offender Supervisor)

Nevertheless, they saw themselves as "an instrument of the court" (officer), whose primary requirement was to treat people equally and not to make their own decisions about what people deserved:

> *To what extent does whether or not they maintain innocence affect how you think about prisoners?*
> I don't think it alters it. Again, it's not for us staff to care—care's the wrong word—but it's not for staff to say if they shouldn't be here. If they appeal it and they win, congratulations, you get to go home and you're not our problem anymore. I don't need to know. If they start the conversation, then I just say, "It's not for me to know. You're here and it's my job to deal with you while you're here." (Officer)

They frequently echoed the famous dictum that people come to prison as a punishment, not for punishment, and they believed that it was for the courts to allocate punishment and for them to deliver it. Engaging with the details of prisoners' offenses would make this task harder.

That officers avoided finding out about the details of prisoners' offenses did not mean that they treated prisoners as their moral equals; rather, they treated all prisoners as equally different to them. Officers felt that prisoners had a lower moral status than they did, but it was defined by their status primarily as a prisoner and secondarily as a "sex offender," rather than by the specifics of what they had done. In order to maintain this status differential and to prevent themselves from being corrupted by prisoners, officers maintained a strict symbolic boundary between themselves and those they incarcerated.[8] They never made cups of tea for prisoners, for instance, and only rarely allowed prisoners to do so for them. They took pride in their uniforms—items of clothing which made their distinction from prisoners clear—and generally preferred to be called by their surnames with the honorific "Mr." or "Miss," while referring to prisoners either by just their surname or their first name.[9] They also made frequent jokes in the office about prisoners as a bloc being "groomers" and warned female officers (and me) to be careful around men they deemed to be predatory. They balanced their reluctance to acknowledge the specifics of prisoners' crimes with the conscious acknowledgment of their stained identities. Doing so prevented them from getting too close to prisoners or from empathizing too strongly with their situation:

> You get the older guys who come and to an extent don't really know what's going on, which is sad to an extent, but I always say to everybody, people don't get sent to Stafford prison because they haven't paid their fishing license. So you can feel empathy to an extent, but they are in jail for a reason, and particularly in Stafford, they're in for a reason. (Offender Supervisor)

> You must not forget the reasons why they're here. They might seem like an OK bloke but they're not. I act like I don't care what they're in for, but I do care. Sometimes I get a bit annoyed and a bit sarcastic and I remind them that I know why they're here and that I'm the officer and they're the inmate and although I might be nice, I haven't forgotten the reason why they're here. I'm not here to persecute them, I'm here to keep them away from the public and do a good job. (Officer)

Deep down, officers believed themselves to be categorically different from the men they imprisoned. They may have aspired to treat prisoners impartially, but they also sought to maintain a clear separation from them, and their interactions were functional but rarely personal. The claim of one Offender Supervisor that "you can have a laugh with them if you take them at face value" was double-edged: working relationships between staff and prisoners were possible because officers held prisoners at a distance, but this distance ensured that these relationships were shallow. Any attempts to breach this boundary, or disrupt the hierarchy which it implied, were seen by officers as a threat.

DANGERS OF COMPLIANCE

> This is a doddle [really easy].
> *Why?*
> Working with YOs [Young Offenders] in particular, it's like a constant battle, it's a war zone.[10] Coming here, when it was mains, it was like semiretirement. Now working with these more elderly, more intelligent gentlemen, it's like full retirement.
> *Are there any ways in which it's harder here?*
> Psychologically it's different. They're more intelligent in lots of ways. With mainstream prisoners, their crimes are based around aggression and taking what they want. These prisoners are in for being nice, for the grooming and petting, so they're much more amenable. (Officer)

Do you think that the fact that they're more compliant affects your work in any way?
Me personally, no, but I think because they are so compliant, people can get complacent and take their foot off the pedal and forget that they are prisoners. These pose just as much risk as the mains.
Can you give me an example?
Just because they always do what you tell them to do, you get into the mindset, "Oh they're alright, these are." You've got to stay in that mindset that they're prisoners, they're here for a reason, you've got exactly the same risk and you need to be dealing with them exactly the same as any other prisoner. (Officer)

Stafford was striking for its calmness and quiet.[11] Whereas in most penal establishments, officers put a great deal of work into the maintenance of order (Sparks, Bottoms, and Hay 1996; Liebling, Price, and Shefer 2011), prisoners in Stafford, like others convicted of sex offenses, were so compliant that order was taken for granted. Prisoners tended to follow, and sometimes preempt, staff instructions: they started to queue to go to work up to fifteen minutes before route began, and they quickly and calmly walked to their cells at the end of association periods, often before they were told to. It was rare for staff to feel the need to challenge prisoners' behavior, and voices were normally raised only when officers shouted prisoners' surnames to summon them downstairs. That prisoners presented fewer control issues than might be expected in a prison of Stafford's size was in part due to the relatively high age of Stafford's population, but it was also a consequence of prisoners' long-standing relationships to authority.[12] Many men in Stafford had never been to prison before, and *repentant* and *resigned prisoners* in particular liked to think of themselves as law-abiding citizens. *Negotiators*, on the other hand, were unlikely to challenge staff because they considered compliance to be in their best interests, and *fatalists* were so vulnerable that they struggled to imagine what resistance would look like.

Despite this apparent calmness, officers frequently complained that prisoners convicted of sex offenses were harder to work with than "mainstream" prisoners had been and stressed that it was important neither to adapt nor to soften their working practices. Officers claimed that their charges posed the same risk to order that their "mainstream" antecedents had, and interpreted their apparent compliance as a mask obscuring inherent dangerousness: "They're very manipulative. These lot are trying to be your friend all the time, they're trying to help you, but really, they're trying to rip your head off" (officer). At the same time, officers thought that there were risks within prisoners' compliance itself, which they felt challenged their professional identities, their ability to hold and exert power effectively, and the boundaried relationships they sought to develop with prisoners. Officers felt that prisoners wanted closer, more intimate relationships with them than they were comfortable with and than "mainstream" prisoners had sought. They described prisoners as "clingy," "needy," and "devious," and complained that "they get in your head" and create a form of "psychological pressure." Officers in all prisons worry that they might be conditioned or manipulated by prisoners (Arnold 2016), but officers in Stafford were intensely sensitive to these risks, largely because of their preconceptions about "sex offenders." All prisoners in Stafford—particularly, but not exclusively, those who had offended against children—were believed to be inherent "groomers": "It's in their nature, it's in their being to be that way inclined" (officer); "the pedophiles and child abusers have been able to condition parents" (nonuniformed staff member). Officers assumed that prisoners would carry these skills and predilections into the prison, and although exaggerated, these risks were not to be discounted. A few female officers described prisoners getting sexual gratification by telling them about their offenses, forming attachments to them and asking them to stay in touch after their release, or trying to persuade them to enter their cells unaccompanied. A couple of prisoners spoke about their desire for "friendship and closeness" with female officers, in ways which clearly threatened professional boundaries. I had one conversation with a young prisoner who complained about the difficulty of maintaining a respectful distance from female officers while repeatedly trying to push his leg against mine.[13]

These risks came from a small minority of men in Stafford, and the majority behaved respectfully and appropriately. However, officers did not use the language of manipulation solely to describe sexual risks. Their belief that prisoners were "groomers" stained staff-prisoner relationships more generally and impacted how officers interpreted prisoners' wider behavior. Officers used the terms "grooming," "conditioning," and "manipulation" interchangeably and defined them nebulously as "small things like we're doing what they want and not the other way around," or behaviors aimed at "testing boundaries" or giving "power to them." These behaviors were united by the fact that they challenged officers' sense of themselves, their expectations of prisoners, and their preferred style of staff-prisoner relationship. Officers favored hierarchical relationships: they wanted to tell prisoners what to do and have prisoners either obey or fight back in ways which were visible and easily definable. Prisoners in Stafford, on the other hand, wanted to engage in and influence the terms of their incarceration, whether through complaints, censoriousness (Mathiesen 1965), or the development of friendly relationships with staff. They thus did not follow the expected script of prisoner behavior and challenged the power of officers in ways which were insidious and difficult to identify, but easy to discount as conditioning, grooming, or manipulation.[14]

Asked to give an example of conditioning, one officer replied:

> So prisoners are having a banter with you. They might be taking the mickey [teasing] and you might be taking the mickey back. But when it gets to the point where they're swearing at you in front of other prisoners and in front of staff, you need to draw a line under it because they're going too far.

Another described calling officers and managers by their first names as "a form of grooming":

> I am not their pal, I am never going to be their pal, I am the person responsible for making sure they comply with the rules and regulations and are behind the door safely at night when they should be, and that's how I see it.

Self-harming was often considered a calculated act: "They're more manipulative, they might not argue to your face, but they'll go to their cell and cut up" (Offender Supervisor). Other officers classed prisoners' apparent willingness to engage with the institution by becoming prisoner representatives or joining the Prisoner Council as symptomatic of their manipulation:

> With sex offenders, they are more manipulative and underhanded in the way they work. They will follow due process to go through the personal officer system, do apps and complaints and stuff, whereas mainstream prisoners, if they don't get their own way, they will sometimes kick off.[15]

It is striking that compliance, following "due process," was seen as devious, and that the violence officers could face from "mainstream" prisoners was considered to be almost preferable.[16]

Officers disproportionately accused older, more middle-class, and more engaged prisoners of manipulation. They believed that these people were particularly unhappy being supervised by "lowly prison officers": "They've got a different level of manipulation, they are the ones who've got a lot outside and they look for positions of responsibility" (officer). Many officers alluded to anxious feelings about working with prisoners they feared were more intelligent than them—"They're ex-teachers, policemen, they're fire officers, and they're bright and influential"—and whose ways of talking and interacting they considered insidious and strategic. Buried within these critiques were negative evaluations of prisoners' masculinity. Several officers compared prisoners to women in terms of their neediness, and they were frustrated that, rather than actively confronting officers, like "mainstream" prisoners or real men, Stafford's more middle-class inhabitants undermined them.[17]

It was certainly the case that prisoners in Stafford had very different relationships with state power and large institutions than is common among "mainstream" prisoners. In their professional lives, a great many had run their own legitimate businesses, and others had worked in large, bureaucratic organizations. Significant numbers of prisoners—more than half of those interviewed—had never been to prison before, and prior to their incarceration they had had little experience of being subjected to the hard edges of state power. They thought of large bureaucracies as institutions which helped you, and which you worked for and with. In many cases, prisoners' prior experiences of work made it harder for them to accept authority, particularly in its heaviest form: "It's unpleasant because the authority as it's exercised is mainly unjust, and I suppose it's the opposite of what I'm used to. I've been the boss and I've exercised authority, but not in an authoritarian way" (Michael). In some cases, this resentment morphed into explicit contempt for staff, as a man I chatted to while walking from one wing to another told me:

> We know exactly where we're going, we know exactly what we're doing. Some of the staff are not so fortunate. That's one of the problems here, the complete lack of organization. The left hand is not only not talking to the right hand, they're not even attached. I've run a few firms and there's very few I'd actually employ.

On first arriving in prison, many prisoners had held unrealistic expectations of what officers could and would do for them. They had imagined officers as service personnel rather than holders of authority, and struggled to adapt to this new way of interacting with workers, as a story told by Kevin about an evening early in his sentence made clear:

> On Fridays there [in my previous prison], I'd always have a salad, not for any reason like I was actually going anywhere, but just so I could eat at a leisurely time. One day I was chopping the salad up and then I went to pull the key back on the pilchards and the key [to the tin] broke. I couldn't get the wretched thing open. So I was sharing a cell then with a guy, a thoroughly nice guy, so I pressed the button for the officer and it was probably about quarter past eight and I waited about ten minutes before he came and he opened the door, big guy, and he said, "What's the matter?"[18] I said, "You couldn't get me a tin opener, could you, to open the pilchards?" And he looked at me and he said . . . I can't repeat what he said. But he said, "Are you taking the piss?" And I said, "No, I've laid all my salad out and I can't get into the pilchards, the key's broke." He said, "I don't believe you. You know what that bell's for, for an emergency." I said, "Well I'm sorry, I'm not going to be able to have my tea!" He just shut the door. [. . .] The next evening the guy was on slightly earlier and he came up to me and he said, "I'm not going to tell you off, but I am going to tell you this. That took an awful lot of bloody nerve, what you did. You're either barking or a bloody fool." I said, "I'm sorry, I do realize, I've had eight hours to digest it. I'm as nervous as hell that I'm going to get into trouble." He said, "No, you're not going to be in trouble, but can I just remind you that this is a prison and not a hotel and we're not bellboys."

While most prisoners had since learned what to expect from officers, some still compared the prison to an "office environment," the atmosphere of which would be improved by chatting with colleagues (in this case, officers) about the weather or what was on television.

Some prisoners actively tried to use their professional expertise to help the prison, in ways which were not always welcomed. One man, for instance, had been rebuffed by management when he volunteered to help with the prison's accounts. Others had frustrated their teachers in Education:

I don't know how true this is, this is a rumor, [but] our tutor left about six or seven weeks ago, she just didn't show up again, and the rumor going round is that we gave her a breakdown! We weren't aggressive or anything, but a lot of us were older blokes, quite a few of us had been in business before, so we just challenged her on some things. She was a business expert but some of the things she said didn't sound right and we just challenged her about it and that caused a lot of problems. (Phil)

At times, prisoners made use of their soft power to attempt to influence the terms of their incarceration. In so doing, they often used social skills they had developed in their professional careers or their lives as consumers. Tony and Steven, both of whom had had professional jobs before their imprisonment, were frequently accused of manipulation:

If you went on the mentor course, for instance, all of the skills that you can learn if you haven't already got them, by going on that course, you could easily say, "That's manipulation, innit. That's manipulative. That's manipulation," if you were inclined to say that. But when it turns out that might just be a good man management skill or a good way of engaging with someone or a good way of earning someone's trust, I think it's a little bit dangerous when people say, "Oh it's manipulation." That might just be something that you do. (Tony)

I don't let things go. When people say no, I don't listen to them [. . .]. But the officers, they'll say, "Oh no, I'm busy," but I'll push it, I'll push it. It's easier for them to dismiss you so you need to get past that barrier, you need for them to see you as a person and not just a blur, and the whole notion as a blur. [. . .] It's the same as going to the shops, sometimes you need more attention, you need sometimes to present yourself as actually person to person, and that's something I do definitely. I fight for that. (Steven)

Prisoners saw these forms of engagement with officers as expressive of their humanity and a result of a desire to have themselves, their ideas, and their needs taken seriously by holders of authority. They resented attempts by staff to label these as acts of manipulation. None of these forms of behavior explicitly or directly challenged order or safety, and they were not actively noncompliant. Nevertheless, they complicated officers' position as powerholders, muddying relationships which officers would have preferred to be deferential and hierarchical.

Officers missed the ontological security (Giddens 1991) of working with "mainstream" prisoners, even if those relationships had been more openly hostile: "That sort of atmosphere is easier to deal with because at least you know where you stand" (officer). Prisoners in Stafford, on the other hand, were able to use soft power, working within the structures of the bureaucratic late-modern prison to challenge the authority of officers. Officers believed that prisoners took advantage of their experience with bureaucracies to "use the system against you" (officer) by regularly and strategically submitting complaints forms. Most officers claimed that prisoners submitted such forms more frequently and more effectively than "mainstream" prisoners had:[19]

These people are very clever, whereas the people we were locking up before, the burglars and the robbers, they were generally less clever. We've got some very intelligent people that we lock up now. That brings different challenges to the staff. Whereas before you could say no to them and just fob them off with an excuse, with these you really have to know your job. They can read and write and they are intelligent so you can't fob them off with bullshit. [. . .] With the mains you'd be more likely to get a mouthful and they'd take a pop at you, where with these, you'll get a "Well I think you're wrong there sir!" [. . .] The complaints now have got more substance and are better constructed. Before, it would be "Mr. Wilson is a prick," now they say why I'm a prick. (Officer)

In some cases, these acts of censoriousness could push officers into more legitimate behavior. In others, the perception that prisoners were more likely to complain made officers uneasy and contributed to a greater distance between staff and prisoners. Astute prisoners like Ahmed recognized that officers were "cautious" around him because "as much as they [officers] have paper power, I have paper power too, because I can write things."

Officers' discomfort with prisoners' apparent tendency to complain was linked to their general feelings of anxiety concerning managerial power, another force which operated behind officers' backs and left them feeling insecure about their positions:

Why do you prefer to deal face-to-face than [with] complaints?
It's easier to deal with because you know what you're dealing with. It's that person with a complaint and it's a valid complaint sometimes. But the other way it's behind your back and the first time you hear of it is when a CM [Custodial Manager] comes and speaks to you. (Officer)[20]

Manipulation, you've just got to nip it in the bud, simple as that. [. . .]
If they're good at it, how can you tell that it's happening?
Because they don't tend to come to officers, they tend to go above us, because the officers know how they work, how the landing works, what's put in the obs [observation] book, we know who's who and what's what.[21] [. . .] They tend to ask for the same Senior Officers or the same CMs or the same governor, because they tend to give them what they want, and again that's where the undermining of staff comes from, and then they wonder why staff get annoyed and the job satisfaction's out the window. (Officer)

Prison sociologist Ben Crewe (2011b) has argued that prisoners in late-modern English and Welsh prisons often complain that power has been decentered from the wings and is instead found in psychologists' offices and management corridors. He suggests that prisoners are frustrated by these changes, which result in a form of power which prisoners describe as both intrusive and opaque. Officers in Stafford shared these annoyances, resenting their loss of control over their territory but often attributing it not just to changes in the way prisons operate but also to the manipulative skill of prisoners. The anxiety which officers felt about their roles had numerous sources, including shifts in how their job was designed, but as I shall argue, it was expressed as moral judgment.

CONTROL AS CONDEMNATION

He shows his power by the way he stares at you and the way he talks to you, and the way he raises his voice and the way he slams your door. Because he does slam it. He doesn't shut it. He pulls it. "That's my authority to you. That's me telling you that you're a dirty inmate, a scumbag, and I'll slam the door in your face because that's my power. I'm up here. You're down there." (Jake)

I think a lot of staff are scared. [. . .] Scared of relationships. So they'll always be, "Smith, behind your door!" instead of going, "Go on Michael," put your hand on his back, "Go on, in your door, you daft bugger." They'll always have a very strict barrier, and I think that's a lack of confidence in them to have relationships with prisoners. Positive relationships, I don't mean being their best mate, but having a relationship with them where they have confidence in you and they feel comfortable with you and you're feeling comfortable about how they're behaving around you. I think a lot of staff don't like to get too close to prisoners, so they will always have their hand up, saying, "That's as far as you're coming Smith." (Officer)

Officers saw prisoners convicted of sex offenses as a threat to their professional identity and to their impartial control. They feared that moral and psychological stain might prompt them to act judgmentally and that manipulation might lead them to behave too liberally, and that either way their authority would be weakened. Prisoners, on the other hand, believed that officers *overused* their power in Stafford, and they believed that this resulted from moral condemnation. They recurrently insisted that their compliance and reluctance to challenge regime decisions meant that they were more tightly regulated than "mainstream" prisoners would be. As Phil said, "that's a big saying in here, 'they wouldn't do that to the mains'".[22] In particular, they complained about the frequency with which periods of association were unexpectedly canceled or shortened:

Half of the stuff the officers do here, they wouldn't do in a mains jail. We're supposed to get banged up at 6:15 every night and sometimes they go, "We can't be arsed, we'll bang them up at 6:00 tonight." That wouldn't happen in a mains jail, because the prisoners would go, "I'm going behind my door at 6:15." "You're not." You've got five officers trying to get 155 lads on the wing behind the door. It's not going to happen, is it? People [here] will go, "Yes, I'll do it," because they don't want to get into trouble. (Owen)[23]

The frequency with which prisoners complained about differential treatment speaks to the frustration they felt at the perceived injustice. But they also found the control which was exerted on them—which Tony described as "being treated like a dickhead by a dickhead"—demeaning and contemptuous. What mattered was not just the nature of the treatment, but what it implied about what you deserved.

Officers did not necessarily intend to treat prisoners contemptuously, but prisoners nevertheless read contempt into their tone and their behavior. Officers spoke to prisoners loudly, abruptly, often bawdily—a communicative style which can feel degrading, and which felt particularly alien and unnecessary to the older men who now inhabited Stafford. Michael, for instance, a *resigned prisoner* in his eighties, complained that he and his friends were spoken to disrespectfully:

> My friend was walking back to his cell to be locked up and Mr. Williams thought he was going too slowly, and he shouted, "Move your arse!," and to his credit he turned around and said, "Show me some respect! I'm old enough to be your grandfather!" He's horrible. Very cruel to us older people.

In a very small number of cases, prison officers' dismissive manner seemed to grow directly out of the stained soil of prisoners' convictions. Nigel—a *redeemed prisoner* who had spent many years in the system—recounted an argument he had had with a member of staff, who had attempted to placate him by alluding to the type of prison Stafford was, and thus the type of prisoner he assumed Nigel to be:

> He said something along the lines of "This is a sex offenders' prison." I think because of my attitude, I'd just had an underachieve [a warning for poor behavior] or something. He went, "You do realize this is a sex offen—." I went, "Before you even finish, what are you making a big point of that for? We all know that, what are you mentioning that for?" I went, "No, let's just change the conversation, because I don't even know why you said that." So I became very forceful in the way I was talking. He got up off his chair and I got up off my chair, and I was kind of like, "Why are you trying to stand over me? Let's stay at the same eye level!"

Other prisoners, though, did not seem to believe that they were treated worse or more dismissively than "mainstream" prisoners would have been. Rather, they thought that their compliance had earned them the right to better treatment, a looser regime, and less authoritarian interactions than "mainstream" prisoners would receive: "They don't need to be as strong with us as they did with the mains. We don't need as much looking after, we're domesticated," one man told me. These men invested their compliance with moral significance, and criticized the regime for failing to live up to it:

> It's not the worst prison in the world but I think the type of people in here, the way we behave—and I put emphasis on the word "behave," because we do—then I think we should be given a bit more time out, time on the yard. You know. Obviously if we were kicking off every five minutes then no, but we deserve it, you know. (Keith)

Repentant and *resigned prisoners*, who thought of themselves as different from "criminals," were most likely to argue that they deserved better treatment than "mainstream" prisoners, but most prisoners shared the belief that they were spoken to and managed in a demeaning way.

On the whole, then, prisoners' perceptions of judgment did not seem to be driven either by what officers said or by their attitudes, and instead lay in the way in which officers used their power and formed relationships with prisoners. The flow of power was the main medium of vertical moral communication in Stafford, and how officers disciplined, policed, provided care for, and formed relationships with prisoners said something to these prisoners about their moral identities. One mechanism by which this happened was that officers' anxieties about manipulation and sexual risk led them to retreat from relationships with prisoners.[24] Anxious officers saw the signs of sexual grooming in even the most innocuous communications: "It starts with 'Have a nice weekend,' and then it's 'Have a nice Christmas,' and then it's 'Have a nice new year,' and then it's 'Have a nice Valentine's Day,' and you're like, 'You what?' They're always seeking some gratification. Weirdos" (officer). Bland social interactions such as these can help to lubricate staff-prisoner relationships (Liebling, Price, and Shefer 2011) and communicate to prisoners that officers see them as human. Concerns about potential sexual manipulation in Stafford meant that interactions such as these came to be seen by some officers as sources of risk rather than potential sources of legitimacy. Some officers avoided these sorts of interactions and policed their colleagues who were friendlier. Female officers were particularly subjected to their lateral surveillance (Ievins 2020a), and they therefore tried not "to come across too friendly" (officer) to protect themselves both from prisoners and from accusations of inappropriate intimacy:

> There's some staff that don't wanna talk at all. I think I'm one of those that's in-between. I'm not one that's, "Oh come in and sit down" and call each other by their first names like some staff do, but I'm also not one that's like, "Oh go away," basically. [. . .] But I also think that because I'm a female though, because you've got to be more careful anyway, I can't just say, "Come in and sit down" because then you've got staff thinking, "Oh is there something going on there?" (Officer)

Women were not the only subjects of this surveillance. The most suspicious officers frequently submitted Serious Information Reports to the Security Department on prisoners they believed were manipulative as well as on colleagues whose more relational working practices were thought to leave them open to conditioning. One highly experienced but quite maverick officer went out of his way to shake hands with prisoners, in an effort to reduce the social distance his role created. I once witnessed him doing this while I was stood next to an equally experienced but more cynical officer, who looked at me, shook his head, and said, "I give up."

Officers' retreat from relationships meant that they did not know their prisoners well, and as a result they struggled to address the issues that mattered to them and to police the risks that did exist.[25] Officers avoided talking to prisoners about anything personal, sexual, or offense-related in order to protect themselves from psychological corruption; as one Offender Supervisor summarized, "you can't get in their head too much or they'll fry yours." Restricting topics of conversation in this way meant that officers rarely had safe conversations with prisoners about the issues that mattered to them, whether their broken relationships with their families, their feelings of guilt and shame, their fears about the future, or their restricted contact with their children. Oliver, for instance, was a vulnerable *fatalist* whose conviction had had severe impacts on his family and had led to his children being taken into care. He self-harmed often, but was unwilling to seek help from staff:

> I try to deal with things myself. Maybe that's the wrong attitude, but I don't really trust staff to open up to, because I'd feel vulnerable.
> *In what way?*
> I don't know how many staff know about my offenses, for example. Say it was about feeling guilty about what I did, or whatever, and I opened up and told one of the officers about it, he might feel the need to look up my OASys [online record] and see what the hell it's about.[26] I don't want that. [. . .] I don't want them to know. Because he might change his attitude. He might turn around and say what he thinks of me.

While officers did see it as their job to manage and care for prisoners in distress, they were reactive rather than proactive. If prisoners did not approach them with their problems, they were likely to remain "under the radar" (Offender Supervisor). The fact that many of the sources of distress experienced by prisoners concerned issues which they and officers found difficult to talk about made this more likely.

Officers' anxieties about being conditioned by manipulative "sex offenders" also pushed them away from exercising discretion and toward acting "by the book" (officer). The exercise of good discretion—judgment about when to enforce rules and when to overlook them in the interest of keeping the peace, of decency, or of care—is often considered one of the most important tasks of the prison officer (Gilbert 1997; Liebling 2000). The confident use of discretion comes with trust in one's own professional skills, and officers' worries about manipulation showed that this trust had been wounded. As a result, they took refuge in the rules and prioritized consistency over discretion:

> *How can you tell when someone's manipulative, and how do you deal with it?*
> I think you have to be aware of it, and that's why you have to have that barrier in terms of not being yourself. I don't know if you would be aware of it. I think you just have to be careful with what you're doing and then make sure you can defend your decision and you would do the same if anyone else had asked you to do it. If you had one decision for one, you have to know in your head that it would be the same for all. (Officer)

Prisoners who had been in the prison before the reroll, or who had spent time on "mainstream" wings in other prisons, insisted that officers in Stafford now leaped more willingly to formal mechanisms of control, choosing to discipline prisoners by adjudicating them rather than talking to them.[27] They offered multiple explanations for this, ranging from the increasing number of young and inexperienced officers to the fact that the prison's relative calm meant that officers were rarely pushed to demonstrate discretion by the requirements of daily peacekeeping: "It's like Mr. Taylor. Gets bored stupid so he'll nick someone. It's like that small guy in the gray, he's always getting nicked. No one talks to him, no one says, 'That's disrespectful,' they just nick him" (Steven). The most professional officers worried that new members of staff might not develop the requisite skills for working with more difficult prisoners and bemoaned their inability to adapt their practice to the specifics of the situation. One experienced, if cynical, officer pointed out a junior colleague to me one day on the wing and told me, "She tried to lock up an eighty-eight-year-old last week. I mean, what's the fucking point? What would it have been like when we had real prisoners?"

Officers' use of power also became morally communicative because the behavioral territory over which they felt able to exert influence had expanded (Ievins 2022). In part, this had happened because officers' reluctance to exercise discretion, combined with the fact that order was taken for granted, allowed them to enforce rules in areas they had previously policed less tightly—or as Peter summarized, "because everyone's under control they can nitpick." Oliver had been in the prison since before the reroll, and complained that officers now monitored the quantity, type, and arrangement of furniture in cells:

> They're more likely to nick you, and more likely to put you down to basic or if you're enhanced, put you down to standard.
> *Do you think they're stricter than they used to be?*
> Damn sight stricter. I mean, all these things up on the doors now that say how your furniture should be, that wasn't there. They'd never do that with the mains, never. They used to shout all the time with the officers, they didn't care.

Prisoners complained that many staff members spent their days disciplining prisoners for having too many pillows in their cells or very strictly controlling the numbers of prisoners in cells during association periods (across the estate, officially only three prisoners are allowed in a cell, although this rule is often not enforced), or even disciplining prisoners for putting photographs up on the walls of their cells rather than on the designated pinboards.

The prison also sought to expand its zone of control by governing prisoners' sexuality and sexual expression. On the one hand, officers were aware that prisoners posed different risks to security and safety than "mainstream" prisoners had, and realized that they had to pay attention to (for example) the forms of contact they were having with women and children outside the prison, or the media they were consuming and sexual relationships they were engaging in inside it. However, officers' instinctive distaste about sexual offenses, and their self-protective desire not to talk about them, meant they struggled to do so meaningfully or consistently. Many prisoners in Stafford were engaged in various forms of sexual behavior with each other, some of which seemed to be consensual, but some of which seemed more troubling. Prisoners spoke to me relatively frequently about the establishment's sexual economy. Young and often debt-ridden men were paid half an ounce of tobacco, equivalent to £5 (around $6.50), for oral sex, or a quarter of an ounce or even a chocolate bar if the person being paid was particularly vulnerable or desperate. Officers, however, never discussed the sexual marketplace in their prison in my presence, although they did discuss the (moribund) drug trade and their (more accurate) belief that some prisoners were bullying older men for their medication. Most officers reacted with unease whenever anyone raised the topic of sexual relationships between prisoners, and showed no interest in finding out more about the dynamics between the participants.

Officers may have underpoliced certain dimensions of prisoners' sexuality, but they tightly policed others, although they still struggled to do so with purpose or clarity.[28] Prisoners who were deemed to pose a risk to children were not allowed to have photographs of anyone under the age of eighteen, but officers did not understand how risk judgments were made and so struggled to explain them to the prisoners whose family photos they confiscated. Officers also monitored the media prisoners consumed, but it was not clear what they were trying to achieve in doing so. John, a life-sentenced prisoner in his sixties who was in bad health, complained that the officers managing the Senior Support Group censored the films they watched:

> If they're [the prisoners] watching a film and there's a woman in her knickers and bra, they [the officers] turn it off. And on the news, they were talking about that Lord Sewell, and as soon as it mentioned prostitution, they turned the news off.[29] If they see two people kissing, the video is ripped out. They make them watch cartoons, kids' films, *Star Wars* and that.

Gay prisoners complained that it was difficult to get access to magazines which depicted images of topless men, but that heteronormative images were more readily available. Other prisoners were able to cut revealing images of women out of magazines and newspapers and stick them on their walls.[30] Officers' inconsistent regulation of prisoners' sexual expression meant that prisoners were not well protected from inappropriate or dangerous sexual behavior, but they still felt stigmatized as "sex offenders."

CONCLUSION: THE INEVITABILITY
OF INAUTHENTICITY

> Furthermore, if punishment is to have the character which it ought to have, much will be demanded not only of the criminals who are punished, but of those who administer the punishments, and indeed of every member of the community. For those who administer punishments must be motivated by a genuine concern for the values which the law embodies, and for the criminal as a moral agent; they must exhibit moral qualities of sensitivity, compassion and understanding: how likely is it that we will be able to staff a penal system with people such as this? (Duff 1986, 293–94)

Reformers and academics often question whether the problems of penal institutions come from bad people or bad structures. Penal theorist Antony Duff implied the former. He believed that the goal of a legitimate penal system would be to communicate to prisoners the censure they deserved for their crimes, in the hope that this would help them repent, reform themselves, and be reconciled with the community (Duff 2001). He imagined that this process would be deeply active and inclusionary, and that it would involve penal administrators—probation officers, perhaps, but also prison officers—keeping prisoners' minds focused both on what they had done and on their processes of moral change. In some of his writing, though, he displayed some pessimism about the capacity of penal administrators to engage in the right sort of inclusionary and reintegrative moral communication, a pessimism which this chapter indicates was well-founded. However, less well-founded was Duff's implication that the fault would lie in the selection of people chosen to work as penal administrators. As we have seen, prison officers did not intend to be judgmental or condemnatory. The fact that they communicated stigmatizing shame, and that they rarely discussed personal issues with prisoners, did not result from their own moral failings, but from the structure of the institution in which they worked.

The professional standards of behavior to which officers in Stafford were committed—impartiality, order, and consistency—discouraged them from acting as morally communicative agents. But one of the ironies undergirding staff-prisoner relationships in Stafford was that it was these very standards of behavior which encouraged them to use power and form relationships in the morally condemnatory ways which I have described. Officers were frightened that they might inadvertently express judgment and contempt toward prisoners and that they might be manipulated by them. Their response to both fears was to keep their relationships with prisoners shallow and distant. That way, they could avoid knowledge which could push them away from acting "by the book" and toward acting either too punitively or too laxly. However, the relational reluctance and heavy forms of control which resulted said something to prisoners about their moral status. Officers had fallen into the trap of becoming agents of moral condemnation.

These processes were not preordained, however, and a handful of officers managed to resist them. These officers were generally experienced enough to be confident in their authority, without having so much experience that they had become tired or cynical. They held tightly on to their belief in the value of care and respect, and often had a special area of responsibility (perhaps a wing, or a particular group of vulnerable prisoners) over which they felt empowered to exercise these beliefs. They thought it was important that concerns about manipulation did not prevent them from speaking to prisoners and recognized that relationships were valuable sources of legitimacy. They saw the value of chatting with prisoners about their lives outside, although they generally avoided talking about details: "It shows that you're a normal person, and if you put yourself on a pedestal, it makes it difficult to talk to people" (Offender Supervisor). Others were sensitive about the ways in which prisoners can feel physically stained by imprisonment, and a few male officers made a conscious effort to touch them:

> I think the most important thing for normal life for a prisoner is touch. Very rarely do prisoners get touched because no one wants to touch them, whether they're mains or they're VPs, so they never get that. But a big part of being human is touch, which is why I do a lot of handshaking. I'll shake prisoners' hands, I'll touch them, I'll put my arms round them, not because of anything other than I think it really does form good strong bonds between people. It forms trust between people. (Officer)

These officers were aware of the genuine risks of inappropriate or inconsistent relationships with prisoners, but they thought that they could manage these risks without retreating from relationships:

> They will try and groom me all the time, and it's about not letting them groom you but being able to help them. The balance between allowing them to have an opinion, to express concerns, to express desires, without that turning into them controlling everything, and it's a fine balance and sometimes you fail and sometimes you don't. Sometimes you get it right. [. . .] For me, that comes with experience. That prisoner over there [pointing] is somebody who likes to control everything. I've learned how to manage his control by talking to him, allowing him to say things, but not allowing him to dictate what goes on. (Officer)

To act in this way required sensitive balancing acts—between giving prisoners a say and retaining authority, between displaying care and humanity and avoiding becoming too intimate—and these officers did not always get them right. What distinguished them, though, was that they saw manipulation and inappropriate relationships as things to be responded to when they happened, rather than risks which should prevent the formation of relationships. One particularly care-oriented female officer, for instance, said that on a couple of occasions in the past six months, prisoners had formed an "attachment" to her, on one occasion suggesting that they stay in touch after release, and on another telling her she was "special." On both occasions, she reported her concerns to her superiors and then spoke to and withdrew from the men—"I wouldn't want them to build on that"— but was reluctant to stop talking to or trying to help prisoners: "when it happens, deal with it then."

Such officers were rare, though, and while prisoners often stated that these officers were the best at their job, they tended to believe that even these officers were judgmental, at least on one level. (It was one of these officers who was the subject of Edward's story, and that was part of what shocked him so much.) Indeed, a second irony shaping staff-prisoner relationships was that both parties complained that the other was inauthentic. Officers felt that prisoners' politeness and compliance masked their manipulative intentions, while prisoners believed that officers' professionalism obscured their true feelings of judgment and hatred. These complaints did not exist because they were correct, although there was, sometimes, a grain of truth in them: a few prisoners were deceptive or sexually inappropriate, and, as Edward's story revealed, officers did sometimes imply that they morally disliked prisoners. However, these mutual complaints of inauthenticity were primarily a result of the difficulty of forming human relationships in an institution which reproduced categorical moral difference. Officers' professional identities may have relied on their ability to treat prisoners equally, but they also needed to maintain a boundary between them and prisoners—after all, they were supposed to hold power, and prisoners were supposed to be subject to it. This boundary was justified by the fact that all prisoners had criminal convictions and reinforced by the fact that their convictions were for sex offenses. The very structure of staff-prisoner relationships in Stafford, then, was built on a foundation of moral difference. It is this which made it difficult for prison officers to work as the sensitive, compassionate, and understanding agents whom Duff wanted to run his morally communicative institutions. It was also this which made the establishment of real, authentic, human relationships between staff and prisoners extremely difficult. In the next chapter, we move on to consider the sorts of relationships which existed between people whose categorization implied that they were morally identical: prisoners.

7

Denying Community

Social Relationships and the Dangers of Acknowledgment

One afternoon about halfway through the fieldwork, I walked onto the wing and was immediately met by George, a *resigned prisoner* I knew well. "Mr. Brown wants to see you in the office. It's nothing you've done," he said, his face stern. I thanked him and found Mr. Brown, an enthusiastic young officer, who awkwardly asked me to read an entry made in the observation book the evening before. While I had been chatting to prisoners queuing for dinner, a man standing in the queue had said to George's best friend, Scott, "Every time I see Alice, I want to rape her." Scott had told George, and together they had reported it to the wing staff, who had in turn reported it to the prison's Security Department and written it in the observation book. Mr. Brown showed me a photo of the man who made the comment and I said I didn't recognize him and had never spoken to him. "That's what's funny, he's really quiet," Mr. Brown said, and his female colleague agreed: "That's when it scares you, when the quiet ones say things like that." They thought I was lucky that the comment had been made to Scott: "George and Scott are decent ones, for prisoners."

The comment made by the man in the queue could have been interpreted in several different ways—as an expression of desire, as a threat, or as a joke—but most people who lived and worked in the prison took it seriously. Officers asked me if I wanted the man who said it to be transferred to a different wing (I didn't), and for the rest of the project they warned me if we were ever seen in the same vicinity. Most prisoners agreed that the comment crossed a moral line. "You don't say things like that, not in here," George told me, and Scott agreed: "You can't even say things like that in jest, but I saw his face, he weren't joking." Several men went as far as suggesting that the speaker should be informally punished. Scott was straightforward: "If I hadn't just got my Cat D [been granted permission to go to an open prison], I would have smashed his teeth in." When Peter found out, he was similarly incensed: "If someone said something like that on this wing, the guys would fucking batter him. So he ought to get moved off to teach him a lesson." The scale of the reaction made me uncomfortable, and at the time I feared that the disciplinary reaction was disproportionate to the wrongness of the comment.[1] Tony, certainly, felt that it had been interpreted through an unjustly distorting lens: "There are things in this prison that may be perfectly appropriate, but they become inappropriate because of the environment. But at the end of the day, they're only words. I hear worse daily."

This chapter offers a description of Stafford as a moral community (Waldram 2012) and considers how much prisoners' stained identities as "sex offenders" mattered to their social relationships.[2] Prison sociologists often describe prisoner society as clearly hierarchical, as though moral judgments about offenses straightforwardly imprint themselves onto social reality (Åkerström 1986; Vaughn and Sapp 1989). As this story and its aftermath indicate, the mark which prisoners' identities left on their social relationships was not solely determined by their convictions.[3] The man who made the rape comment was convicted of grooming offenses against a teenage girl, but the opprobrium was directed at his public statement of intent rather than at his earlier crime. The reaction was all the more outraged because he was a socially isolated and conventionally unattractive man, and he made the comment to two prisoners with more social capital, who better met the ideal set by heteronormative masculinity, and who neither saw themselves nor were seen as "sex offenders." George was a *resigned prisoner* whose claims of innocence for raping two young women were believed by staff and by most prisoners on his wing, and Scott was currently serving a sentence for a nonsexual offense, allowing him to place a firm moral boundary between himself and other men and present himself as a *"mainstream" prisoner*: "I'm not a sex offender, I don't think like them," he had told me when explaining his decision to report the comment.

Prisoners' convictions—or at least, prisoners' stories about their convictions—clearly mattered to life in Stafford, but their effects were compounded and distorted by factors like prisoners' appearance, behavior, and demeanour.[4] One reason for this indirect relationship was that prisoners simply did not know what their peers had been convicted of, and so were forced to make social judgments based on information that was more immediately discernible to them. As this chapter will argue, though, one reason for prisoners' ignorance about their peers was that they, like officers, went out of their way to avoid finding out about people's convictions. Prison researchers have argued that "mainstream" prisoners in integrated prisons respond to the fear that they might be living among "sex offenders" by demanding to see other people's paperwork, so they can find out what everyone is in prison for (Schwaebe 2005; Ugelvik 2014). In Stafford, however, prisoners knew that everyone else was a "sex offender," and so reading prisoners' paperwork would not be able to purify them of the staining connotations. They also knew that reading prisoners' convictions would not provide the information which mattered much more to them: whether people were guilty, and what their guilt said about their moral and sexual identities. Faced with this epistemologically and morally confusing situation, they tried to dilute the relevance of each other's convictions.

This does not mean that prisoners in Stafford approved of the crimes for which their peers were in prison. John Braithwaite (1989) feared that people who are stigmatized by shaming punishment processes might form a deviant subculture, and that this subculture would reinforce an oppositional moral worldview and allow people to live as though their exclusion were unjust. In our case, that would involve stigmatized men in Stafford coming together and stating that sexual violence (or at least some forms of sexual violence) is morally acceptable, and thus that their punishment was illegitimate. As the widespread disapproval of the comment made about me suggested, though, the fundamental moral framework underpinning social life in Stafford was very similar to that which existed outside the prison, and most prisoners thought that sexual violence was wrong. During the fieldwork, I never heard anyone openly articulate their support for nonconsensual sex with adults, and I only spoke to one person who implied that sex with prepubescent children was ever acceptable (he had dementia, which may have made him less able or likely to control what he disclosed).[5] Most prisoners, however, did believe that many sexual offenses were more nuanced than denunciatory public and legal discourse implied, and their belief in this moral gray zone made it easier for people to tell stories about their offending which challenged or neutralized the narratives which had been crystallized into their criminal convictions.

Prisoners in Stafford did not live in a different moral universe to those living outside the prison, although as this chapter will argue, they did live in a distinct moral microclimate. Prisoners had been sent to Stafford because of their convictions, but in the prison these convictions were impossible to see. Prisoners' victims—the recipients of the real harm which many prisoners had caused—were absent from the prison, veiling the social world from the harm on which it was built (Ievins 2019). The prison was spatially and temporally bounded, a fact which allowed people to live their lives inside differently from how they would outside, knowing that the people they met in prison were unlikely to meet and endanger their families.[6] As a result, the environment became somehow unreal, and prisoners in Stafford were able to make moral and social judgments on different grounds than would have applied outside: "A lot of the people that you meet in here, would you trust them to babysit your kids? Maybe not. Would you trust them to do a lot of things that you would trust your average friend to do? The answer is probably not, in a lot of cases" (Tony).

Immoral offenses were still considered immoral, but information was controlled and managed in such a way that their social consequences were reduced. Prisoners in Stafford had been sent there because of their convictions, but imprisoning them both drew attention to and obscured what they had done, and all that remained visible was the indistinct stain left by the "sex offender" identity. Prisoners responded to this situation by deliberately trying to ignore their stain and avoid finding out about the details of their peers' convictions. They engaged in forms of "tactical collusion" (Cohen 2001, 146), working together to resist the "sex offender" label. Overlooking their stigmatization in this way could be read as a rejection of the seriousness of their offenses, but it could also be read as an attempt to move on from their staining pasts and to try to control what shaped their current reality. Wiping the slate clean of their convictions allowed them to be judged not just on what they had done, but on who they were—or at least, who they were able to present themselves as being. What was formed was a new moral community, and this community was built on a foundation of denial.

EATING RAT AND MOSQUITOES: DENIAL AND ITS LIMITS

Harry's approach to other prisoners' offenses was typical of men in Stafford. He was deeply interested in psychology and anthropology and was curious about his peers, and he had a list of people he wanted to google when he was released so that he could find out what they had been convicted of. However, he had decided against asking his girlfriend to look them up while he was in prison, explaining this with the following analogy:

> You're in China, you're having a meal. "That's lovely, what's that?" The Chinese man says, "It's rat and mosquitoes." "Fucking hell, I'm not having that again!" But you've still got to live there for another week and there's not a McDonald's in sight. But when you get home, you're like, "Christ, what was that meal I was eating? Rat and mosquito? Fucking hell! I wouldn't start to eat it tomorrow!" It's one of them for me. I don't wanna know now because I've got to live with them and if I find out something really gruesome, I'm gonna find it really hard to walk away from my clan. There might be five people in here that I really get on with, but I've just found out that the sex assaulting person that's accidentally just touched someone in the club, it turns out he's not, he's actually raped his niece. I'm gonna struggle then.

Harry, like other men in Stafford, was not indifferent to his peers' convictions. He said that he would not want to be close friends with someone he knew was convicted of what he called a "grisly" offense—a crime against a ten-year-old, for instance, or multiple stranger rapes. He was also protective of female staff and said that he intervened when he heard people talking about them in a sexualized way: "I don't know what you're in for, you could be in for rape or stalking or something, and you're sitting there going, 'She's fit.'" Nevertheless, the requirements of the situation he found himself in had prompted him to restrain his naturally inquiring mind and keep his knowledge of other people's offenses as abstract as possible. By avoiding firm and verified information, Harry engaged in a deliberate act of denial.

In his influential work *States of Denial: Knowing about Atrocities and Suffering*, Stan Cohen (2001) describes the many ways in which different societies either hold at bay, overlook, or neutralize knowledge about injustice which is either too disturbing or too anomalous to be taken in. Cohen's focus is knowledge about mass suffering and political atrocities, and he draws on the work of psychoanalyst Christoper Bollas to argue that the impulse to denial is often driven by the "need to be innocent of a troubling recognition" (25). The denial he describes can be maintained through many different strategies. In some cases, denial involves a deliberate desire to avoid knowledge; in others, it involves a reluctance to change one's life in the light of this knowledge. It can involve saying and believing something that is not factually true, and it can also involve accepting that something is true but thinking that it is not important or that its implications are different from what they seem. Central to the state of denial, though, is the individual or collective effort to control both the flow of information and the ability of that information to penetrate the social world and change the way it is lived.

Prisoners in Stafford had many motivations for engaging in acts of collective denial, and they followed diverse strategies in doing so. Many men said that they avoided hearing or thinking about each other's convictions because they found them too upsetting.[7] Many said that they had overheard distressing and sometimes detailed sexual conversations in Stafford, whether about people's own offenses or about their ongoing sexual interest in children; others had overheard people having conversations imagining deviant sexual acts with women they saw on television or in the prison. Some men told stories about being locked up overnight with cellmates who refused to stop talking about what they had done. They had strong emotional reactions to these conversations, using physical language which was indicative of disgust (Miller 1997): they described feeling "physically sick" (Tony), and hearing stories that "make my skin crawl" (Phil) or make "your head fall off" (Owen). The mental images produced were intrusive and shocking, with many prisoners saying that they shook their view of the world—"things you can't believe can physically be true" (Ricky)—although their taboo nature meant that they sometimes struggled to articulate precisely what they had heard:

> I was affected when I was a Listener, with the stories I got told.[8] But I wouldn't even tell you now, Alice, because they were that bad. They were horrific. I had nightmares. I didn't realize things like that happened in the world, I just didn't, especially as I'd just come into prison. (George)

> When I was cleaning down in the SOTP room the other week, on the board there was a little box like that on there that said, "My preference is three- to four-year-olds." That was on the board. [. . .] There was all the boxes from each different person, and that was one of the things that I seen. And after that, when I read that . . . I just went and mopped up somewhere. Now, I ain't gonna forget that. I can remember how the board was set up, how it was cut up into different divisions. So that's only one thing I've read, and I ain't forgot that. (Frank)

Prisoners only needed to have had these experiences once to be disturbed by them, and so they avoided exposing themselves to this corruption. They rarely asked people questions about their convictions, and either walked away or tried to change the topic when such conversations started. Similarly, many prisoners said that their unwillingness to hear these stories meant that they were unwilling to participate in the SOTP, where they would have to listen to detailed accounts of other people's offending.

Prisoners had other motivations to avoid learning about offenses. As Harry suggested, and as other prisoners confirmed, people in Stafford required a degree of human contact, whether for recreation, trading, or emotional intimacy, and they had very little choice of whom to talk to. The environment in which they lived also provided them with a very specific form of information: prisoners knew that almost all their peers had been convicted of a sex offense, but they did not know which one, nor did they know if they had done it, or if what they had done said anything about their current characters. Prisoners' own experiences told them that criminal convictions did not accurately describe what happened, and that not everybody who was stained as a "sex offender" met the stereotypes implied by that term. On the other hand, prisoners also did not know if the stories their peers told them were true, and if they were as innocent as they sometimes claimed to be. In such a context, it made sense to live as though convictions did not matter:

> People generally tend to ignore a lot of stuff for harmony. They can't be bothered. To be honest most people don't care. They don't care. They don't care about each other. One or two people bond, and it's surprising how caring some people can be, but no matter how far that goes, I think they're very selective in that. But I think people ignore a lot of what we're in for, because it's in our face constantly, isn't it? The guy you could be talking to or having a game of chess or cards or having a chat with or being friendly with, he could be in for something that on the outside you'd be prepared to kill him for. [. . .] You can't live under those stresses, no. So a lot is forgiven or ignored. (Steven)

One way of ignoring offenses was by limiting the flow of information so that people only knew what needed to be known. Conversations about offending were described as simultaneously invasively unpleasant—"I don't wanna know too much about it because you can't get it out of your head then" (Vince)—and "boring to listen to" (Tommy). It was better to avoid such topics in favor of the relevant and entertaining:

> I think if everyone in here, if they could just say, like, "Hello, how are you?" "Good, fine, how are you?" Walk away. "Oh, I need this, do you know anything about this?" "Oh yeah, good, good." And then he tells me a story about what happened once in his past and I say, "Oh really?" and I find it really interesting. OK, he's telling me about an experience, that's interesting. "So how did you get to there? Oh really, OK." And then, "OK, I'll see you later, alright, bye." That's it. If everyone could carry themselves like that on a day-to-day basis, that's fine. Without bringing any of them horrors in, you know. (Ahmed)

Such a community might only involve shallow and pragmatic interactions, but the lack of intimacy was worth it as it would protect people against facing unnecessary or unwanted stories. The goal was to construct a community which engaged in deliberate and knowing acts of denial, and this aspiration was underpinned by the normative claim that people should be assessed on their characters rather than their offenses. According to this moral norm, people's pasts should become irrelevant as soon as they pass through the prison's gates and are reborn as prisoners. "I want to judge a person in here as I see them," Kevin said, and most of his peers agreed: "The way I see it is, everybody's committed a crime, that's fair enough. They've done something wrong in their life. People deserve a chance. I'm not one of those people that see the person for the crime, I see the person for the person" (James).

In practice, prisoners found this norm difficult to live up to, and they tended to assume that what their peers were like as people said something about their offenses. Initial social bonds were formed based on who seemed like a good person to have in your life and to be "on your wavelength" (George), and prisoners frequently said that they were a "good judge of character" (Darren) who would not become friends with a truly problematic person. In practice, these decisions were often made based on physical appearance, and people who resembled the stereotypical image of a pedophile—who were White, old, disabled, wore glasses, had evident learning difficulties, or had bad hair—were more rarely befriended. Kieran told me that he made judgments on the basis of "stereotypes," but he was nevertheless confident about their accuracy: "I could stand down at the servery and I could practically tell you what everybody is in for and I could, hand on my heart, say if I were wrong on more than twenty people on this wing, I'll give you everything in my cell."

Such judgments relied on ignorance and were therefore vulnerable to the stains of knowledge. Even those who most wanted not to let offenses matter to them said that condemnatory impulses were instinctive and thoughts about offending were invasive. John, a *redeemed prisoner* who carried deep feelings of guilt about his own crime, said, "I couldn't judge them, they've been judged. It's difficult. I can't judge them. You can like the person and not like the crime, you know what I mean? But the crime keeps coming back into my head." Phil, a *resigned prisoner*, also found it extremely difficult not to be affected by "the thought that they can do things like that." In order to avoid being placed in this situation, people in Stafford went out of their way to sidestep talking or thinking about convictions, to the extent that they complained more often about those who talked about their offenses than they did about the severity of said offenses. Ian described the protective qualities of the veil of ignorance, and the damaging effects which unwanted information could have on friendships:

> I don't think anyone really talks about it. I think everyone just wants to . . . Because . . . See, if . . . This sounds wrong, this, but say if I start talking to some lad, a decent

lad, but then he was like, "Oh yeah, my sentence is, it's with a five-year-old, and I did do it. I got my jollies off on it." Then I'd be thinking, "You were a great lad till you tell us that."

Despite prisoners' best efforts, it was not possible to prevent all information about offending from entering Stafford. In some cases, the details of people's convictions were unexpectedly revealed by stories in the newspaper or on television; in others, people were forced to tell their stories in treatment and then to live alongside each other on the wing. Some men resisted the normative pressure not to talk about their convictions on the wing, and others—like the man whose inappropriate comment opened this chapter—spoke and acted in ways which drew attention to the stained nature of the environment. In this context of semi-ignorance, many men, particularly *negotiators* and *"mainstream"* prisoners, struggled to resist the voyeuristic pull which objects of disgust can exert (Miller 1997). Many admitted to speculating about other people's offenses—George said, "You instantly see a creepy old man and you're like, 'I wonder what he's in for?' but you shouldn't be"—and some said they enjoyed testing people's stories and gossiping about what people were in prison for, with Ahmed saying, "You've got to have a hobby in here" and Noah comparing it to "fishing."

The inevitability of knowledge meant that men in Stafford had to find other ways of absorbing their peers' convictions without allowing them to threaten the prison's equilibrium or their social relationships, and they followed five key strategies in doing so. First, they distinguished between mistakes, which they saw as foolish one-off acts which could be discounted in the social and moral reckoning, and actions which they thought reflected people's true characters. The difference between these two categories was partly determined by the offenses themselves, and acts which prisoners believed were symptomatic of pedophilia were taken particularly seriously as a sign of having a faulty sexuality and a stained character. Terry, for instance, said that sexual acts against children were categorically different from those committed against adults: "Everybody's entitled to make a mistake, but when they start to go with kids and things, that's not a mistake, that's an illness." Tony agreed:

> There's definitely a buffer. If you know someone who's twenty, twenty-one, twenty-four, whatever, who's slept with a girl who was fifteen, in honesty, fifteen-year-old girls can look significantly older than that, and I can see why it would be a genuine mistake. Or if someone did it honestly and said, "You know, she was fucking fit [attractive], I knew she was fifteen, I shouldn't have done it," yeah, there is a sort of acceptance of that.

Prisoners also interpreted the way their peers told their stories as a sign of their character. Remorse indicated that the offense was an error of judgment:[9]

> I'm not interested in other people['s offenses] because that's their private life, their personal life. It doesn't affect me, unless a person is proud of it and laughing about

it. [. . .] If somebody has done it and is feeling bad about it, they don't want to do it, that person's alright, I'm alright to talk to you. (Shezad)

As character was what truly mattered, prisoners used the idea of "mistakes" to justify continuing to be friends with people who had done bad things but whom they knew to be good people.

Second, when people learned things about their peers which were harder to neutralize as a mistake, they interpreted this information in line with their preexisting assumptions about their characters in ways which made it possible for relationships to continue. These interpretations were facilitated by prisoners' established doubts about the legal system, their instincts about which offenses were more serious, and their awareness that the prison's rehabilitative regime incentivized the false admission of guilt. Ian, for instance, told me that he had assumed that a friend of his—a man with significant prison experience serving an indeterminate sentence—was not guilty. When his friend told him that he was about to start the SOTP, a requirement of which was the admission of guilt, Ian concluded that his motivations were instrumental and that the admission was misleading: "He's opened up saying, 'I'm doing the SOTP course.' I don't think any the worse of him for doing it. The guy's on a parole sentence, he wants to get out as fast as he can by doing this." However, his friend told me that he was guilty of his offense, and that while his motivations for participating in the SOTP were partly pragmatic, they were also indicative of his growing feelings of regret and shame about his offending.

Third, prisoners' offenses and stained identities were often discussed and defused as jokes. Humor about offenses and offenders was frequent and took different forms, including comments about people's appearances, exaggerated stories about other people's offenses and sexual predilections, and referring to the SOTP course as "Stay Out the Park" and the wing band as the Pedophonics. In many cases, prisoners said that they tried to find the humor in situations as a way of redirecting their attention from the horror (Morreall 1987; Palmer 1994; Sanders 2004; Zijderveld 1968). Tony recounted a story he had heard about someone in the prison who had raped his brother and put him in the washing machine to destroy the evidence, and had killed him in the process:

> That's pretty bad, innit. But it's like, what were you thinking? Do you know what I mean? Get over the bit where a rape and a murder have gone on—
> *Just ignore that! [laughs]*
> Just move past that bit! Let that bit go! What were you thinking with the washing machine, you fucking idiot? That's another level that, isn't it! There's a part of you that thinks, "Fucking hell, I wish I'd never had to know stuff like this!" but I think there's a morbid sort of humor attached to it where you think, "What were you thinking? What was it, when that was going on? How did you get to the bit where you thought, 'Yeah, I'll put him in the washing machine, that'll solve all my problems!'"

Jokes also allowed people to demonstrate that they did not approve of their friends' offenses without threatening the relationship. Owen was a *"mainstream" prisoner* who insisted that "you're not going to want to be friends with someone who's a fucking pedo," but he was also "close to," in his words, a man who was convicted of multiple counts of grooming teenage girls. Owen frequently teased his friend about his convictions, and his friend, perhaps reluctantly, joined in:

> I think sometimes it does get to him, but he knows it's all in jest, and he knows he's done wrong. He's put his hands up and said, "I fucked up." Maybe two or three times, but he fucked up and he put his hands up, so you have a laugh with him to let him know that he's done wrong.

At times, Owen's teasing of his friend seemed to creep beyond the boundaries of friendship. On one occasion, Owen tried to persuade his friend to tell me a funny story about his unusual masturbation technique, but his friend, embarrassed, stormed off. On such occasions, jokes seemed to function more as a way of establishing a barrier between Owen and his friend than as a way of absorbing the shock posed by their differences.

The fourth strategy was to ignore what people were told. This strategy was primarily deployed in cases where people repeatedly insisted on their innocence, as people who accepted that they were guilty discussed their offenses less frequently. Many men, even *activists* and *resigned prisoners*, were suspicious of some claims of innocence, but they rarely challenged them, as Ahmed explained: "Ain't polite, is it. You don't want to. Nah. That's what he believed. But to me it's like, 'Oh bloody hell!' You know? Probably in the back of my mind I'm saying, like, 'Yeah, sure, right.'" In such cases, prisoners tried not to let their suspicions and incredulities affect their actions. Tommy said you just "blank them out" if they keep talking about their case; James said it was easy to "switch off to it," and Paul said, "Someone could tell me summat [something] and it could go in one ear and out the other."

The fifth strategy involved ignoring people, rather than ignoring information. If people were believed to be convicted of offenses against younger children and if they had few social and economic ties to other prisoners, they were sometimes avoided and ignored by their peers. Darren said, "I'm not saying I'm better than anyone in here, not for a minute, but I just don't want to associate with them," and Zac took this one step further: "I don't look down on anyone, I just blank them out of my head." The judgment implied by this avoidance was rarely made explicit, and it was expressed as discernment rather than condemnation. Its targets would sometimes be discussed by other prisoners but rarely to their face:

> Nothing happens in here, nothing. I mean, prisoners have come in here before now and people like Noah and that, they'll go, "There's that one that was in the newspaper for raping them kids." That's it. But if it was on the mains wing, it would have been slice slice slice, stab stab stab. On here it's just sort of like, "There's Joe Bloggs, the pedophile of the town. You alright? Pot of sugar?" Acceptance. (Harry)

Such judgment was expressed so discreetly that those who were subjected to it were often oblivious. *Fatalists* often expressed anxiety that if their offenses became public knowledge, they would be at risk from other prisoners. In reality, their offenses were often widely known—because a friend had broken their trust or through someone who knew them in a previous prison—without this having much effect on their daily experience.

Through these mechanisms of denial, prisoners in Stafford managed to maintain their friendships, trading relationships, and psychological equilibrium against the pressure of their peers' convictions. In doing so, they produced a moral order which tried and partially succeeded to stop people's convictions from mattering and to mitigate the stain that marred the prison. Precisely how people lived within this moral order varied greatly, however. Prisoners were not just corrupted by Stafford, they were contaminants themselves, and how they thought about and interacted with other people was inextricably linked to their understanding of why and how their own criminal convictions mattered. Closer examination of the social relationships of the different "types" reveals how prisoners' social relationships, their inclination to condemn other prisoners, their willingness to discuss offenses, and their precise concerns about contamination were knitted together with their adaptations to their own convictions and sentences. How people made sense of their position as imprisoned "sex offenders," and how they thought about living with other imprisoned "sex offenders," were two sides of the same ethical coin.

THE HALL OF MIRRORS: JUDGING
AND BEING JUDGED

Imprisonment in Stafford was like being in a hall of mirrors: prisoners were "looking at themselves, looking at others, and looking at others looking at them, with these reflected images bouncing off each other *ad infinitum*" (Ievins and Crewe 2015, 497). People in Stafford felt differently about their guilt, but almost everyone felt that they had been unjustly labeled "sex offenders" and resented the assumption that their convictions said everything about who they were and who they could be. They also lived in a confined space with hundreds of other people who shared the same label, and despite their best efforts, their social interactions with and judgments of these people were certainly marked by their awareness of it. Prisoners' attempts at maintaining collective denial were not enough to stop their peers' convictions and labels from mattering to their social world, albeit in a reduced and distorted way. But precisely *how* these convictions and labels mattered—what they said to people and how they shaped social relationships—varied depending on prisoners' ways of thinking about their own responsibility for their crime and approaches to their sentence. Everyone in Stafford saw other prisoners as potential sources of contamination, but the nature of their concern about contamination said something about the type of project they believed they were engaged in.

Repentant and *redeemed prisoners* were fixated on their individual moral journeys, and this intense preoccupation meant that they rarely judged other prisoners for the specific acts which had brought them into custody. Through their own experiences, they had learned "that everybody's got the capability to do a bad thing" (Keith), and they were reluctant to reproach anyone else for what they had done, or even to talk about offenses: "In a place like this, you're in here for something and it's gonna be a topic of conversation at some point I suppose, but again, it's something I've learned, you deal with your own stuff, it's personal to you, and you just get on" (Peter). They were generally sociable and had often developed close friendships with a small number of fellow prisoners, particularly if they had participated in treatment together. Jake had two close friends on his wing, whom he had known in a previous prison and who had completed treatment courses at a similar time to him. These were the only people in the prison who knew about Jake's offense:

> I've told them openly, yeah.
> *Did they ask or did you . . . ?*
> I think one of them asked me. He says, "I've known you so long now. I've known you three years. I don't even know why you're here." But I knew him so long that I could trust him, you know what I mean? We were like that, sort of thing.
> *He's a good guy.*
> Same with the other one, we're really good friends. So, yeah, he knows what I'm in for. I know what he's in for. So, the first one is in for the same thing as me. Stepdaughter, so, yeah. Actually, the other one's the same. He's in for his stepdaughter. But we've talked about how it came about, what was going on, where your head was at, sort of thing. The only difference is that I was abused as a child, where they weren't.

In Jake's case, at least, the similarity of the offenses made them easier to talk about, and talking about them solidified the relationship: "I think it brought us closer together because the offenses were similar. But it gave us a talking point to build up trust and a good friendship. [. . .] We have a sort of understanding of what we're about and where we're from." *Repentant* and *redeemed prisoners* did not need to have committed the same offenses as their friends to understand them, though; what mattered more was that they responded to them in the same way and had a similar approach to their sentence. William, for example, took a great deal of comfort from his relationship with a man on his wing whom he described as "on the same sort of path as me." Despite the closeness of these friendships, prisoners were highly aware that they were temporary, not least because they were unwilling to break license restrictions preventing them from remaining in contact on release.

These close friendships were the only context outside SOTP courses in which *repentant* and *redeemed prisoners* discussed offending. They normally considered such conversations to be gratuitous and unpleasant and were particularly condemnatory of those who spoke about women, children, or sex in explicit or aggressive ways. As moral crusaders, they responded to stain by demanding purity from those who surrounded them, and their forgiveness of other prisoners' pasts did not extend into exoneration of their current behavior:

> I hear people saying, like, "I could crack her spine." It's like I just can't believe . . . It's like, wow. I get angry, but it makes me feel physically sick as well at the same time. Because I've bettered myself now, it's making . . . I can understand why I've done what I've done to better myself, but [. . .] what people say can make me feel bad. And it's like, wow, you need to sort yourself out. It's just wrong. It's not right. It's not right anymore. It's like, it makes me think about my victim, like I should never have made her do these things. I should never have made her feel that way. I should have been more in control of my own self to stop doing this shit. But people are quite happy to talk about their offenses, in quite graphic detail sometimes as well. I just walk away, like I can't be bothered with this. But I walk away because one, I could say something, two, I could blow my top, and three, it could send me back into that pattern of thoughts. And I just don't want to know. (Jake)

In part, these feelings were straightforward moral judgments, an understandable reaction to hearing conversations which were troubling and objectionable. Identity work was also at play: positively comparing oneself to others helped *repentant* and *redeemed prisoners* reinforce their sense of themselves as moral actors and reminded them of how far they had come. William had come to Stafford with a friend from a more rehabilitatively minded prison. He described them as being like "two goldfish and we've been dropped in a piranha's pond," but he saw some advantages in seeing how "manipulative and controlling" other prisoners could be:

> I know it might sound a bit distasteful, but it made me feel happy knowing that I've never been in that kind of role, to be overselfish or overcontrolling and all these things, and it helped me to see, thinking, well, if I don't correct myself, that's what I'm going to be like. I'm thinking, woah, no, I don't want to even go near that.

These processes of identity work were complex and in some respects contradictory. On the one hand, *repentant* and *redeemed prisoners* saw themselves as good people who had repaid their moral debts, in stark contrast to many of those they lived with; on the other hand, their atonement would never be complete and they were required to continually monitor themselves and other people. Their purity put them at risk of contamination, and they worried about being dragged back, both in terms of being forced to remember an offense which disgusted them and of being influenced and corrupted by the "horrible thought patterns" (Louis) which other prisoners demonstrated and which they had worked so hard to move on from.

Fatalists were vulnerable, ashamed, and aware that their convictions were the most disdained in Stafford. They primarily focused on getting through their sentence with the minimum of damage. Of all the groups, they were the most steadfast in their insistence on the norm of equality, strategically limiting conversations around offending and claiming that everyone in Stafford was the same:[10]

> *How do you feel about living with people convicted of sex offenses?*
> Well, it's not really a problem in here. I don't know what their sex offense is. I don't want to ask them. They don't ask me, I don't ask them. It doesn't really bother me. To me, I don't think of them as sex offenders. I think they're just people who've made a mistake, simple as that.
> *Why don't you want to know?*
> Well, for one thing, it might be something really nasty, and I don't want to know because if they tell me theirs, I'll feel obligated to tell them what I'm in for, and they'll make me feel like I'm a nasty person. So I know I'm not a nasty person, and hopefully they're not nasty. [. . .] I try to forget what I'm in here for. It makes my life easier, and it makes me talk to people more. (Samuel)

These claims of equality had two aims, the first of which was common among all prisoners in Stafford: to allow prisoners to continue to interact with people who had committed troubling crimes. The second was more specific to *fatalists*. They hoped to protect themselves from judgment on similar grounds and were thus reluctant to condemn other prisoners.

They had small and relatively distant groups of friends, mostly other *fatalists* and sometimes *resigned prisoners*, with whom they were unlikely to discuss their offenses. They were unwilling to remain in contact on release, aware that to do so would be a breach of license restrictions, might put them at risk of reoffending, and would extend an experience which had been profoundly unpleasant:

> Some people might not want to be friends with me [if they knew about my offense]. I wouldn't say [they'd be] violent because they know they shouldn't do that or they might get shipped out [transferred], but they might discard you as a friend. But I don't class this lot as my friends. It's like my sister and my probation officer said, "They're associates in here, they're not friends.[11] You're not going to meet all these on the outside and have a laugh together because you've got to start afresh. Associates." While you're in here you're friendly, people are nice, but then you go "Ta-ra." (Barry)

In some cases, *fatalists* circumvented conversations about offending to avoid their sexual desires being awakened. Several *fatalists* either admitted or alluded to being sexually attracted to children, and they said that their main strategy for managing this attraction was to avoid thinking about it. Conversations about offending could stir bad thoughts, as Oliver said:

> I don't like those kind of people, because they're never going to get out, because if they get off on that, they'll get off on it when they get out. And I want to move on from that. I know I've got an illness. I don't need to be triggered.

As the medical language used by Oliver implies, *fatalists'* concerns about contamination were different from those expressed by *repentant* and *redeemed prisoners*, but in a way which was consistent with their approaches to their sentences. *Redeemed* and *repentant prisoners* were engaged in a project of ethical self-construction and feared sexually explicit conversations might morally debase them. *Fatalists*, on the other hand, genuinely feared that they might be unable to control other people's impact on their sexuality, and that this might disrupt their goal of practical self-management.

Negotiators and *"mainstream" prisoners* were less vulnerable and more pragmatic in their approach to both their sentences and their peers. They acknowledged that they were forced to live in prison with people convicted of sexual offenses and that some degree of association was practically, emotionally, and economically necessary, and they were the men who most consciously limited their knowledge about their peers to allow these relationships to continue. Their friendships were often quite strategic, based on shared interests and backgrounds, and they were generally emotionally distant from their associates. While they were often quite open about their own offenses, they generally eschewed asking too directly about other people's, avoiding only those whose convictions were generally known (or more accurately, those whose reputations were generally known) and those whose appearances implied that they might be convicted of particularly serious offenses. They justified this avoidance on practical grounds: "It's better not to know, and just carry on not seeing what we've done" (Ahmed). While they rarely openly abused them, they disapproved of those they knew were convicted of offenses against young children (and those whose appearances, in their eyes, indicated that they were), and they were reluctant to associate with them more than was necessary: "I'm very choosy with who my friends are, and I don't see that because we're all in the same boat in here that we're all the same people" (Frank).

These distinctions were largely a consequence of identity work. *Negotiators* and *"mainstream" prisoners* were frustrated with their imprisonment and sensitive to the stigma of the "sex offender" label, and they managed this situation by suggesting that those they lived with deserved this situation more than they did:

> That was probably the lowest I've ever been in my entire life, when I was waiting for that trial, waiting for that to all come through. That was probably the lowest, scummiest I've ever felt, and that's the truth. I've got used to it a bit more now. I've come to this place, like I say, we're all classed as sex offenders, but I've labeled it, and you've got this, you've got that. And I class myself—whether I'm right, whether I'm wrong—but I class myself as up here [in the moral hierarchy]. I'm not down there. (Frank)

This differentiation was also socially reinforced. Younger *negotiators* and *"mainstream" prisoners* were aware that their prison friends might find them guilty by association if they spent time with someone known to have offended against a child: "If you make a friendship with one of the bacons [someone in for a child sex offense], then you're an outcast" (Noah). Their concern with contamination was thus symbolic. Their priority was protecting their reputation, and they were aware that they might further damage it by spending time with the wrong people, and this preoccupied them more than any fear that they might be sexually or morally infected by them. As long as the reputational impact of their relationships was managed, and they did not overhear graphic descriptions of offenses, they were willing to socially engage with other prisoners.

Resigned prisoners were less concerned with stigmatization and reputational damage within the prison. They coped with their imprisonment by ignoring its illegitimacy and focusing on dealing with their daily life within the institution. Their interactions with other prisoners employed a complementary style, and they preferred neither to discuss their own offenses, nor to talk about other peoples':

> It's not interesting to me. There are so many more interesting things to talk about. Prisoners come and go in these places. I don't want to spend the rest of my time enlightening the next one that comes in, enlightening the next one that comes in. No thanks. Because that way, I'm missing out on something. I've got to make the best of what it is in here. That, to me, is off the radar unless I've really got to talk about it. (Kevin)

Resigned prisoners tried to cope with their imprisonment by simply not seeing their conviction as part of the interior world of the prison. This was not always easy. Other prisoners sometimes talked about their offenses, and judgmental instincts were able to pierce through protective exteriors:

> When you hear what some of them are convicted of . . . Some of them are very open about it, they'll tell you themselves. As a parent and a husband, some of them absolutely disgust me. I have to be careful, I have to try and balance things because I'm in their club now, but I think some of them should be locked away forever and I don't want to engage with them on any level. You know, I'd be the same on the outside, but like I say, in here you have to make allowances. (Phil)

They saw themselves as fundamentally different from those who were guilty of the most serious offenses, and yet they were forced by unjust circumstance to spend time with them. Balancing these two competing needs—for protection from unfairly imposed stain and for social engagement to make imprisonment easier—was central to how *resigned prisoners* adapted to their sentences. They often formed quite close friendships within the prison, primarily with other *resigned prisoners*, and they talked mainly about their shared experiences of employment, family, and "normal life" (Shezad), rather than a mutual feeling of injustice.

Activists, on the other hand, powered themselves with discussions of injustice, although like other prisoners they avoided directly discussing offenses in order to maintain social relationships. They considered the legal system to be corrupt, and this belief made them open to the idea that other people had also been the victims of a miscarriage of justice. Cain, for instance, said, "If I can come in here on an innocent thing, then how many people can come in on an innocent thing?" He, like other *activists*, preferred to socialize with people he believed to be innocent, but he felt forced by circumstance to lower his moral standards: "I only stick around not guilty people. Don't get me wrong, there are a few what are guilty, I'll probably talk to one or two, and I'll probably think, 'Bloody hell man, what am I doing?' [. . .] But look at the jail I'm in, what can I do?" Nevertheless, *activists* came closest to replicating the "mainstream" offense hierarchy in Stafford. They regularly and openly discussed their distaste for many of those they lived among, and they distinguished between those who were guilty and those who were innocent, and between those convicted of offenses against adults and those convicted of offenses against children. Like other prisoners, they preferred to minimize contact with those they condemned and rarely confronted them directly, but they assigned responsibility for this to those they sought to avoid: "As long as they keep out of my way, I keep out of their way" (Cain). This moral hierarchy served a symbolic function, just as it did for *negotiators*:

> Some of these people are child molesters, gays, who knows what they are. No. Pedophiles, whatever. They put all of us in the same category, but there's pedophilia and there's rape, but the worst of the worst is the pedophiles. I cannot—urgh. I can't understand how a man can get off on a child. I can't relate to it, put it that way. I cannot relate to it. I can't see where they're getting off on a child. (Terry)

Activists disparaged the masculinity of those convicted of offenses against children as much as they criticized them morally: they were not just bad people, but also bad men who were sexually aroused by unacceptable stimuli, and *activists'* voluble disgust illustrated their dissimilarity from pedophiles. The revulsion they felt also fed into their general cynicism about the justice system, with several *activists* complaining that they had received longer sentences for (allegedly unfair) convictions relating to adults than other prisoners had received for offenses against children. They considered the formal system to be as corrupt as the informal social world.

CONCLUSION: MAKING SEXUAL VIOLENCE MATTER

> One way, though, that communities bring themselves into existence, sustain themselves, and define and refine their identities is by the progressive articulation and the enforcement of their norms and of their membership. When individuals take up the role of judges, invoking norms and affirming membership, they make use of something that is common property, the moral authority of a community. (Walker 2006, 33)

Philosopher Margaret Urban Walker argues that communities have three responsibilities when moral norms have been breached: to reiterate the broken standards, to make the wrongdoer accept responsibility, and to validate victims and their needs. Punishing the wrongdoer is one way of achieving all three of these goals, Walker argues, as punishment can show that the standards are so significant that we are willing to change our world in response to a breach of them, that the wrongdoer is part of the community who should obey them, and that the victims are members of the community who should be protected by them (30–32). However, Walker suggests that such punishment should not simply be contracted out to formal legal systems. Instead, all members of a community should "take up the role of judges" and show that wrongdoing matters by choosing not to ignore it, but instead allowing it to change our relationships.

Increasingly, imprisonment is the method we use to show that sexual violence matters, but in so doing we professionalize and bureaucratize the delivery of punishment, making it the job of the state and not of the moral community. When we do this, we forget that prisons create communities as well as exclude people from them. These communities inevitably engage in their own forms of moral communication which do not always align with those intended by the state, and which demonstrate the different ways in which sexual offenses can matter to people. In Stafford, other people's offenses mattered to prisoners in a way which was determined more by how prisoners approached their own sentences than it was by the moral seriousness of the offense in question. Imprisonment removed people from the harm they had caused and from their communities, and subjected them to a painful experience, pushing them to focus their attention on themselves. As a result, for most prisoners in Stafford, other people's offenses represented a threat to themselves more than it did a harm to others: for *repentant* and *redeemed prisoners*, the threat was to their moral integrity; for *fatalists*, it was to their futures; for *negotiators*, their reputation; for *resigned prisoners*, their coping strategies; and for *activists*, their masculine morality.

The primary goal of most prisoners in Stafford was to guard themselves against the threats these offenses represented rather than to make these offenses matter. As a result, they, like prison officers, were reluctant to "take up the role of judges" and allow prisoners' convictions to become the primary factor shaping their relationships. Rather than amplifying the messages of denunciation which they knew their peers' sentences represented, they closed their ears to them. They had been marked as "sex offenders" and were surrounded by people sharing the same stain, and their response to this pressure was to try to ignore it as much as possible. They therefore engaged in complex acts of collective denial to stop themselves from finding out what their peers had been convicted of and to absorb the knowledge which they gained so that it did not become the dominant factor governing their lives inside.

Just as there is no evidence that individual offense denial makes reoffending more likely (Ware and Blagden 2020), there is no reason to believe that these forms of collective denial would increase participants' chances of offending again. Indeed, one way of thinking about Stafford's moral community is as a model of reintegration. It may be the case that the only way for society to accept people who have committed acts of sexual violence, or other serious wrongs, is by deliberately limiting our awareness of their offenses, and thereby choosing to stop thinking about them as "sex offenders" or "criminals."[12] However, Stafford's moral community did not control this knowledge in a way that made it a tempting model. Prisoners' attempts to suppress knowledge about other people's worst acts were more an attempt to ignore knowledge which would be distressing than a meaningful ethical claim about the relevance of these acts to future social interactions. Mechanisms of denial also had the effect of promoting troubling ways of thinking about sexual offending. Prisoners' reluctance to challenge and question their peers' stories of innocence encouraged the belief that miscarriages of justice were common and reinforced rape myths. Most prisoners estimated that between a third and a quarter of their peers were not guilty, and others questioned the seriousness of other people's offenses by drawing on victim-blaming tropes. Also, the decision to avoid knowledge about offending meant that prisoners made judgments about their peers on the basis of people's appearances and demeanors, and never challenged the common stereotyped assumption that sexually violent acts are only enacted by sexually inadequate men (Temkin, Gray, and Barrett 2018).

Feminists have long argued that we should pay more societal attention to sexually violent acts and actors that do not fit our stereotypes. Stafford, however, encouraged its prisoners to simultaneously pay too much and too little attention to sexually inappropriate behaviors. Its stain was so absolute and so all-encompassing that it was difficult to see through it clearly, and so only that which was immediately visible was acknowledged. The comment which opened this chapter provides a clear illustration of this. The statement, while deeply unpleasant, was not qualitatively dissimilar to sexually explicit comments made in other contexts, and the man who made it was far from the first to make graphic sexual comments to or about me. What differentiated this remark, as Tony recognized, was its phrasing: "It's the 'rape' thing. If he'd said, 'She's pretty' or 'I'd fuck her,' that'd be OK." By using a criminal label, this man made clear that what he desired was wrong. Had he used a less condemned term to express the same wish, the message would have been heard differently.

8

Judging Prisons

The Limitations and Excesses
of Denunciatory Punishment

After leaving the wing at lunchtime on my last day of fieldwork, I went to a staff office and logged into the computer's online system to find out what the people I had interviewed had been convicted of and what sentences they were serving.[1] I was interested in how people adapted to and made sense of their sentences and their convictions, and to understand that, I needed to know what their sentences and convictions were. Although I had asked interview participants to tell me what they had been convicted of, I had also stressed that they did not need to; although most did, they often spoke in vague terms which did not align with legal categories, and I had no way of verifying their stories. I deliberately waited until the last day of fieldwork to look people up on the online system, for three key reasons. First, I wanted to allow people to control what they told me. My thinking here was partly strategic, and partly principled. I thought that some people might feel more comfortable talking to me if they knew I didn't know what they were in for, and certainly a few men told me they were happy with me accessing their records as long as I only did it at the end of the project. I also believe that, unless there is a strong reason to the contrary, people should be able to choose what they tell people about their pasts. Until there was a reason for me to read the records, I was uncomfortable doing so. Second, I was worried about what I might find out. I liked most of the people I met, and the project was dependent on my being able to form trusting relationships with them, and I didn't want to learn anything which might jeopardize that. While I did not intend to be morally judgmental, and while in principle I believe that all people are more than their worst actions, disgust is instinctive and I didn't want to risk awakening it. Third, I didn't want to know anything that might contradict the stories prisoners were telling their peers, as I feared accidentally giving something away and endangering their relationships.

For the same reasons, I deliberately never googled anyone, and so for the course of the fieldwork period all I knew about people's convictions and sentences was what I was told by people in the prison.

After taking quick and sparse notes on prisoners' convictions and sentences, which I wrote in a separate notebook from the rest of my fieldwork notes, I went to the town McDonald's to wait for my train home. I was uncomfortable and restless, sad about leaving the prison and saying goodbye to people I cared about, but also confused by some of what I had just learned. It was clear that a few "*mainstream*" *prisoners*, who had claimed to be convicted of nonsexual offenses and who had insisted that they were fundamentally different from the "sex offenders" they lived among, had previously served sentences for serious sexual offenses. Several people had been charged with more offenses than they had told me about. Others were charged under both the 1994 Criminal Justice and Public Order Act and the 2003 Sexual Offences Act, which implied their offending had covered a span of years and complicated their attempts to neutralize their crimes as "mistakes." Even when looking at the official records hadn't revealed new information, reading lists of convictions presented in cold legal language was unnerving, and I struggled to connect the inventories of offenses to the men I had just said goodbye to.

Impulsively, I picked up my phone and googled a few of the men I had known best. I justified myself by thinking that if I wanted to understand how people responded to stigmatization, it was worth knowing how their convictions had been publicly disseminated, but I also thought that more knowledge might help me make moral sense of what I had read. It didn't. I found out that two of the men I most liked were convicted of crimes that were significantly more serious than I had assumed. Both had told me they were guilty of the rape of someone under the age of sixteen, and, because I liked them and because they seemed normal, I had automatically imagined that they must have once raped someone just under sixteen, an offense which is of course deeply immoral and damaging, but which felt comprehensible. I read that both had been convicted of offending against children under the age of ten, and in one case the abuse had involved a close family member and had gone on for years. I cried in McDonald's, and again on the train, and again when I got home.

While I was in the field, I had followed similar strategies of information control to prison officers and prisoners: I had feared that I would be unable to hold specific information about people's sexual convictions in the forefront of my mind while also having the sorts of relationships I needed to have, so I accepted the stories I was told, deliberately tried to avoid finding anything out which might contradict them, and interpreted them in line with my preexisting instincts and prejudices. My emotional response to learning the details about these offenses indicated that my caution had not been groundless. Sitting in the Stafford McDonald's, I wept out of confusion and horror. I struggled, and struggle, to integrate what I was reading with the other things I knew about the men I met: that they were thoughtful, respectful, generous people who spoke with principle about what was owed to them and their peers, and what they owed to the wider community. I feared that this new knowledge would infect my memories of men I had truly liked and that by reading and thinking about this information I was being disloyal to them. I also worried that I had been wrong to like them, and that by doing so I had somehow been tricked into betraying the children they had hurt and putting my own moral integrity at risk.[2]

In 1967, sociologist Howard Becker wrote a famous article, "Whose Side Are We On?", in which he discussed the tendency of sociologists of deviance to sympathize with the underdog. He said that sociologists were often accused of bias for exploring the perspectives of those with a low position in the *"hierarchy of credibility"* (241, emphasis in original), even if their sympathy did not infect their findings. Sitting in that Stafford McDonald's, my confusion stemmed from the fact that not only did I not know whose side I had been on, I also did not know whose side I should be on. Wherever I placed my sympathy, it cast a shadow—over the victims whose stories had been obscured or over the prisoners whose moral identity had been stained—and I couldn't even decide who was placed lowest in the hierarchy of credibility. I didn't want to betray my participants by allowing their offenses to shape how I saw them, but I also worried that liking someone who had been convicted of such serious sex offenses implied that I thought their offenses didn't matter.

It was so difficult to work out how to incorporate my new knowledge about people's offenses because being convicted of and imprisoned for a sex offense functions as what American sociologist Harold Garfinkel (1956) called a status degradation ceremony. Such ceremonies are ways of expressing denunciation, and denunciation involves assigning someone a new identity, in our case, that of the "sex offender":

> The other person becomes in the eyes of his condemners literally a different and *new* person. It is not that the new attributes are added to the old "nucleus." He is not changed, he is reconstituted. The former identity, at best, receives the accent of mere appearance. In the social calculus of reality representations and test [sic], the former identity stands as accidental; the new identity is the "basic reality." What he is now is what, "after all," he was all along. (421–22, emphasis in original)

In other words, once someone has been successfully denounced as a "sex offender," a "sex offender" is all we accept they can be. Any attributes which appear to contradict the implications of this stained identity cannot be acknowledged, and if we do acknowledge them, then the "sex offender" label must have been inaccurately applied. Either people are guilty and therefore "sex offenders," with all of the discrediting attributes which go with that label, or they do not fit properly into the "sex offender" category and therefore their offending either didn't happen or wasn't serious.

During fieldwork, I had tried to control what I knew about the men I interviewed in order to stave off the effects of the denunciation which their conviction and imprisonment had imposed on them, and to see them as they were—as people who had, in most cases, done awful things, but who were not reducible to them. Blocking out this knowledge had only provided temporary relief, however, and as soon as I found out what people were in for, I was confronted with the false choice imposed by the denunciatory label. I was unwilling to do what some officers had done and interpret people's visible respectability and kindness as acts of manipulation. At the same time, I didn't want to follow in the footsteps of some prisoners and, at best, minimize the offenses these men had committed, and at worst, assume that their decency to me meant that they must be innocent. I tried to find a different path, one which took the middle ground between the two sides and allowed me to take the convictions and the harm seriously without allowing that acknowledgment to overrule everything else which I could learn about life in Stafford. While I am sure I have stumbled while writing this book, I hope I have done so equally in each direction.

In the remainder of this concluding chapter, I explore the relationship between denunciation and justice, and argue that I was not the only dupe of the false choice the denunciatory label created. I draw on empirical research on what victims of sexual violence think justice is, as well as on the normative work of penal theorists about the messages that imprisonment could and should send, to argue that a just response to sexual violence would involve people who have committed sexual offenses acknowledging their acts and recognizing their wrongness—in other words, realizing that rape means rape. I then summarize the research presented in this book and argue that imprisonment in Stafford and the denunciation it entailed made such acknowledgment harder and was more likely to shame wrongdoers than to focus their attention on the wrongness of their acts. I end by briefly considering how to generate more effective moral communication, both by looking beyond prisons and by changing them.

RAPE MEANS RAPISTS: HMP STAFFORD AS A DENUNCIATORY INSTITUTION

Antiviolence activist and playwright Eve Ensler (2019a) was sexually and physically abused by her father from a young age. Decades after his death, she wrote the apology he would never make. The book which contained it is both brutal and generous. In her father's voice, she describes his childhood, the abuse he perpetrated, and its devastating effects on her. In a TED talk which accompanied the release of the book, Eve says that she used to want her father to be punished, to go to prison, or to die (Ensler 2019b). By writing the apology, she realized that she had actually wanted her father to repent and change:

The apology I wrote—I learned something about a different lens we have to look through to understand the problem of men's violence that I and one billion other women have survived. We often turn to punishment first. It's our first instinct, but actually, although punishment sometimes is effective, on its own, it is not enough. My father punished me. I was shut down, and I was broken. I think punishment hardens us, but it doesn't teach us. Humiliation is not revelation. We actually need to create a process that may involve punishment, whereby we open a doorway where men can actually become something and someone else.

In this TED talk, Eve suggests that apologies might be the route by which both perpetrators and survivors can be liberated. She says that successful apologies allow people to take responsibility and make amends, but they start with people saying what they did, saying why they did it, and feeling the pain that they caused. Her book ends with her father living "in the torturous limbo" he made inside her and realizing the harm he has done and how he harmed himself in the process: "I am nothing. I have no family. I have no place. I have no father. I have no mother. I am badness. I am shame. I am disgraced." Prompted by this awareness, and by seeing the stars "breaking through this dark" (2019a, 111), he apologizes to his daughter:

Eve,
Let me say these words:
I am sorry. I am sorry. Let me sit here at the final hour. Let me get it right this time. Let me be staggered by your tenderness. Let me risk fragility. Let me be rendered vulnerable. Let me be lost. Let me be still. Let me not occupy or oppress. Let me not conquer or destroy. Let me bathe in the rapture. Let me be the father.
Let me be the father who mirrors your kindheartedness back to you. Let me lay no claims. Let me bear witness and not invade.

Eve,
I free you from the covenant. I revoke the lie. I lift the curse.
Old man, be gone. (112)

Imagined by Eve, this apology is not intended "to elicit understanding or forgiveness" (9), nor is it intended as a precursor to personal reconciliation. Shortly after publishing the book, Eve decided that she no longer wished to be known by her father's name and took the name V, demonstrating her wish to no longer feel bound to him (Akbar 2020). One effect of the apology is to liberate V: in the preface to the book, and in her own voice, she describes the letter as "my attempt to endow my father with the will and the words to cross the border, and speak the language, of apology so that I can finally be free." But her father is also freed by it, released from the agony of being the man who did those things to his daughter and to himself.

In her creative response to the sexual violence she experienced, V shared with other victim-survivors a desire to have the wrong which had been done to her recognized, and a skepticism about the ability of punishment and the legal system to fully deliver this recognition. In recent years, a small but significant amount of research has been conducted on how victim-survivors of sexual and gender-based violence imagine justice.[3] These studies suggest that, to victim-survivors, justice is multifaceted, and includes the ability to have a voice, to control what happens to you, and to have the wrong acknowledged. This acknowledgment often includes the perpetrator receiving a conviction, but it is not reducible to it. A criminal conviction symbolically marks that the state understands what happened and that it was wrong, but the recognition which victim-survivors seek is fuller than this. It involves being "taken seriously" (McGlynn and Westmarland 2019, 188) as a person who matters and needs support, and recognition can be granted by the perpetrator, family members, and the community as well as by the state. This desire for acknowledgment is often accompanied by a desire for the perpetrator to face consequences, but it is rarely expressed as a desire for harsh punishment. These studies suggest that victim-survivors often do not even want their attacker to go to prison; when they do, it tends to be because they believe that incapacitating the person who hurt them is the only way they can be protected from them, and not because they desire them to suffer.[4] There is even some anecdotal evidence that their desire to avoid the person who hurt them being sent to prison actively discourages them from reporting their victimization (Sered 2019), although it is not clear if this reaction is widespread.

Some normative penal theorists have also suggested that the right response to crime is to acknowledge it, and that punishment could be justified if its aim was to declare that the crime was wrong and that it mattered. As discussed in chapter 2, many morally communicative penal theorists suggest that punishment should focus its expressive energies at people who have committed crime and tell them either "what you did was wrong" or "you should feel guilty about what you have done." In the case of people convicted of sex offenses, this would involve sending the message that "rape means rape," and teaching perpetrators to align their personal moral evaluations of the past with those made by the state and by their victims.

If it were successfully sent and received, this message should result in remorse, which is defined by philosopher Miranda Fricker (2016, 167) as "a pained moral perception of the wrong one has done."[5] Remorse is both cognitive and emotional. It involves accepting intellectually that one did wrong and feeling the appropriate guilt and distress about it. Margaret Urban Walker has argued that remorse "is the minimal condition for those who have harmed or offended against others to 'set things right' with them" (2006, 191).[6] She states that this is the case because morally adequate social life can only take place when people are confident that they share standards with others, when they trust others to live in accordance with these standards, and when they hope that people merit the trust we place in them. Our confidence, hope, and trust are all damaged when we are the victims of injustice and violence, but when responsibility is placed with wrongdoers, when remorse is expressed by them, and when the community attempts to reinstate standards, trust, hope, and moral repair can take place.[7] The expression of remorse would make clear that the wrongdoer is responsible, and would contribute to the reinstatement of standards, trust, and hope, as it would involve the person who has committed the harm painfully recommitting themselves to shared moral norms.[8] Remorse could therefore be generative and bring us closer to the sort of moral repair which Walker describes and which V and other victim-survivors desire. By demonstrating that the wrongdoer now sees the past in the same way as the state and the victim, this remorse would make it possible for the wrongdoer to continue to live in a moral community with the people they have hurt.

The empirical research discussed in this book suggests that Stafford failed to produce or nurture remorse. Only one person interviewed for this project said that he started his sentence believing that he was innocent and shifted to see himself as guilty, and very few said that they felt more guilty about their crimes as their sentences continued. While many prisoners were deeply remorseful, it was rare for these emotions to have been generated by, or even birthed in, the prison. That Stafford failed to persuade people that "rape means rape" does not mean it said nothing, however. As this book has described, it was a denunciatory institution which sent the message "rape means rapists," declaring to prisoners that "you should be ashamed of yourself." The individual actors working in Stafford or for the Prison Service did not intend for the prison to send these messages. Instead, they resulted in part from the institutional distortions described in chapter 3. Stafford only held people convicted of an especially stigmatized category of offenses, and thus it stained them in a way which was profoundly visible and potentially permanent, but which also adhered to all aspects of prisoners' behavior and character and carried implications which were both mortifying and unspecific. It appended this stain to them following a legal process which felt both alienating and capricious, and which therefore made it easier for prisoners to distract themselves from the moral connotations of what they had done (if they had done it) and instead to focus their attention on the fairness of their convictions and imprisonment. The prison then attempted to coerce moral transformation, pushing them to prioritize the performance of change rather than genuine engagement in it, and providing them with the alibi of incentivization to excuse any behaviors which implied guilt.

The denunciatory message also resulted, paradoxically, from the efforts of people living and working in the prison to avoid expressing condemnation and to live as though offenses did not matter. In chapter 6, I showed that prison officers attempted to de-moralize punishment in Stafford, and to avoid thinking or talking about prisoners' offenses in order to prevent unnecessary punitiveness. However, this strategy reinforced officers' sense that the prisoners in Stafford were a different category of person, and thus inadvertently deepened the stigmatizing message which the prison sent. Similarly, chapter 7 described prisoners' collective attempts to ignore offenses so that they could continue to form social relationships with each other. Their efforts at overlooking offenses were more successful than those of prison officers, but in doing so, they promoted dangerous myths about sexual violence and supported and upheld individual acts of denial.

Prisoners responded differently to the messages the prison sent, as I described in chapters 4 and 5. Those I classed as *repentant prisoners* had started their sentence pained by remorse and were desperate to use their imprisonment as an opportunity for atonement and change. As they realized that the institution would not live up to its symbolic promise and that it would never recognize how they felt they had transformed, they grew frustrated. The most discouraged of these men, *redeemed prisoners*, did not change how they felt about their offending past, but they became increasingly cynical about the state, its agents, and the integrity of institutions of punishment. Most other prisoners felt much less strongly about their convictions and were much more focused on themselves. *Fatalists* were frightened of the dangerous effects of being treated as a pariah by people outside and inside the prison, and were preoccupied by avoiding that fate rather than by reckoning with their pasts. *Negotiators* wanted to avoid the implications of their stain, whether by trying to make their sentence as bearable as possible or by arguing that they weren't like other stained people. Some *negotiators* went as far as rejecting the label altogether: *"mainstream" prisoners* insisted, sometimes incorrectly, that they had not been convicted of a sex offense and thus that they were not "sex offenders." *Resigned prisoners* and *activists* also resisted their denunciation, insisting on their innocence when speaking to others, and seeking to embody it in their interactions with morally communicative penal power.

The message which was sent by Stafford took this denunciatory form for two key reasons. The first was that the symbolic function of punishment was "submerged" (Garland 1990, 73) by the bureaucratized and professionalized form which modern imprisonment takes. Prison officers, the members of staff with the most frequent contact with prisoners, actively avoided speaking to them about their offenses. These discussions were hived off to specialist staff like probation officers, psychologists, and treatment providers, and took place in a rehabilitative context which turned prisoners' conversations about offending into a target of penal power. The second reason was that the social and legal connotations of being convicted of a sex offense meant that it permanently, personally, and painfully stained them. Research on shaming discussed in chapter 2 suggests that people are more likely to feel remorse when they know what they have done wrong, when they do not fear that their identities will be overwhelmed by it, when they feel like they can do something to make amends, and when they feel that they will be reintegrated (Ahmed 2001; Harris 2001). Being convicted of a sex offense in England and Wales in the twenty-first century does not create these conditions. The result is that people have very little motivation to accept their moral responsibility and lots of reasons to resist it.

The denunciatory context in which men are punished for sex offenses may mean that accepting responsibility for one's offenses makes desistance from offending *less* likely. This claim contradicts many of our instincts about how people give up crime. V was not alone in her belief that true acknowledgment of the wrong that one has done is the first step to change. This principle was shared by the early reformers of the penitentiary, has formed the basis of rehabilitation programs, has influenced penal theorists' attempts to justify punishment (Duff 2001; Hampton 1984), and lies at the heart of the modern insistence that people who have done wrong should take accountability.[9] Nevertheless, there is very little empirical evidence that taking responsibility for the wrongs we have done helps us stop committing crimes (Ievins forthcoming; Maruna and Mann 2006). The very small amount of research conducted into desistance processes among men convicted of sex offenses suggests that neutralizations are common among people in the early stages of desistance from sexual violence (Hulley 2016), and that desistors are more likely to externalize blame for their offenses onto causes like substance abuse and mental health problems (Kras and Blasko 2016) or other situational causes (Farmer, McAlinden, and Maruna 2016) than they are to insist that the responsibility was their own. Other research has suggested that those who maintain that they are not guilty of their sexual offenses are no more likely to commit further offenses (Yates 2009), and may even be less likely to do so (Hood et al. 2002; Ware and Blagden 2020).

This finding puts penal theorists and penal practitioners in a difficult position. Which is a more important goal for punishment: reduced reoffending, even if it means people do not take responsibility for their crimes, or remorse and acknowledgment, at the possible cost of increased recidivism? The answer is that the choice exists because of the way we punish and the messages we send in doing so. The admission of guilt has the social meaning and effect which it does because of the framework we have for understanding the relationship between sexually violent acts and moral identity. In Europe and North America, taking responsibility for a sex offense is tantamount to admitting being a "sex offender." Excuses and denials, however, enable people to absorb the blow of the conviction without surrendering their identities. Desistance scholar Shadd Maruna (2001) argues that it is by making excuses for our offenses that we avoid internalizing them and living as though they are the part of our history which determines who we are. We thereby protect ourselves from depression, low self-esteem, and the fear that we cannot do anything about our identities. In a different cultural and punitive context—one in which we made space for change, avoided denunciation, and designed systems of punishment which communicated more clearly—taking responsibility for sexual offenses could hypothetically have a different relationship to desistance.

FROM DENUNCIATION TO REPAIR: HOW TO COMMUNICATE BETTER?

This book has described how conviction and imprisonment discourage people convicted of sex offenses from focusing on the wrongs that they have done. It ends by making a few suggestions about how we could more effectively respond to sexual violence, first by looking beyond prisons, and then by changing them. One way of responding to the communicative weaknesses outlined in this book would be to join with the growing calls to abolish prisons and replace them with institutional arrangements which might speak more clearly about the wrongness of sexual violence, such as transformative and restorative justice.[10] These calls are strengthened by the fact that state punishment as it is currently envisaged fails to come close to condemning violence, vindicating victims, or engaging in meaningful or desirable moral communication with people who commit sexual violence. In England and Wales, it is estimated that 128,000 women are raped every year, but in only 1.6 percent of cases is someone *charged*, let alone convicted (HM Government 2021). Even when people are charged, it is unlikely that the wrongs will be officially recognized. The fear of conviction and imprisonment incentivizes people to plead "not guilty," and evidentiary requirements make it extremely difficult to find people guilty (K. Daly 2006).[11] If people are convicted, the research described in this book suggests that imprisonment does little to talk people out of the dishonest claims of innocence promoted by the legal process. There is also simply no realistic chance that all the sexual assaults which take place in England and Wales will ever lead to imprisonment. No one is charged following 98.4 percent of rapes each year, or 125,952 in raw numbers. Supposing (for argument's sake) that each man who committed one rape was actually responsible for an average of five, that would mean that 25,190 men are not charged with rape each year. For each of them to be imprisoned for just one year would require thirty-four new prisons of the size of Stafford to be built each year to contain them—an unimaginable prospect.

The impossibility of a mechanized and bureaucratic system of punishment ever being able to adequately respond to sexual violence at the scale it currently takes place is one reason why those who advocate for the abolition of imprisonment have suggested alternative mechanisms of justice. Proponents of different forms of informal, alternative, or transformative approaches have suggested that responses to crime which are rooted in community, and which therefore permit an "organic rather than a bureaucratic approach" (Bottoms 2003, 102), might promote accountability more effectively than the responses enacted by the state. Transformative justice and community accountability "toolkits" are proliferating, promoting responses such as naming the violence as violence, facilitating personal change on the part of the perpetrator, and providing physical and psychological safety for the victim.[12] Social justice and abolitionist activists have provided numerous anecdotal accounts of the process and its success at protecting victims and encouraging change.[13] Nevertheless, I am not aware of any rigorous evaluations of the effects of transformative forms of justice. The approach's success depends on the person who committed the act being willing to cooperate (Ansfield and Colman 2012) and on the community in question being "thick" enough to follow through, neither of which will always be possible. Proponents of transformative justice have asked important questions about whether we can find responses to crime which honor the wrongness of the offense, but which do not reproduce violence. However, the alternative to state punishment which they offer has not yet fully answered these questions.

Other scholars and activists have suggested that part of the answer might be found in restorative justice conferences, which they argue provide a form of moral communication which is more meaningful than that offered by retributive punishment (Bottoms 2003; Duff 2011). While courtrooms speak in professionalized abstractions and prisons distract people from the realities of what they have done, restorative conferences bring the operations of justice closer to the people involved. The conversations they facilitate should be more direct than those created in courtrooms, as they require perpetrators to face the victim-survivor and hear their experiences in their own language, and thus come closer to the sort of recognition which victim-survivors need. They should also be less distorted than those enabled by prisons, as well-trained facilitators should ensure that people are unable to take refuge in denial and minimizations. The approach is not without its critics, though, and the past twenty-five years have seen a significant debate about the appropriateness of restorative approaches for cases of sexual and gendered violence.[14] Opponents have argued that bringing together victim-survivors and perpetrators risks retraumatizing victims and perpetuating damaging power differentials, particularly in cases of intimate-partner and interfamilial violence. They have also argued that restorative justice lacks the symbolic power to replace conviction and imprisonment. These debates have proved difficult to resolve due to a lack of rigorous evidence about the nature and effectiveness of restorative justice conferences in cases of sexual violence, and a recent systematic review of evaluations of restorative justice in such cases found only one study which met their inclusion criteria (Gang et al. 2021). However, as several advocates of restorative justice have argued, many of the arguments against it fall apart if we don't think of it as an alternative to state punishment. Instead, we can treat it as something which takes place along a different trajectory and which can be pursued either as a supplement to more conventional forms of punishment or in cases where criminal convictions are either not pursued or not achieved (B. Hudson 2002; McGlynn, Westmarland, and Godden 2012; Pali and Sten Madsen 2011).

The appeal of restorative justice speaks to the communicative failures of imprisonment. However, since there is no reason to expect the imminent replacement of prisons as our primary method of moral condemnation, it is worth considering how they could be reformed to make them speak more effectively. The findings discussed in this book point us toward two potential areas of change. First, we should pay more attention to the relationship between the pains which prisons exert and the messages they send. As eighteenth-century reformers of the prison knew, the experience of excessive suffering distracts people from thinking about what they have done and pushes them to focus on their own agony. If we want prisons to send a message which is conducive to genuine reflection, repentance, or accountability, there might be good reasons to be parsimonious with the pain we inflict, and to speak more loudly about the harm we do by lengthening prison sentences, hardening conditions, and permanently staining people.

Second, prisons should provide spaces in which intimate and honest conversations about offending can be facilitated, and in which people can come closer to the form of recognition which V imagines her father reaching. As this book has described, the professional identity of prison officers in Stafford pushed them away from talking to prisoners about their offending, and the forms of rehabilitation and treatment provided were so tied up with systems of incentivization that prisoners often did not engage with them authentically. Deliberately engineering spaces in which offending could be discussed without the risk that it would affect the length or conditions of people's confinement might help promote more meaningful moral communication. One way of doing this could be through greater provision of restorative justice conferences while people are in prison. Another might be through the forms of therapy and discussion facilitated by Therapeutic Community prisons, which people convicted of murder often describe as providing them their first opportunity to process and make sense of their crimes (Crewe, Hulley, and Wright 2019). People may also benefit from participating in creative endeavors (Crockett Thomas et al. 2021), from speaking to chaplains (R. Williams 2003), or from having the opportunity for longer, more private, and more meaningful conversations with family members and loved ones. The goal of these conversations should not be to push people to take responsibility, but it should enable them "to talk of their actual history without fear" (R. Williams 2003, 3), and create the conditions in which people can express and feel remorse.

To make these changes would be difficult and any intervention should be cautious. Ever since the penitentiary was introduced as a penal technology, prison reformers have sought to reorganize prisons so that they produce the desired moral effects (Throness 2008). They have rarely been successful. More recently, decades of prison sociology have taught us that prisons are extraordinarily complex environments, and that well-meaning reforms often have damaging consequences. It is for these reasons that prison sociologists, as experts in the effects and texture of imprisonment, should be engaged in this discussion, and should take more seriously the roles which prisons play as morally communicative institutions.

1. PUNISHING RAPE: FEMINISMS AND THE CARCERAL CONVERSATION

1. A transcript of the program is available at BBC News (2011).

2. Between 2010–2011 and 2019–2020, the budget of the Ministry of Justice was cut by around 25 percent, although initially the plan was to cut it by more (Sturge et al. 2019).

3. Clarke was legally incorrect. Sex with a fifteen-year-old is illegal in England and Wales, as the age of sexual consent is sixteen. However, sex with a fifteen-year-old is not automatically considered to be rape and is instead covered by the Section 9 provisions in the 2003 Sexual Offences Act, which cover "Sexual activity with a child." Sex with a child under thirteen is rape, and this is a strict liability offense (which means that *mens rea*, or a guilty mind, does not need to be proven).

4. England and Wales is a separate legal jurisdiction to both Scotland and Northern Ireland, and Clarke's proposal would have only applied to England and Wales.

5. For a sympathetic examination of the achievements, and some of the limitations, of feminist rape law reform in England and Wales, see McGlynn (2010). McGlynn herself has a complex and nuanced view about the relationship between the criminal legal system and justice; see McGlynn (2011) and McGlynn and Westmarland (2019). For much less sympathetic analyses of the effects of feminist law reform in the United States, see Goodmark (2018a), Richie (2012), and Gruber (2020), although for balance see also Nussbaum (2021). For an exploration of the influence of the feminist push for punishment outside the Global North, see Houge and Lohne (2017).

6. Feminist scholar Catherine MacKinnon sees expanding the legal definition of rape, "so that some of the most common rapes in life become rapes in law" (2005, 125), as a necessary task. On the whole, however, she is not optimistic about the capacity of legal reform due to the essentially masculine nature of the law.

7. The rate of increase was even starker in the United States, where the proportion of the prison population serving time for sexual offenses increased by 675 percent between 1990 and 2013 (Gruber 2020, 146).

8. This fall was exacerbated by the COVID-19 pandemic but continues preexisting trends.

9. The Victims' Commissioner of England and Wales is a government appointee whose role is to promote the interests of victims and witnesses of crime, encourage good practice when dealing with them, and review the government's Code of Practice for Victims.

10. McGlynn (2010) recounts that the blanket ban on the use of sexual history evidence in England and Wales was successfully challenged under the Human Rights Act 1998 as working against the defendant's right to a fair trial. Other challenges to feminist legal reforms based on human rights legislation—such as the challenge to the introduction of the strict liability offense of "child rape" in 2003, which was challenged under the same act— have been unsuccessful. Gruber (2020, 165–66) also cites several US-based feminist activists condemning procedural protections during campus rape cases.

11. In the United States, Black men and men of color are less overrepresented among men imprisoned for sex offenses than they are among men imprisoned for other offenses (Levine and Meiners 2020). In England and Wales, the Lammy Review (2017) found that the CPS was more likely to prosecute Black and Chinese men, as well as those listing their ethnic background as "other," for rape and domestic abuse than they were White men. However, ethnic minorities were no more likely than White British men to be found guilty or to receive a prison sentence for a sexual offense.

12. Throughout this book, I use gendered pronouns to describe perpetrators of sexual violence. While women and nonbinary people do commit sexual violence, the vast majority of people who are convicted are men. On December 31, 2021, 125 people listed as "females" were serving an immediate custodial sentence for a sex offense, and 12,005 listed as "males" (Ministry of Justice 2022b).

2. COMMUNICATING BADLY: PRISONS AS MORALLY COMMUNICATIVE INSTITUTIONS

1. For relevant works, see Durkheim ([1893] 1997; [1902] 1992; [1925] 1961), and chapters 2 and 3 in Garland (1990).

2. This section owes a significant debt to Michael Ignatieff's (1989) description of the birth of the modern prison, *A Just Measure of Pain: The Penitentiary in the Industrial Revolution 1750–1850*, as well as to Ian O'Donnell's (2014) account of the emergence of solitary confinement in *Prisoners, Solitude, and Time*.

3. For a discussion of the Auburn system of "separate but silent" prisons and the Pennsylvania system of solitary confinement, see Rubin (2021).

4. This argument builds heavily on Garland's (1990) account of the rationalization of punishment in chapter 8 of *Punishment and Modern Society*.

5. Although see Robinson (2008), who argues that late-modern rehabilitation takes a morally expressive form.

6. "The disciplinary measures and rational institutions of the modern penal system may be morally neutral and unemotive in their operational style, but they exist within a

context which has been socially and authoritatively defined as a punitive one. Prisons, re-
formatories, probation orders, fines, and so on operate within a symbolism of the punitive
because they are evoked as sanctions within a condemnatory ritual and they derive their
social meaning from this use. The social significance of these institutions, as well as the subjective meaning which they hold for those who occupy them, is largely fixed by this punitive usage, even though the institutions tend to deny or play down this punitive intent. The
punitive, condemnatory sign thus throws a long shadow over everything the penal system
does" (Garland 1990, 191; see also 260–62).

7. Sparks, Bottoms, and Hay (1996, 75–76) describe the prison as an organization which
manages people's time and behavior: "Organizations (offices, factories, schools, hospi-
tals, prisons) direct the activities of their members via the precise control of time; their
hierarchies are reflected and sustained in their 'zoning' of space; they monitor their own
activities through surveillance considered both as the collation and storage of information
(files, records, inventories, accounts) and through 'direct supervision,' especially of subordinate members. Organizations use 'specially designed locales' (Giddens 1987, p. 157) to
facilitate their continuous activity. Such buildings (of which prisons are an obvious instance
. . .) are 'power containers: physical settings which through the interaction of setting and
social conduct generate administrative power' (Giddens 1987, p. 157)."

8. Alison Liebling (assisted by Arnold 2004) has described the moral climates of prisons, using the term to describe the ways in which different forms of order, expressions of
power, and styles of staff-prisoner relationship enact different values. Her work does not
explore how different prisons shape ways of thinking about prisoners' convictions.

9. Exceptions include Crewe, Hulley, and Wright (2019), Jarman (2020), Ugelvik (2012),
and Wright, Crewe, and Hulley (2017).

10. Among European prison sociologists, "prisoner" continues to be a more commonly
used term than "incarcerated person." My research participants comfortably referred to
themselves as "prisoners" and none referred to themselves using person-first language
of the kind popular among abolitionists or in progressive American discourse. I prefer to
use the language used by my participants, and while I avoid using the stigmatizing term "sex
offender," I do use the term "prisoner" in this book.

11. "Privatization is an especially contentious aspect of criminal justice politics because
it crystallizes a conflict of world-views between a managerialist outlook concerned with
utilities (the best prison is the one that most efficiently and correctly performs its allocated
tasks) and one which emphasises the moral and constitutional dilemmas of imprisonment
(punishment is at best a necessary evil; it involves the exercise of power in imposing a painful deprivation and is hence a unique kind of *public* obligation)" (Sparks, Bottoms, and Hay
1996, 22, emphasis in original).

12. Penal theorists are moral, political, and legal philosophers who consider the conditions under which punishment could be justified.

13. The quotation in the subtitle for this section comes from Feinberg (1965, 402). The
idea that punishment is morally communicative has a long history, and legal theorists like
Henry M. Hart (1958) have also argued that the criminal law is condemnatory. It is also
worth noting that many of the theorists whom I will discuss in this section would not
self-define as moral communication theorists, nor would they necessarily see themselves
as forming a coherent tradition. Von Hirsch (1993) would probably describe himself as a

desert theorist. Hampton's (1984) early work stressed the value of moral *education*, rather than moral communication; her later work, however, was more conventionally retributive. Morris (1981) called his theory of punishment paternalistic rather than communicative. However, everyone whom I will discuss here described punishment as a form of *expression*, as something which carries meaning through the delivery of pain. As my intention is to use these scholars to suggest ways of thinking and raise questions, and not to provide a thorough review of the concept of moral communication, I am prepared to take some definitional liberties.

14. Feinberg is not the only critical moral communication theorist. Duff (2001), Hampton (1984), and Christopher Bennett (2008) call for imprisonment to be used more sparingly, and for moral communication to be expressed more effectively. Braithwaite (1989) could be described as a moral communication theorist who has given up on the institution of punishment.

15. Penal theorists often distinguish between expression, which is not necessarily directed at a recipient, and communication, which is more of "a *reciprocal* and *rational* engagement" with an active participant (Duff 2001, 79, emphasis in original). Criminologist Rob Canton (personal communication) says that expression can be compared to a "cry of pain," one which may be made impulsively without much attention being paid to the form it takes. Communication, on the other hand, should be compared to a "cry for help," something which is deliberately directed at an imagined recipient, and which should therefore be shaped such that the message is successfully sent. This distinction makes sense if we are describing punishment in the abstract or if we are prioritizing the actions and intentions of the message-sender. This book, however, describes the messier messages which are sent in practice, and it is key to its arguments that many are unintentionally sent. For this reason, the difference between communication and expression is not useful to our purposes, and in most cases I use the terms interchangeably.

16. For a complementary description of the narratives of offending given by men imprisoned for sexual violations in Norwegian prisons, which argues that the extent to which prisoners acknowledge the harm they have caused depends in part on the way other people respond to them and their stories, see Kruse (2020). Kruse conceptualizes these responses as a form of "friction" and identifies three types: productive or reintegrative friction, destructive or stigmatizing friction, and the absence of friction. Productive friction carries some similarities to the second message I identify ("you should feel guilty about what you have done"), and destructive friction to the third ("you should be ashamed of yourself").

17. See, for instance, Duff (2001) and Von Hirsch (1993).

18. Von Hirsch writes that "[b]ecause the prescribed sanction is one which expresses blame, this conveys the message that the conduct is reprehensible, and should be eschewed. It is not necessarily a matter of inculcating that the conduct is wrong, for those addressed (or many of them) may well understand that already. Rather, the censure embodied in the prescribed sanction serves to *appeal* to people's sense of the conduct's wrongfulness, as a reason for desistence" (1993, 11, emphasis in original). Duff (2001, 142) says that one goal of punishment is to "bring offenders to face up to the character and the significance of what they have done," and he sees this as a process of "correction or persuasion rather than of education" (92).

19. Von Hirsch (1993), whose main interest is in proportionate punishment, calls for this sort of balance, prompting debate among penologists about precisely how to measure the severity of a penal sanction (Hayes 2018).

20. "By forcibly removing the offender from the standing temptations and routines of his daily existence, by subjecting him to hard treatment as a response to his wrongdoing, the punishment can be not only a *constitutive* component of his repentance, but also an instrumental *means* of stimulating the process of repentance. That is, punishment can help spark in the offender the remorseful recognition of his wrongdoing that leads him to undergo his punishment as a penance, as something he willingly embraces as justified" (Tasioulas 2007, 496, emphasis in original). See Crewe, Hulley, and Wright (2019) for an empirical description of this sort of reflection.

21. Tavuchis offers an authoritative account of the "miraculous" (1991, 8) power of apologies, which allow us to live almost as though wrongful actions have not happened while simultaneously acknowledging that they have.

22. Von Hirsch (1993, 2003) argues that it is inappropriately invasive for the state to demand repentance, and Duff (2001, 2003a, 2003b) and Tasioulas (2007) disagree. See Bottoms (2019) and Ievins (forthcoming) for an attempt to call a truce.

23. "To coerce, dominate or manipulate an offender into feeling guilt, apologizing and reforming his conduct and character is not to bring about genuine repentance" (Tasioulas 2007, 510). Similarly, Morris (1981, 268–69) argues that "the goal is not repentance at all costs, if that has meaning, but repentance freely arrived at and not merely a disposition toward conformity with the norms. [. . .] What must be aimed at is that the afflicted become autonomous not automatons."

24. The discussion about the role of repentance in punishment also raises questions about the justification of punishing the already repentant wrongdoer; see Christopher Bennett (2008), Von Hirsch (1993), and Duff (2001).

25. The argument advanced in this discussion of the relationship between shame and guilt is expanded in Ievins (forthcoming).

26. For an alternative perspective on shame, see Bernard Williams (1993).

27. Harris (2001) calls constructive guilt "Shame-Guilt-Remorse," and destructive shame "Unacknowledged Shame."

28. Ahmed (2001) calls constructive guilt "Shame Acknowledgement," and destructive shame "Shame Displacement."

29. This term was made famous by Jack Abbott (1991) and was also used by Crewe (2015) to title his article arguing that "big picture" penal scholarship should reflect more seriously on what happens inside prisons.

30. For a brief overview of the history of prison sociology, see Crewe (2016).

31. For descriptions of the violence facing people convicted of sex offenses, see Crewe (2009), Hogue (1993), O'Donnell and Edgar (1999), Sparks, Bottoms, and Hay (1996), Ugelvik (2014), Vaughn and Sapp (1989), and Winfree, Newbold, and Tubb (2002).

32. As Adam Sampson (1994) recounts, prisoners were held on these separate units under Rule 43 (now Rule 45), which allowed the prison to isolate prisoners for the purposes of good order and discipline. In the 1980s, it was estimated that 70 percent of the prisoners held on Rule 43 were convicted of sex offenses. In such units prisoners faced a restricted regime, were offered worse facilities than "mainstream" prisoners, faced verbal and physical

abuse if they crossed paths with a "mainstream" prisoner, and were still held alongside "mainstream" prisoners.

33. When a prison rerolls, its purpose or category changes and the prisoners who live there are often transferred elsewhere and replaced with new prisoners. At the time of the fieldwork, a few prisoners had been there since before the reroll, but most had come more recently. All but a handful were currently serving a sentence for a sex offense.

34. Category C prisons hold those whom the Prison Service would not trust in open conditions, but who are deemed unlikely to escape. In practice, this tends to cover people on custodial sentences of longer than a year but will rarely include those at the beginning of long and indeterminate sentences. At the time of the fieldwork, prisoners serving sentences for sex offenses were ineligible for open conditions, although this policy has since changed.

35. For a discussion of prison officer cultures in England and Wales, see Liebling (2007) and Liebling and Kant (2018).

36. Benchmarking was a mechanism by which prison regimes were standardized in the pursuit of efficiency and cost-saving (Mulholland 2014).

37. When prisoners are "released on temporary license," they can leave the prison for a small amount of time. It enables prisoners to work, visit their families, or resettle in the community after a long sentence, and is most commonly granted to prisoners toward the end of long and indeterminate sentences. At the time of the fieldwork, "release on temporary license" had been nationally banned for prisoners convicted of sex offenses after a high-profile nonsexual offense was committed by someone who was on day release.

38. In most cases, people serving determinate sentences serve the first half in prison, and the second half "on license" in the community. While they are "on license," they must abide by certain restrictions which are intended to manage their risk of reoffending. If they breach these conditions, they can be recalled to prison.

39. In England and Wales, almost everyone who receives a life sentence is given a tariff which they must serve before they are considered for release (the exception is the very few people who are given "whole life" sentences). IPP sentences are slightly different. They were introduced in 2005 and designed to protect the public from "dangerous offenders" whose crimes did not merit a life sentence. People were given a minimum tariff (of, for example, five years), after which they were eligible for parole and had to prove that they were no longer a risk to the public. The sentences proved highly controversial and were abolished in 2012, but thousands of people continue to serve them.

40. In the United Kingdom, the term "Asian" is normally used to describe people of South Asian descent.

41. Stevens (2016) found that prisoners in institutions which hold lots of men convicted of sex offenses tend to be more sexually active.

42. At the time of the fieldwork in Stafford, each wing was managed by a Supervising Officer (previously called a Senior Officer).

43. In prisons in England and Wales, meals are normally distributed on the wings from a servery, rather than in a central cafeteria or mess hall.

3. DISTORTING INSTITUTIONS: STRUCTURING THE MORAL DIALOGUE

1. For a critical discussion of the cognitive distortion literature, see Maruna and Mann (2006) and Maruna and Copes (2005).

2. For examples of methodological texts, see Blagden and Pemberton (2010), Cowburn (2005, 2007), Scully (1990), and Waldram (2007).

3. "Anyone accused of committing a sexual crime should be expected to initially deny culpability. The list of potential negative consequences to those individuals is wide-ranging and might arise at the time of being accused (e.g. fear of losing the support of family), during the judicial processes (in an attempt to avoid conviction), or after being incarcerated (e.g. fear of being physically harmed)" (Ware and Blagden 2020, 1).

4. For an ethnography of the crown court system in England and Wales, the system through which almost all prisoners in Stafford had passed, see Rock (1993). Rock describes trials as entailing "an antagonism that was so commonplace, widely presumed, and routine in the courtroom that it is almost necessary to be reminded of its significant features: that trials were fought by two opposing sides ('fight,' 'side,' and 'opponent' being words in common use), one prosecuting and one defending, and each having its own retinue and clients; that the system was conceived not as an inquiry into the final truth of a matter but as a struggle, a 'trial of strength,' between two competing, partial, and incomplete cases made out in public by advocates; and that judge and jury acted as arbiters rather than as inquisitors, necessarily leaving much that was unquestioned, unsaid, and unresolved" (30–31). For other ethnographies of the adversarial court system, see Feeley (1979) and Merry (1990). For an encyclopedic argument that the justice system in England and Wales is uninterested in the pursuit of truth, see Hillier and Dingwall (2021).

5. As Summers (1999) highlights, formal legal truth is not the same as substantive truth, and the attempt to determine the former may obscure the latter.

6. Ian Dennis argues that for a verdict to be legitimate, it is not enough that it reflects the factual truth, as "a decision may be factually correct [he gives the example of a confession obtained through torture] and yet lack the elements of moral authority and expressive value necessary for the further [legitimating] functions of the verdict" (2017, 56, quoted in Nobles and Schiff 2019, 101).

7. Plea bargaining is not official practice in England and Wales, and although it does sometimes take place (Hillier and Dingwall 2021), it does so to a much smaller degree than it does in the United States (Hessick 2021).

8. The age of sexual consent in England and Wales is sixteen, but the age when one can legally purchase alcohol is eighteen.

9. Legally, hearsay is "a statement not made in oral evidence in the proceedings" (section 114 (1) Criminal Justice Act 2003), for example, "I heard her say that he raped her." However, prisoners often used the word "hearsay" to refer to a victim serving as a witness in court and stating their own experiences ("he raped me"). George illustrated this misunderstanding when he claimed to have been convicted of rape on hearsay, "just through someone saying something," but to be unable to use hearsay evidence to support his appeal. The evidence which contributed to his conviction was not hearsay evidence and was instead his victim's account of what had happened which had been given in oral evidence at the trial. The evidence he wanted to use to support his appeal—his former partner saying that the victim had told her she was lying—was hearsay and was therefore inadmissible.

10. The metaphor builds on Mary Douglas's (2002) work on the moralization of dirt and cleanliness.

11. This fear was not unrealistic. Years after finishing this project, I was in a "mainstream" prison when I bumped into a man whom I had first met when he was held on a

VPU. At first, and in front of other people, he pretended not to know me. When he got the chance to speak to me privately, he asked me to be extremely careful not to reveal where we had first met as being exposed could put him in danger.

12. These latter categories were further fixed by the panic about sexual psychopathy which developed in the United States in the 1920s and 1930s (Meiners 2016).

13. Rates of reoffending are likely to be higher than reconviction data suggests (Falshaw et al. 2003).

14. The term "sex offender" is in more widespread use in England and Wales than in countries which do not separate people based on their offense (Ievins 2020b; Ievins and Mjåland 2021).

15. For research on the experiences of the family members of those convicted of sex offenses in England and Wales, see Brown (2017) and Duncan et al. (2022).

16. For a discussion of the experience of reentry in a jurisdiction which does not have such restrictive policies, see Ievins and Mjåland (2021) and Sandbukt (2021).

17. Garland goes further and argues that the figures of criminality on which the criminology of the other rests are not "representative of the real dangers that crime undoubtedly involves, since its inventory of risks focuses almost exclusively on street crime and forgets the serious harms caused by criminal corporations, white-collar criminals or even drunk drivers. Each figure is, instead, selected for its usefulness as a 'suitable enemy'—usefulness not just for the criminal justice state in its sovereign mode but also for a conservative social politics that stresses the need for authority, family values, and the resurrection of traditional morality" (2001, 136). It is easy to see how the figure of the "sex offender" serves both the criminal justice state and conservative social politics (see also Wacquant 2009).

18. It is possible to appeal indefinite placement on the Register after fifteen years. For a discussion of the fear of the Register in England and Wales, see Ievins and Reimer (forthcoming).

19. Jimmy Savile was a famous British children's entertainer who, after his death, was accused of hundreds of sexual offenses, particularly but not exclusively against children.

20. In England and Wales, all people who are released from prison are assigned a probation officer. Most should also have a probation officer (known as an offender manager) during their prison sentence, who is supposed to help them complete their sentence plan (the list of requirements for their sentence) and help assess and prepare them for release. Ideally, people should have the same probation officer during their sentence as they have postrelease, but this is often not the case.

21. The "new penology" thesis has been critiqued (Cheliotis 2006; Liebling and Crewe 2013; Lynch 1998; Robinson 2008), and it is certainly not a full description of modern penality.

22. Different risk assessment tools were used at different parts of the process, and some were based on actuarial risk calculations and some on the judgment of professionals. Curiously, a different risk assessment—one based on static rather than dynamic factors—was introduced after release, frustrating prisoners who had been low risk during their sentence but whose risk would be raised as soon as they got out.

23. See Robinson (2008) for an analysis of rehabilitation as risk management, and Crewe (2011a, 2011b; Crewe and Ievins 2021) for an account of the impact of this understanding of rehabilitation on the operation and experience of penal power in England and

Wales. See also Alford (2000), who argues that much less disciplinary power flows in prisons in the United States.

24. For a discussion of the distinction, see McNeill (2012).

25. For a discussion of incentivization in prisons in England and Wales, see Crewe (2009, 2011a) and Crewe and Ievins (2021).

26. During my time in the prison, risk assessment procedures for work changed and prisoners' attitudes to their offense were no longer considered relevant.

27. Nine percent of prisoners were serving an IPP sentence or a life sentence. Other prisoners in Stafford would also be eligible for early release after a parole hearing: the small number serving Extended Determinate Sentences, who would be eligible for parole two thirds of the way into their custodial sentence; those who were convicted of serious offenses committed before 2005 and who were therefore subject to discretionary conditional release; as well as those who had been released from prison but recalled into custody while they were on license and thus were only eligible for release before the end of their sentence if approved by the Parole Board.

28. Research suggests that program completion plays a more complicated and moderating role in Parole Board decisions than many prisoners think (Lackenby 2018). However, research conducted in the 1990s suggested that the Parole Board was less likely to approve the release of people convicted of sex offenses who maintained that they were innocent, even though the same research found that this group was less likely to reoffend (Hood et al. 2002).

29. That said, it was relatively easy for prisoners who were deemed to pose a "low risk" of reoffending to get away with maintaining their innocence as they were never asked to participate in treatment.

30. Waldram (2012) provides a useful discussion of the interaction between treatment narratives and those produced through legal processes.

31. Denial or minimization of planning is one of the seven forms of denial identified by Marshall, Anderson, and Fernandez (1999, 63).

32. While prisons in England and Wales do sometimes provide one-on-one interventions for people convicted of sex offenses, these interventions were not available in Stafford at the time of the fieldwork.

33. For a description of how prisoners in another institution reacted to the report, see Ievins (2017).

4. MANAGING GUILT: LIVING AS A "SEX OFFENDER" IN PRISON

1. The project was titled "Penal Policymaking and the Prisoner Experience: A Comparative Analysis," and it was led by Professor Ben Crewe. The project was envisaged as an empirical test of the Nordic Exceptionalism thesis (Pratt 2008a, 2008b), and it involved fieldwork in prisons in England and Wales and Norway. One substudy of this project included an exploration of power and social relationships in prisons holding men convicted of sex offenses. For more details, and for some of the findings from this project, see Crewe et al. (2022), Crewe and Ievins (2021), Ievins (2020a, 2020b), and Ievins and Mjåland (2021).

2. Prisoners serving life sentences are assigned a tariff, a period of time which they have to serve in custody before they are eligible for release. They can only be released if they

manage to convince a Parole Board that they do not pose a risk of reoffending. One common way of doing this is by spending time in an open prison prior to release.

3. In Stafford, Offender Supervisors were Supervising Officers who worked with prisoners on their sentence plans.

4. For the most significant examples, see Sykes ([1958] 2007), Irwin and Cressey (1962), Cohen and Taylor (1972), Kruttschnitt and Gartner (2005), and Crewe (2009).

5. In what follows I draw on the typology which Crewe (2009) developed following fieldwork in another category C English prison, ten years before I conducted research in Stafford.

6. I do not want to imply that the proportions of my sample which each group represents are likely to be replicated. My sample was not fully randomly selected, and it was relatively small.

7. One man was not placed in the typology. He had dementia and his attitude to his conviction and description of his orientation toward his sentence was inconsistent.

8. Their actions were reminiscent of those of Christopher Bennett's "*virtuous offender*," the figure he uses to describe "what someone would do if they were properly affected by the fact that they have done wrong" (2008, 103, emphasis in original). The extreme guilt which they felt predated their punishment and was a direct response to "having failed as a qualified moral agent" (100), to the damage they had done, and to the relationships they had broken. As a result of this guilt, they felt a deep responsibility to make things right, and embraced their punishment as an opportunity both for penance and for moral transformation.

9. In this sense, they were like the "enthusiasts" identified by Crewe (2009, 157–67).

10. The R-SOTP was a cognitive behavioral intervention for people deemed to pose a low risk of sexual recidivism. The intervention normally took twelve weeks to complete and was decommissioned in 2014 (Ministry of Justice 2014).

11. The idea that punishment should both acknowledge the past and build to something better is central to much moral communication theory. Hampton (1984) and Duff (2001) suggest that this is why punishment should be understood as penance, something which shows the offender and the victim that the wrong was serious and provides the wrongdoer with a structure for change. Helping the wrongdoer change is one way of stopping them from getting stuck in the past, Hampton suggests: "For how is it that one overcomes shame? Is it not by becoming a person *different* from the one who did the immoral action?" (1984, 234, emphasis in original). The fact that penance can help people change is one reason given by both authors for punishing people who are already repentant.

12. For a discussion of reasons for compliance, see Bottoms (2002).

13. The power acting on them thus had strong echoes of the "performative regulation" that Scott (2011) sees as the central mode of power operating within reinventive institutions. Scott argues that performative regulation occurs whenever groups of people "submit themselves to the authority of an institution, internalise its values and enact them through mutual surveillance in an inmate culture" (242). In reinventive institutions, power is not simply exerted from above on those who participate; it works through them, and they are agents who can channel, resist, and redirect the institution's power. While coercion was undoubtedly present within Stafford, it rarely acted visibly on *repentant prisoners*; rather they voluntarily engaged with the institution, willingly made use of its moral discourse, and interpreted official judgments of them as a signal that they had "reached the required threshold of a trajectory towards self-improvement" (40). Stafford was not a true reinventive

institution—prisoners were not there voluntarily—but *repentant prisoners* were willing to be transformed by their time there, and their incarceration was experienced as an opportunity rather than an imposition. For an expanded version of this argument, see Crewe and Ievins (2020).

14. They bore some similarity to the "crusaders" identified by Crewe: "their fixation on personal integrity [had turned] them from committed supporters of the regime to its most rabidly censorious critics" (2009, 222).

15. For "release on temporary license," see chapter 2, note 37.

16. William, a *repentant prisoner* who was teetering on the edge of joining Nigel as a *redeemed prisoner*, similarly complained that Stafford was "stagnant," and that it did not do enough to encourage change.

17. If a prisoner is alleged to have broken a prison rule, they can receive an adjudication, also known as a "nicking." Adjudications are small hearings which take place within the prison. If the rule infraction is proven, the prisoner can receive a punishment, which might include a period of cellular confinement or even having extra days added to their sentence.

18. In this case, the term "IEP" refers to a formal recording of an infraction which could lead to the prisoner's IEP status being downgraded. For a general discussion of the IEP scheme, see chapter 3, page 53.

19. *Fatalists* may have constituted a greater proportion of the prison population: they were particularly anxious and unlikely to spend time in public spaces in the prison, and I suspect they were disproportionately likely to turn down my requests for an interview.

20. A Sexual Offences Prevention Order (now a Sexual Harm Prevention Order) is a civil order which aims to inhibit sexual offending by preventing the individual from engaging in certain forms of behavior, which can include accessing the internet or having contact with under-eighteens.

21. Probation officers write pre-sentence reports to provide judges or magistrates with a view of the person's background and what the probation officer thinks a suitable sentence would be. Recommendations are not always followed, but they do have some effect on the sentence which is handed down (Gelsthorpe, Raynor, and Robinson 2010).

22. Crewe (2009, 83, emphasis in original) calls this *"fatalistic resignation."*

23. The Healthy Sex Programme is an accredited program which aims to help high-risk and very high-risk prisoners manage their offense-related sexual thoughts and fantasies.

24. For a discussion of "mainstream" prison culture in England and Wales, see Crewe (2009).

25. Paul was an exception. He admitted having "interfered with" his sister, who was a young child, but he challenged his conviction for rape. He nevertheless showed no signs of guilt, and spoke about this offense straightforwardly and without emotion, justifying it by saying that he had not had sex in a long time.

26. Similar metaphors were used by Crewe's "players" (2009, 206), but *negotiators* used them differently. Rather than signifying that they were competing with the system and that officers were their opponents, *negotiators* used these metaphors to indicate their acquiescence to the terms of the situation.

27. Many prisons run "family visits," special visiting sessions for prisoners with young family members. These visits are often longer than normal visits and are supposed to be more relaxed.

28. "Bang up": the time at which prisoners were locked in their cells.

29. I have chosen not to use these men's pseudonyms to protect their confidentiality.

30. Travelers, often known as Irish Travelers, are a traditionally peripatetic ethno-cultural group.

31. Apps, or applications, are forms prisoners submit to make requests from staff.

32. TAB—tackling antisocial behavior—procedures are put in place by officers in response to perceived bullying by prisoners. The behavior of prisoners put on a TAB 2 is formally monitored, those on a TAB 1 are informally monitored, and those on a TAB 3 are normally moved off the wing.

33. See also the story about Edward which opens chapter 6.

34. As Murphy (2012) argues, hurting people and seeing the harm we have caused produces more guilt than breaking abstract rules does.

35. This is also consistent with Maruna's (2001, 143) reflection on Leibrich's (1993, 1996) finding that shame is the main reason given for desistance from crime. Maruna highlights that most of Leibrich's sample had only a few convictions and had never been to prison, and so for them, labeling could be a helpful deterrent. Maruna argues that shame and labeling function less helpfully when offending has become a lifestyle, as it had for the men in his sample.

36. See Sullivan (2007), who argues that public attitudes toward the rape of sex workers have become more condemnatory over recent years and that this is reflected in the increasing numbers of prosecutions and convictions of men who rape sex workers. Nevertheless, she acknowledges that the rape of sex workers is still taken insufficiently seriously by the public. See also Waites (2016), who historicizes and complicates the fact that sixteen is the legal age of sexual consent. He cites a study which found that only 30 percent of teenage boys and 37 percent of teenage girls thought that sexual intercourse under the age of sixteen is always wrong (McGrellis 2000, 14, quoted in Waites 2016, 85).

37. Tasioulas acknowledged the dangers of forms of punishment which do not treat people as moral agents: "there is also the fact that subjection to the scornful gaze of others—which threatens either to crush the offender's spirit or else counter-productively encourage him to brazen out the ordeal—is more likely to inhibit, rather than facilitate, the offender's development of a penitent understanding of his deed" (2007, 496–97).

5. MAINTAINING INNOCENCE: CONTESTING GUILT AND CHALLENGING IMPRISONMENT

1. For a discussion of the law of rape in England and Wales, see chapter 1, note 3.

2. Marshall, Anderson, and Fernandez (1999, 63), for instance, identified seven different types of denial and minimization, including complete denial (e.g., claiming not to have been there), partial denial (e.g., claiming that a consensual sexual encounter took place), minimizing the offense (e.g., claiming that an offense took place, but it was neither serious nor harmful), and minimizing responsibility (e.g., arguing that drunkenness meant a failure to understand what you were doing). The account which William gave in prison would be classified as minimizing the offense. All interview participants, including those whom I considered to be *repentant prisoners*, demonstrated some aspects of the denial and minimization identified by Marshall, Anderson, and Fernandez.

3. There is some indication that being wrongfully convicted alters, and perhaps exacerbates, the pains of imprisonment by prompting prisoners to doubt the legitimacy of authority figures in general and the criminal justice system in particular (Campbell and Denov 2004; Grounds 2005; Hoyle, Speechley, and Burnett 2016). Research on life-sentenced prisoners has also found that prisoners who deny their guilt often lash out against the institution (Crewe, Hulley, and Wright 2019). Digard has also argued that people convicted of sex offenses who maintain innocence challenge the legitimacy of their probation officers' authority: "in order to attribute legitimacy to a figure of power, one must first consider oneself to be a legitimate target of governance" (2010, 197–98).

4. I met other *activists* whom I did not interview, and many *resigned prisoners* who used to be *activists*.

5. The sole exception was James, who was convicted of a nonpenetrative offense against a child and who insisted that he had not had any sexual contact with her.

6. In their rejection of the institution, they were reminiscent of Crewe's "players" (2009, 200–220), but I did not see much sign of them being heavily involved in Stafford's lackluster drugs trade.

7. In England and Wales, juries are asked to reach a unanimous verdict. If they are unable to do so, they may seek permission from the judge to reach a majority verdict of at least ten people.

8. The Criminal Cases Review Commission is an independent public body which is responsible for investigating possible miscarriages of justice in England, Wales, and Northern Ireland. The Commission cannot quash a conviction or reduce a sentence, but it can refer a case to an appeals court. It normally only refers a case if significant new evidence is presented or if a successful legal argument is made.

9. These claims are echoed by proponents of "false allegation discourse" (Naughton 2019)—campaigners who argue that false allegations of sexual abuse are frequent and often lead to wrongful convictions.

10. Compensation for victims of sexual violence is calculated based on the physical and psychological damage done to victims, and not based on the number of years the person who hurt them spends in prison. See Ministry of Justice (2012).

11. Despite the fact that most *activists* were Black or from a minority background, they never suggested that their imprisonment had racial dynamics, although this may have been because I am White and I did not ask.

12. James Gilligan argues that "the purpose of violence is to diminish the intensity of shame and replace it as far as possible with its opposite, pride, thus preventing the individual from being overwhelmed by the feeling of shame" (2000, 111). Similarly, Scheff argues that unacknowledged shame can combine with anger to form rage: "One way to deal with the feeling that one has been rejected as untrustworthy is to reject the rejector, rather than to blame one's self as untrustworthy" (2006, 152; see also Scheff 1995; Scheff and Retzinger 1991; Sykes and Matza 1957).

13. This was the way the term was used by Crewe's "players" (2009, 206).

14. Prison Service Instructions (PSIs) are statements of Prison Service policy. They should be accessible to all prisoners and are normally available in the prison library.

15. Kieran was correct. PSI-02–2012, point 2.1.11, which was in force during the fieldwork, opens: "If a prisoner continually submits complaints to such an extent that it is viewed

as an abuse of the process, the prison has the authority to intervene and use its discretion to determine how to manage the situation. One of the ways that this can be done is to impose a limit of one complaint per day. This can include appeals and confidential access complaints at the discretion of the prison. Such a restriction would allow other prisoners to have their complaints investigated and answered."

16. I took notes during these interviews. One man asked to see and approve the transcript before I analyzed it.

17. George had received a nine-year sentence, of which he had served four-and-a-half years before being released on license. He was now in prison following his second recall into custody.

18. This hope was not always achieved. Prison officers often derided *resigned prisoners* as snobbish, demanding, and "in denial."

6. MORALIZING BOUNDARIES: STAFF-PRISONER RELATIONSHIPS AND THE COMMUNICATION OF DIFFERENCE

1. "Wrong-uns": a slang term to mean people who commit sex offenses, particularly against children.

2. Previous research supports the idea that prison officers have been influenced by this discourse, and that they have a worse attitude toward prisoners convicted of sex offenses than they do toward other prisoners (Kjelsberg and Loos 2008; Ricciardelli and Spencer 2018).

3. Eriksson (2021) and Garrihy (2022) have described how prison officers respond to the taint of prison work, drawing on Hughes's (1958) concept of "dirty work" and later developments of it by Ashforth and Kreiner (1999). Dirty work can be tainted in three different ways: physically (by association with bodies, waste, death, and danger), socially (by contact with stigmatized groups or by performing servile work), or morally (because it involves work that goes against our moral and civil instincts). Prison officers in Stafford were clearly subjected to social taint.

4. Doing work which deliberately inflicts punishment could be understood as a morally tainted form of work (see note 3). The occupational morality I am describing is one response to doing this sort of tainted work, which allows officers to reframe it as morally worthwhile (see Ashforth and Kreiner 1999).

5. For a discussion of prison officer "presence," see Crewe, Liebling, and Hulley (2014).

6. The argument made in this book thus complements and develops Sparks, Bottoms, and Hay's (1996, 204–26) argument that power was systematically overused on the VPU at HMP Albany because the officers assumed prisoners were so compliant that they didn't need to think about how they would respond to staff behavior.

7. Sociologist Stan Cohen (2001) argues that acknowledgment is about more than knowledge. It involves knowing that something is true, choosing to think about it, caring about it, and letting it affect your actions.

8. Lamont and Molnár (2002, 168) define symbolic boundaries as "conceptual distinctions made by social actors to categorize objects, people, practices, and even time and space. They are tools by which individuals and groups struggle over and come to agree upon definitions of reality. [. . .] Symbolic boundaries also separate people into groups and generate feelings of similarity and group membership (Epstein 1992, p. 232)." Symbolic boundaries are "a necessary but insufficient condition for the existence of social boundaries" (Lamont

and Molnár 2002, 169), which are defined as "objectified forms of social differences manifested in unequal access to and unequal distribution of resources (material and nonmaterial) and social opportunities. They are also revealed in stable behavioral patterns of association" (168). See also Jacob, Gagnon, and Holmes (2009, 157–58), who argue that "symbolic and tangible boundaries" can help maintain psychological safety and keep "the abject at a safe distance."

9. This final distinction was partly generational, and it is a typical marker of traditional public-sector staff culture. While highly experienced officers, particularly those who had been in the military, were dedicated to these naming patterns, less experienced officers or those with a more rehabilitative orientation were more comfortable being known by their first names or calling prisoners by theirs.

10. This officer used to work in a Young Offender Institution, a type of prison which holds people aged between fifteen and twenty-one (those under eighteen are held in a separate building from those over eighteen).

11. In the five-month fieldwork period, I was aware of restraint procedures being used on two prisoners. One had serious mental health problems and assaulted a staff member with a weapon and was restrained first by other prisoners and then by officers. Another had a verbal altercation with a member of staff about eating on the landing, which was against the rules; the incident escalated and staff restrained him because they said they felt threatened. I was aware of a few other violent incidents. One prisoner threw a chair, which narrowly avoided hitting an officer and was caught by a prisoner. On a couple of occasions, I heard about scuffles between prisoners as they were walking to and from work. I heard the alarm bell on a few occasions, but mostly it had been pressed by mistake. It was easily the calmest and safest prison I have ever spent time in.

12. The evidence suggests that younger prisoners are more likely to be involved in disorder and violence in prison (Ditchfield 1990).

13. He then spent the next few days following me around the wing. Eventually I spoke to him and reminded him that I was there to work and asked him to give me some space, which he did. His interest had been noted by other prisoners. Several months later, another man told me, "It got to the point where a few of the lads were calling him your shadow and saying he'll have that many SIRs [Serious Incident Reports] on him that he'll never leave prison!" Serious Incident Reports were forms submitted to the prison's Security department, detailing concerning prisoner or staff behavior.

14. Many thanks to my colleagues Ryan Williams and Ruth Armstrong for helping me clarify this point.

15. At the time of the fieldwork, every prisoner was assigned a personal officer, who was supposed to be their main point of contact during their sentence. For apps, see chapter 4, note 31.

16. See Waddington, Badger, and Bull (2005), who found that police officers and care workers considered malicious complaints to be an act of violence.

17. Officers described men convicted of sex offenses similarly to female prisoners. Female prisoners are often seen by officers as "emotional, manipulative, impulsive, and resistant to taking orders," as well as being "less dangerous but more troublesome" than male prisoners (Kruttschnitt and Gartner 2003, 32).

18. All cells have buttons ("cell bells") which are intended to attract officers' attention in an emergency.

19. Unfortunately, I was unable to access information on the numbers of complaints forms submitted in recent years. However, a report by HM Chief Inspector of Prisons conducted a year after my fieldwork found that the number of complaints submitted in Stafford was relatively low, and lower than at similar prisons (HM Chief Inspector of Prisons 2016).

20. Custodial Managers were one rank above Supervising Officers (previously known as Senior Officers), and a Custodial Manager had responsibility for each unit in the prison. Supervising Officers were an active presence on the wing, whereas Custodial Managers appeared less frequently.

21. Each wing has an observation, or obs, book, which is kept in the staff office and in which officers write down incidents which might be of interest or importance to their colleagues.

22. The cross-sectional study design means that it is not possible for me to reliably assess whether staff policed prisoners more strictly than they had before the reroll. However, it is worth noting that although prisoners' claims were undoubtedly mythologized, they were made by those who had been in the prison before the reroll as well as by those who had spent many years in "mainstream" prisons. They are also consistent with Sparks, Bottoms, and Hay's (1996) finding that power was systematically, sometimes dangerously, overused in the VPU at HMP Albany.

23. Officers attributed the frequent periods of "bang-up" to the need to escort many prisoners to hospital and sometimes accompany them for long stays. Those staffing these "bed watches" were not replaced on the wings, and staff did not unlock prisoners without the officially detailed ratio of staff-to-prisoners being met. This does not mean that prisoners were wrong, however. Stafford was unusual in how rigidly they adhered to the ratio, and in many prisons, staff would have unlocked prisoners anyway. See chapter 2, page 25.

24. Liebling, Arnold, and Straub (2011) found similar dynamics at HMP Whitemoor. They found that the changing makeup of the prison's population meant that officers no longer understood or trusted their prisoners (see also Liebling 2013). Officers therefore kept their distance from prisoners, trying to do their work and keep order through systems rather than through relationships.

25. As Liebling (2013) has argued, knowing your audience is a central component of legitimate power in prisons.

26. "OASys": the Offender Assessment System, a computerized system to measure the risks and needs of prisoners and probationers in England and Wales.

27. Research has found that officers working on the VPU at HMP Whitemoor were disproportionately likely to formally sanction prisoners for threatening, abusive, or insulting words or behavior, whereas "mainstream" prisoners "were 'allowed' a certain amount of 'resistant language'" (Liebling, Price, and Shefer 2011, 60).

28. See Rios (2011) on the "overpolicing underpolicing paradox."

29. Lord Sewell was a member of the UK upper legislative chamber, the House of Lords, who was filmed by the newspaper *The Sun* snorting cocaine with sex workers.

30. I once spent an uncomfortable morning chatting to an officer while he read through prisoners' newspapers and made lascivious comments about some of the pictures, interspersed with asking me what my boyfriend thought about my research.

7. DENYING COMMUNITY: SOCIAL RELATIONSHIPS
AND THE DANGERS OF ACKNOWLEDGMENT

1. On reflection, I think I was so uncomfortable with the scale of the reaction because it publicized the initial comment and encouraged discussion about the propriety of my presence in the prison. I was embarrassed by what had been said, but I was more deeply embarrassed by the prolonged public conversation about my potential rape, and by my lack of control over the story. Some officers implied that I had provoked the comment by my outfits and my demeanor, and I felt both ashamed of the comment and guilty for eliciting it. Looking back, I realize that I blamed myself for what the man said about me, and I felt it to be a sign of my failure to live up to the gendered standards of the "perfect academic" (Schneider 2020, 182). I worried that my physical existence and gendered readings of me would damage my credibility in an academic and professional world in which "[a]nthropologists don't get harassed or raped. Women do" (Moreno 1995, 246, quoted in Schneider 2020, 186).

2. Prison sociology has a long tradition of describing social relationships among prisoners, with a particular focus on norms, hierarchies, and friendship. For an introduction, see Sykes ([1958] 2007), Cohen and Taylor (1972), Kruttschnitt and Gartner (2005), and Crewe (2009).

3. Waldram (2012) has usefully described the many different norms which shape social relationships in a therapeutic prison for men convicted of sex offenses, in particular the clash between the therapeutic norms of the institution, which encouraged people to see each other as equals, and the hierarchy of offenses implied by the prisoner morality. Genders and Player (1995) and Stevens (2013) describe similar dynamics in English prisons run as Therapeutic Communities.

4. Tynan (2019, 149–52) argues that the stigma attached to young men imprisoned for sex offenses is mediated by factors like other prisoners' knowledge and their trust in the stigmatized person.

5. Several prison officers and a few prisoners told me that they had heard people openly support and even advocate for the morality of sex with children, although these stories never involved details and may have been mythologized. The fact that I never heard anyone advocate for child sex abuse, and the fact that people rarely gave concrete examples of hearing others doing so, indicates that it was not a significant part of public discourse.

6. This knowledge was reinforced by the fact that license conditions prevented people convicted of sex offenses from meeting people with similar convictions after release.

7. A significant literature suggests that psychiatrists and treatment providers working with people convicted of sex offenses experience vicarious traumatization (McCann and Pearlman 1990; Pearlman and Saakvitne 1995; Rich 1997; Way et al. 2004). They report changes in their interpersonal relationships, experiences of sexuality, and affect regulation and management, and experience symptoms of psychological trauma including nightmares and intrusive imagery. To the best of my knowledge, no similar research has been conducted with prisoners like those in Stafford, all of whom involuntarily lived in a confined space with people convicted of sex offenses, and many of whom found the experience traumatic. Kotova and Akerman's (2022) recent work on the experiences of men who had both been victims and perpetrators of sexual abuse and were currently held in a Therapeutic Community prison comes closest.

8. Listeners are prisoners trained by the Samaritans, a UK- and Ireland-based suicide prevention charity, to provide emotional support to their peers.

9. See Ievins (forthcoming) for a discussion of remorse and repentance.

10. Their attitude to their peers was very similar to that described in Ievins and Crewe (2015).

11. It is common for prisoners in England and Wales to distinguish between "friends" and "associates" (Crewe 2009).

12. This is one of the goals of "ban the box" campaigns.

8. JUDGING PRISONS: THE LIMITATIONS AND EXCESSES OF DENUNCIATORY PUNISHMENT

1. I gained permission from the institution and from individual prisoners to do this. I only read prisoners' sentences and formal charges ("rape," "sexual assault," and so on) and did not read a narrative account of what had allegedly happened. A few interview participants showed signs of discomfort when I raised the idea of me reading their charges, and in these cases I said I did not need to. When people had left the institution—because of being transferred or because of being released—I was no longer able to access the information.

2. I discuss similar emotions in Ievins (2019).

3. For research on victim-survivors' perspectives of justice, see Clark (2015), Kathleen Daly (2017), Herman (2005), Jülich (2006), McGlynn, Downes, and Westmarland (2017), and McGlynn and Westmarland (2019).

4. More research on how victims of crime experience the imprisonment of the person who hurt them would be extremely valuable, especially if it considered how they hear morally communicative punishment.

5. This paragraph draws on Ievins (forthcoming).

6. Walker does not use the word *remorse*, but the minimal conditions she identifies— "Accepting responsibility for one's actions and their consequences, and acknowledging that those actions or their consequences are wrong or harmful" (2006, 191)—could be described as remorse. Walker's minimal conditions do not explicitly name the emotional dimensions of remorse, but it is not clear that one could properly acknowledge the wrong and harm of the wrongs one has done without feeling guilt about them.

7. Walker defines moral repair as "*restoring or creating trust and hope in a shared sense of value and responsibility*" (2006, 28, emphasis in original). Moral repair is not the same as restoring relationships to what they were before the wrong was committed. It instead involves "repairs that move relationships in the direction of *becoming morally adequate*, whether or not they have been adequate before" (209, emphasis in original).

8. As Fricker argues, one effect of remorse is "an increased alignment of the wrongdoer's moral understanding with that of the blamer" and thus a regenerated "shared moral consciousness" (2016, 167).

9. *Accountability* is a term which is used more often than it is defined, but there are exceptions. Abolitionist campaign organization Philly Stands Up (2012) developed an "Accountability Road Map," which has five main processes: accountability involves identifying your own behaviors, accepting the harm you have done, looking for patterns outside of the initial event, unlearning old problematic behaviors, and learning new ones. Restorative

justice theorist Howard Zehr (1990, 42) maintains that genuine accountability "includes an opportunity to understand the human consequences of one's acts, to face up to what one has done and to whom one has done it. But real accountability involves more. Account-ability also involves taking responsibility for one's behavior. Offenders must be allowed and encouraged to help decide what will happen to make things right, then to take steps to repair the damage."

10. For influential arguments for penal abolition even in the case of sexual violence, see Angela Davis (2013, 2017), as well as the 2001 statement made by the abolitionist and feminist organizations Critical Resistance and Incite! (2003).

11. See Cossins (2008) for an alternative interpretation of Daly's data, and Kathleen Daly (2008) for a response to Cossins.

12. For examples of transformative justice toolkits, see Generation Five (2007), Russo (2013), and the Philly Stands Up (2012) Accountability Road Map.

13. For accounts of transformative justice in action, see Ansfield and Colman (2012) and the Chrysalis Collective (2011). For a history of transformative justice, see Kim (2018).

14. For overviews of the debates about the appropriateness of restorative justice for cases of gendered violence, see Kathleen Daly (2006), Goodmark (2018b), Barbara Hudson (1998, 2002), McGlynn, Westmarland, and Godden (2012), and Zinsstag and Keenan (2017). For an account of victim advocates' views of restorative justice, see Curtis-Fawley and Daly (2005).

REFERENCES

Abbott, Jack Henry. 1991. *In the Belly of the Beast: Letters from Prison*. New York: Vintage Books.

Ackerman, Alissa R., and Jill S. Levenson. 2019. *Healing from Sexual Violence: The Case for Vicarious Restorative Justice*. Brandon, VT: Safer Society Press.

Adler, Zsuzsanna. 1987. *Rape on Trial*. London: Routledge and Kegan Paul.

Ahmed, Eliza. 2001. "Shame Management: Regulating Bullying." In *Shame Management Through Reintegration*, edited by Eliza Ahmed, Nathan Harris, John Braithwaite, and Valerie Braithwaite, 211–314. Cambridge: Cambridge University Press.

Akbar, Arifa. 2020. "'It's Time for White Women to Listen': Writers V and Aja Monet on What Will Replace the Vagina Monologues." *Guardian*, November 20, 2020. https://www.theguardian.com/culture/2020/nov/20/v-eve-ensler-aja-monet-voices-campaign.

Åkerström, Malin. 1986. "Outcasts in Prison: The Cases of Informers and Sex Offenders." *Deviant Behavior* 7 (1): 1–12. https://doi.org/10.1080/01639625.1986.9967691.

Alford, C. Fred. 2000. "What Would It Matter If Everything Foucault Said about Prison Were Wrong? *Discipline and Punish* after Twenty Years." *Theory and Society* 29 (February): 125–46. https://doi.org/10.1023/A:1007014831641.

Ansfield, Bench, and Timothy Colman. 2012. "Confronting Sexual Assault: Transformative Justice on the Ground in Philadelphia." *Tikkun* 27, no. 1 (January): 41–44. https://doi.org/10.1215/08879982-2012-1018.

Arnold, Helen. 2007. "The Experience of Prison Officer Training." In *Understanding Prison Staff*, edited by Ben Crewe, Jamie Bennett, and Azrini Wahidin, 399–418. Cullompton, UK: Willan.

———. 2016. "The Prison Officer." In *Handbook on Prisons*, 2nd ed., edited by Yvonne Jewkes, Jamie Bennett, and Ben Crewe, 265–83. London: Routledge.

Ashforth, Blake E., and Glen E. Kreiner. 1999. "'How Can You Do It?' Dirty Work and the Challenge of Constructing a Positive Identity." *Academy of Management Review* 24, no. 3 (July): 413–34. https://doi.org/10.5465/amr.1999.2202129.

Auty, Katherine M., and Alison Liebling. 2020. "Exploring the Relationship between Prison Social Climate and Reoffending." *Justice Quarterly* 37 (2): 358–81. https://doi.org/10.108 0/07418825.2018.1538421.

Baird, Vera. 2020. *2019/20 Annual Report*. London: Victims Commissioner. https://s3-eu -west-2.amazonaws.com/victcomm2-prod-storage-119w304kq2z48/uploads/2020/07 /Victims-Commissioners-Annual-Report-2019-20-with-hyperlinks.pdf.

Bales, William D., and Alex R. Piquero. 2012. "Assessing the Impact of Imprisonment on Re-cidivism." *Journal of Experimental Criminology* 8, no. 1 (March): 71–101. https://doi.org /10.1007/s11292-011-9139-3.

Baumeister, Roy F., Arlene M. Stillwell, and Todd F. Heatherton. 2001. "Interpersonal As-pects of Guilt: Evidence from Narrative Studies." In *Emotions in Social Psychology: Es-sential Readings*, edited by W. Gerrod Parrott, 295–305. Hove, UK: Psychology Press.

BBC News. 2011. "In Full: Ken Clarke Interview on Rape Sentencing." Last modified May 18, 2011. https://www.bbc.co.uk/news/uk-politics-13444770.

Becker, Howard S. 1967. "Whose Side Are We On?" *Social Problems* 14, no. 3 (Winter): 239–47. https://doi.org/10.2307/799147.

Bennett, Christopher. 2008. *The Apology Ritual: A Philosophical Theory of Punishment*. Cambridge: Cambridge University Press.

Bennett, Jamie. 2016. *The Working Lives of Prison Managers: Global Change, Local Culture and Individual Agency in the Late Modern Prison*. Houndmills, UK: Palgrave Macmillan.

Bentham, Jeremy. (1791) 1995. *The Panopticon Writings*. Edited by Miran Božovič. London: Verso Books.

———. 1830. *The Rationale of Punishment*. London: Robert Heward.

Bernstein, Elizabeth. 2007. "The Sexual Politics of the 'New Abolitionism.'" *differences* 18, no. 3 (Fall): 128–51. https://doi.org/10.1215/10407391-2007-013.

Blagden, Nicholas, and Sarah Pemberton. 2010. "The Challenge in Conducting Qualitative Research with Convicted Sex Offenders." *Howard Journal of Criminal Justice* 49, no. 3 (July): 269–81. https://doi.org/10.1111/j.1468-2311.2010.00615.x.

Blagden, Nicholas, and Christian Perrin. 2016. "'Relax Lads, You're in Safe Hands Here': Experiences of a Sexual Offender Treatment Prison." In *Experiencing Imprisonment: Re-search on the Experience of Living and Working in Carceral Institutions*, edited by Carla Reeves, 27–45. Abingdon, UK: Routledge.

Blagden, Nicholas, Christian Perrin, Sam Smith, Faye Gleeson, and Laura Gillies. 2017. "'A Different World': Exploring and Understanding the Climate of a Recently Re-Rolled Sexual Offender Prison." *Journal of Sexual Aggression* 23 (2): 151–66. https://doi.org/10.1 080/13552600.2016.1264633.

Blagden, Nicholas, Belinda Winder, Kerensa Hocken, Rebecca Lievesley, Phil Banyard, and Helen Elliott, eds. 2019. *Sexual Crime and the Experience of Imprisonment*. Houndmills, UK: Palgrave Macmillan.

Blagden, Nicholas J., Belinda Winder, Karen Thorne, and Mick Gregson. 2011. "'No-One in the World Would Ever Wanna Speak to Me Again': An Interpretative Phenom-enological Analysis into Convicted Sexual Offenders' Accounts and Experiences of

Maintaining and Leaving Denial." *Psychology, Crime & Law* 17 (7): 563–85. https://doi .org/10.1080/10683160903397532.

Bosworth, Mary. 1999. *Engendering Resistance: Agency and Power in Women's Prisons.* Hampshire, UK: Ashgate.

Bottoms, Anthony. 2002. "Morality, Crime, Compliance and Public Policy." In *Ideology, Crime and Criminal Justice: A Symposium in Honour of Sir Leon Radzinowicz*, edited by Anthony Bottoms and Michael Tonry, 20–51. Cullompton, UK: Willan.

———. 2003. "Some Sociological Reflections on Restorative Justice." In *Restorative Justice and Criminal Justice: Competing or Irreconcilable Paradigms*, edited by Andrew von Hirsch, Julian V. Roberts, Anthony E. Bottoms, Kent Roach, and Mara Schiff, 79–114. Oxford: Hart.

———. 2019. "Penal Censure, Repentance and Desistance." In *Penal Censure: Engagements Within and Beyond Desert Theory*, edited by Antje du Bois-Pedain and Anthony E. Bottoms, 109–40. Oxford: Hart.

Boutellier, Hans. 2019. *A Criminology of Moral Order.* Bristol: Bristol University Press.

Braithwaite, John. 1989. *Crime, Shame and Reintegration.* Cambridge: Cambridge University Press.

Brown, Michelle. 2017. "An Exploration of the Challenges Families Experience When a Family Member Is Convicted of a Sex Offence." *Prison Service Journal* 233 (September): 34–41. https://www.crimeandjustice.org.uk/sites/crimeandjustice.org.uk/files/PSJ%20 233%20September%202017.pdf.

Burt, Martha R. 1980. "Cultural Myths and Supports for Rape." *Journal of Personality and Social Psychology* 38, no. 2 (February): 217–30. https://psycnet.apa.org/doi/10.1037/0022 -3514.38.2.217.

Butler, Judith. 1997. *Excitable Speech: A Politics of the Performative.* New York: Routledge.

Campbell, Kathryn, and Myriam Denov. 2004. "The Burden of Innocence: Coping with a Wrongful Imprisonment." *Canadian Journal of Criminology and Criminal Justice* 46, no. 2 (January): 139–64. https://doi.org/10.3138/cjccj.46.2.139.

Cheliotis, Leonidas K. 2006. "How Iron Is the Iron Cage of New Penology?: The Role of Human Agency in the Implementation of Criminal Justice Policy." *Punishment & Society* 8, no. 3 (July): 313–40. https://doi.org/10.1177%2F1462474506064700.

Christie, Nils. 1981. *Limits to Pain.* Oxford: Martin Robertson.

———. 1986. "The Ideal Victim." In *From Crime Policy to Victim Policy: Reorienting the Justice System*, edited by Ezzat A. Fattah, 17–30. London: Macmillan.

Chrysalis Collective. 2011. "Beautiful, Difficult, Powerful: Ending Sexual Assault through Transformative Justice." In *The Revolution Starts at Home: Confronting Intimate Violence within Activist Communities*, edited by Ching-In Chen, Jai Dulani, and Leah Lakshmi Piepzna-Samarasinha, 188–205. Brooklyn, NY: South End Press.

Clark, Haley. 2015. "A Fair Way to Go: Justice for Victim-Survivors of Sexual Violence." In *Rape Justice: Beyond the Criminal Law*, edited by Anastasia Powell, Nicola Henry, and Asher Flynn, 18–35. Houndmills, UK: Palgrave Macmillan.

Cohen, Stanley. 2001. *States of Denial: Knowing about Atrocities and Suffering.* Cambridge: Polity Press.

Cohen, Stanley, and Laurie Taylor. 1972. *Psychological Survival: The Experience of Long-Term Imprisonment.* Middlesex, UK: Penguin Books.

Cossins, Annie. 2008. "Restorative Justice and Child Sex Offences: The Theory and the Practice." *British Journal of Criminology* 48, no. 3 (May): 359–78. https://doi.org/10.1093/bjc/azn013.

Cowburn, Malcolm. 2005. "Hegemony and Discourse: Reconstruing the Male Sex Offender and Sexual Coercion by Men." *Sexualities, Evolution & Gender* 7, no. 3 (July): 215–31. https://doi.org/10.1080/14616660500231665.

———. 2007. "Men Researching Men in Prison: The Challenges for Profeminist Research." *Howard Journal of Criminal Justice* 46, no. 3 (July): 276–88. https://doi.org/10.1111/j.1468-2311.2007.00474.x.

CPS. 2017. *Violence Against Women and Girls Report, Tenth Edition, 2016–17*. London: CPS. https://www.cps.gov.uk/sites/default/files/documents/publications/cps-vawg-report-2017_0.pdf.

Crawley, Elaine. 2004. *Doing Prison Work: The Public and Private Lives of Prison Officers*. Cullompton, UK: Willan.

Crewe, Ben. 2009. *The Prisoner Society: Power, Adaptation, and Social Life in an English Prison*. Oxford: Oxford University Press.

———. 2011a. "Depth, Weight, Tightness: Revisiting the Pains of Imprisonment." *Punishment & Society* 13, no. 5 (December): 509–29. https://doi.org/10.1177%2F1462474511422172.

———. 2011b. "Soft Power in Prison: Implications for Staff–Prisoner Relationships, Liberty and Legitimacy." *European Journal of Criminology* 8, no. 6 (November): 455–68. https://doi.org/10.1177%2F1477370811413805.

———. 2015. "Inside the Belly of the Penal Beast: Understanding the Experience of Imprisonment." *International Journal for Crime, Justice and Social Democracy* 4 (1): 50–65. https://doi.org/10.5204/ijcjsd.v4i1.201.

———. 2016. "The Sociology of Imprisonment." In *Handbook on Prisons*, 2nd ed., edited by Yvonne Jewkes, Jamie Bennett, and Ben Crewe, 77–100. Abingdon, UK: Routledge.

Crewe, Ben, Susie Hulley, and Serena Wright. 2019. *Life Imprisonment from Young Adulthood: Adaptation, Identity and Time*. London: Palgrave Macmillan.

Crewe, Ben, and Alice Ievins. 2020. "The Prison as a Reinventive Institution." *Theoretical Criminology* 24, no. 4 (November): 568–89. https://doi.org/10.1177%2F1362480619841900.

Crewe, Ben, and Alice Ievins. 2021. "'Tightness', Recognition and Penal Power." *Punishment & Society* 23, no. 1 (January): 47–68. https://doi.org/10.1177%2F1462474520928115.

Crewe, Ben, Alice Ievins, Simon Larmour, Julie Laursen, Kristian Mjåland, and Anna Schliehe. 2022. "Nordic Penal Exceptionalism: A Comparative, Empirical Analysis." *British Journal of Criminology*. https://doi.org/10.1093/bjc/azac013.

Crewe, Ben, Alison Liebling, and Susie Hulley. 2014. "Heavy-Light, Absent-Present: Rethinking the 'Weight' of Imprisonment." *British Journal of Sociology* 65, no. 3 (September): 387–410. https://doi.org/10.1111/1468-4446.12084.

Critical Resistance and Incite! 2003. "Statement on Gender Violence and the Prison-Industrial Complex." *Social Justice* 30 (3): 141–50. https://www.jstor.org/stable/29768215.

Crockett Thomas, Phil, Fergus McNeill, Lucy Cathcart Fröden, Jo Collinson Scott, Oliver Escobar, and Alison Urie. 2021. "Re-Writing Punishment? Songs and Narrative Problem-Solving." *Incarceration* 2 (1): 1–19. https://doi.org/10.1177%2F26326663211000239.

Curtis-Fawley, Sarah, and Kathleen Daly. 2005. "Gendered Violence and Restorative Justice: The Views of Victim Advocates." *Violence Against Women* 11, no. 5 (May): 603–38. https://doi.org/10.1177%2F1077801205274488.

Daly, Ellen. 2022. *Rape, Gender and Class: Intersections in Courtroom Narratives*. Basingstoke, UK: Palgrave Macmillan.

Daly, Kathleen. 2006. "Restorative Justice and Sexual Assault: An Archival Study of Court and Conference Cases." *British Journal of Criminology* 46, no. 2 (March): 334–56. https://doi.org/10.1093/bjc/azi071.

———. 2008. "Setting the Record Straight and a Call for Radical Change: A Reply to Annie Cossins on 'Restorative Justice and Child Sex Offences.'" *British Journal of Criminology* 48, no. 4 (July): 557–66. https://doi.org/10.1093/bjc/azn034.

———. 2017. "Sexual Violence and Victims' Justice Interests." In *Restorative Responses to Sexual Violence: Legal, Social and Therapeutic Dimensions*, edited by Estelle Zinsstag and Marie Keenan, 108–40. Abingdon, UK: Routledge.

Davis, Angela. 2013. "Feminism and Abolition: Theories and Practices for the Twenty First Century." Lecture presented at the Center for the Study of Race, Politics and Culture and the Center for the Study of Gender and Sexuality Classics in Feminist Theory series, University of Chicago, June 5, 2013.

———. 2017. "Abolition Feminism: Theories and Practices for Our Time." Lecture presented at the Eleventh Annual Nicos Poulantzas Memorial Lecture series, Athens, Greece, December 11, 2017.

de Vel-Palumbo, Melissa, Laura Howarth, and Marilynn B. Brewer. 2019. "'Once a Sex Offender Always a Sex Offender?' Essentialism and Attitudes towards Criminal Justice Policy." *Psychology, Crime & Law* 25, no. 5 (October): 421–39. https://doi.org/10.1080/1068316X.2018.1529234.

Digard, Léon. 2010. "Sex Offenders and Their Probation Officers' Perceptions of Community Management in England and Wales." PhD diss., University of Cambridge.

Digard, Léon. 2014. "Encoding Risk: Probation Work and Sex Offenders' Narrative Identities." *Punishment & Society* 16, no. 4 (October): 428–47. https://doi.org/10.1177/1462474514539536.

Ditchfield, J. 1990. *Control in Prisons: A Review of the Literature*. London: Her Majesty's Stationery Office.

Douglas, Mary. 2002. *Purity and Danger: An Analysis of Concept of Pollution and Taboo*. London: Routledge.

Duff, R. A. 1986. *Trials and Punishments*. Cambridge: Cambridge University Press.

———. 2001. *Punishment, Communication, and Community*. Oxford: Oxford University Press.

———. 2003a. "Appendix: Response to Von Hirsch." In *Debates in Contemporary Political Philosophy: An Anthology*, edited by Derek Matravers and Jon Pike, 423–27. London: Routledge.

———. 2003b. "Penance, Punishment and the Limits of Community." *Punishment & Society* 5, no. 3 (July): 295–312. https://doi.org/10.1177%2F1462474503005003004.

———. 2011. "Responsibility, Restoration, and Retribution." In *Retributivism Has a Past: Has It a Future?*, edited by Michael Tonry, 63–85. Oxford: Oxford University Press.

Duncan, Katie, Andrea Wakeham, Belinda Winder, Nicholas Blagden, and Rachel Armitage. 2022. "'Grieving Someone Who's Still Alive, That's Hard': The Experiences of Non-Offending Partners of Individuals Who Have Sexually Offended—An IPA Study." *Journal of Sexual Aggression*. https://doi.org/10.1080/13552600.2021.2024611.

Durkheim, Emile. (1893) 1997. *The Division of Labour in Society*. Translated by W. D. Halls, with an Introduction by Lewis A. Coser. New York: Free Press.

——. (1902) 1992. "Two Laws of Penal Evolution." In *The Radical Sociology of Durkheim and Mauss*, edited by Mike Gane, 21–49. London: Routledge.

——. (1925) 1961. *Moral Education: A Study in the Theory and Application of the Sociology of Education*. Translated by Everett K. Wilson. New York: Free Press of Glencoe.

Elias, Norbert. (1939) 1994. *The Civilizing Process: The History of Manners and State Formation and Civilization*. Oxford: Blackwell.

Elison, Jeff. 2005. "Shame and Guilt: A Hundred Years of Apples and Oranges." *New Ideas in Psychology* 23, no. 1 (April): 5–32. https://doi.org/10.1016/j.newideapsych.2005.07.001.

Ensler, Eve. 2019a. *The Apology*. New York: Bloomsbury.

——. 2019b. "The Profound Power of an Authentic Apology." Filmed December 2019 at TEDWomen, Palm Springs, CA. Video, 8:14. https://www.ted.com/talks/eve_ensler_the _profound_power_of_an_authentic_apology.

Eriksson, Anna. 2021. "The Taint of the Other: Prison Work as 'Dirty Work' in Australia." *Punishment & Society*. https://doi.org/10.1177%2F14624745211047534.

Falshaw, Louise, Andrew Bates, Vaneeta Patel, Carmen Corbett, and Caroline Friendship. 2003. "Assessing Reconviction, Reoffending and Recidivism in a Sample of UK Sexual Offenders." *Legal and Criminological Psychology* 8, no. 2 (September): 207–15. https://doi.org/10.1348/135532503322362979.

Farmer, Mark, Anne-Marie McAlinden, and Shadd Maruna. 2016. "Sex Offending and Situational Motivation: Findings from a Qualitative Analysis of Desistance from Sexual Offending." *International Journal of Offender Therapy and Comparative Criminology* 60, no. 15 (November): 1756–75. https://doi.org/10.1177%2F0306624X16668175.

Feeley, Malcolm M. 1979. *The Process Is the Punishment: Handling Cases in a Lower Criminal Court*. New York: Russell Sage Foundation.

Feeley, Malcom M., and Jonathan Simon. 1992. "The New Penology: Notes on the Emerging Strategy of Corrections and Its Implications." *Criminology* 30, no. 4 (November): 449–74. https://doi.org/10.1111/j.1745-9125.1992.tb01112.x.

Feinberg, Joel. 1965. "The Expressive Function of Punishment." *Monist* 49, no. 3 (July): 397–423. https://www.jstor.org/stable/27901603.

Fleetwood, Jennifer, Lois Presser, Sveinung Sandberg, and Thomas Ugelvik, eds. 2019. *The Emerald Handbook of Narrative Criminology*. Bingley, UK: Emerald.

Foucault, Michel. 1991. *Discipline and Punish: The Birth of the Prison*. Translated by Alan Sheridan. London: Penguin Books.

——. 1998. *The Will to Knowledge: The History of Sexuality*. Vol. 1. Translated by Richard Hurley. London: Penguin Books.

Fox, Kathryn J. 1999. "Changing Violent Minds: Discursive Correction and Resistance in the Cognitive Treatment of Violent Offenders in Prison." *Social Problems* 46, no. 1 (February) : 88–103. https://doi.org/10.1525/sp.1999.46.1.03x0243i.

Freedman, Estelle B. 2013. *Redefining Rape: Sexual Violence in the Era of Suffrage and Segregation*. Cambridge, MA: Harvard University Press.

Fricker, Miranda. 2016. "What's the Point of Blame? A Paradigm Based Explanation." *Noûs* 50, no. 1 (March): 165–83. https://doi.org/10.1111/nous.12067.

Gang, Daye, Bebe Loff, Bronwyn Naylor, and Maggie Kirkman. 2021. "A Call for Evaluation of Restorative Justice Programs." *Trauma, Violence, & Abuse* 22, no. 1 (January): 186–90. https://doi.org/10.1177%2F1524838019833003.

Gannon, Theresa A., Mark E. Olver, Jaimee S. Mallion, and Mark James. 2019. "Does Specialized Psychological Treatment for Offending Reduce Recidivism? A Meta-Analysis Examining Staff and Program Variables as Predictors of Treatment Effectiveness." *Clinical Psychology Review* 73 (November). https://doi.org/10.1016/j.cpr.2019.101752.

Garfinkel, Harold. 1956. "Conditions of Successful Degradation Ceremonies." *American Journal of Sociology* 61, no. 5 (March): 420–24. https://doi.org/10.1086/221800.

Garland, David. 1990. *Punishment and Modern Society: A Study in Social Theory.* Oxford: Clarendon Press.

———. 2001. *The Culture of Control: Crime and Social Order in Contemporary Society.* Oxford: Oxford University Press.

Garrihy, Joe. 2022. "'That Doesn't Leave You': Psychological Dirt and Taint in Prison Officers' Occupational Cultures and Identities." *British Journal of Criminology* 62, no. 4 (July): 982–99. https://doi.org/10.1093/bjc/azab074.

Geertz, Clifford. 1998. "Deep Hanging Out." *New York Review of Books*, October 22, 1998. https://www.nybooks.com/articles/1998/10/22/deep-hanging-out/.

Gelsthorpe, Loraine, Peter Raynor, and Gwen Robinson. 2010. "Pre-Sentence Reports in England and Wales: Changing Discourses of Need, Risk and Quality." In *Offender Supervision: New Directions in Theory, Research and Practice*, edited by Fergus McNeill, Peter Raynor, and Chris Trotter, 471–91. London: Routledge.

Genders, E., and E. Player. 1995. *Grendon: A Study of a Therapeutic Prison.* Oxford: Clarendon Press.

Generation Five. 2007. *Toward Transformative Justice: A Liberatory Approach to Child Sexual Abuse and Other Forms of Intimate and Community Violence—A Call to Action for the Left and the Sexual and Domestic Violence Sectors.* June 2007. http://www.generationfive.org/wp-content/uploads/2013/07/G5_Toward_Transformative_Justice-Document.pdf.

Giddens, Anthony. 1991. *Modernity and Self-Identity: Self and Society in the Late Modern Age.* Cambridge: Polity Press.

Gilbert, Michael J. 1997. "The Illusion of Structure: A Critique of the Classical Model of Organization and the Discretionary Power of Correctional Officers." *Criminal Justice Review* 22, no. 1 (Spring): 49–64. https://doi.org/10.1177%2F073401689702200105.

Gilligan, James. 2000. *Violence: Reflections on Our Deadliest Epidemic.* London: Jessica Kingsley.

———. 2003. "Shame, Guilt, and Violence." *Social Research* 70, no. 4 (Winter): 1149–80. https://muse.jhu.edu/article/558608/pdf.

Goffman, Erving. 1961. *Asylums: Essays on the Social Situation of Mental Patients and Other Inmates.* New York: Anchor Books.

———. (1963) 1990. *Stigma: Notes on the Management of Spoiled Identity.* London: Penguin Books.

Goodmark, Leigh. 2018a. *Decriminalizing Domestic Violence: A Balanced Policy Approach to Intimate Partner Violence.* Oakland, CA: University of California Press.

———. 2018b. "Restorative Justice as Feminist Praxis." *International Journal of Restorative Justice* 1 (3): 372–84. https://doi.org/10.5553/IJRJ/258908912018001003003.

Grounds, Adrian T. 2005. "Understanding the Effects of Wrongful Imprisonment." In *Crime and Justice: A Review of Research*, Vol. 32, edited by Michael Tonry, 1–58. Chicago: University of Chicago Press.

Gruber, Aya. 2020. *The Feminist War on Crime: The Unexpected Role of Women's Liberation in Mass Incarceration*. Oakland, CA: University of California Press.

Hall, Maggie. 2016. *The Lived Sentence: Rethinking Sentencing, Risk and Rehabilitation*. Houndmills, UK: Palgrave Macmillan.

Hampton, Jean. 1984. "The Moral Education Theory of Punishment." *Philosophy & Public Affairs* 13, no. 3 (Summer): 208–38. https://www.jstor.org/stable/pdf/2265412.pdf.

———. 1991. "Correcting Harms versus Righting Wrongs: The Goal of Retribution." *UCLA Law Review* 39, no. 6 (August): 1659–702. https://heinonline.org/HOL/P?h=hein.journals /uclalr39&i=1673.

Hanson, R. Karl, Arthur Gordon, Andrew J. R. Harris, Janice K. Marques, William Murphy, Vernon L. Quinsey, and Michael C. Seto. 2002. "First Report of the Collaborative Outcome Data Project on the Effectiveness of Psychological Treatment for Sex Offenders." *Sexual Abuse: A Journal of Research and Treatment* 14, no. 2 (April): 169–94. https://doi .org/10.1177%2F107906320201400207.

Harris, Nathan. 2001. "Shaming and Shame: Regulating Drink-Driving." In *Shame Management Through Reintegration*, edited by Eliza Ahmed, Nathan Harris, John Braithwaite, and Valerie Braithwaite, 73–210. Cambridge: Cambridge University Press.

Hart, Henry M., Jr. 1958. "The Aims of the Criminal Law." *Law and Contemporary Problems* 23 (Summer): 401–41. https://scholarship.law.duke.edu/lcp/vol23/iss3/2.

Hawker-Dawson, Thomas. Forthcoming. "Penal Communication in Crown Court Sentencing." PhD diss., University of Cambridge.

Hayes, David. 2018. "Proximity, Pain, and State Punishment." *Punishment & Society* 20, no. 2 (April): 235–54. https://doi.org/10.1177%2F1462474517701303.

Herman, Judith Lewis. 2005. "Justice from the Victim's Perspective." *Violence Against Women* 11, no. 5 (May): 571–602. https://doi.org/10.1177%2F1077801205274450.

Hessick, Carissa Byrne. 2021. *Punishment Without Trial: Why Plea Bargaining Is a Bad Deal*. New York: Abrams Press.

Hillier, Tim, and Gavin Dingwall. 2021. *Criminal Justice and the Pursuit of Truth*. Bristol: Bristol University Press.

HM Chief Inspector of Prisons. 2015. *Annual Report 2014–15*. London: Her Majesty's Stationery Office. https://www.justiceinspectorates.gov.uk/hmiprisons/inspections/annual-report -2014-15/.

———. 2016. *Report on an Unannounced Inspection of HMP Stafford*. London: Her Majesty's Stationery Office. https://www.justiceinspectorates.gov.uk/hmiprisons/wp-content /uploads/sites/4/2016/06/Stafford-Web-2016.pdf.

———. 2020. *Report on an Unannounced Inspection of HMP Stafford*. London: Her Majesty's Stationery Office. https://www.justiceinspectorates.gov.uk/hmiprisons/wp-content /uploads/sites/4/2020/05/Stafford-web-2020.pdf.

HM Government. 2021. *The End-to-End Rape Review Report on Findings and Actions*. London: HM Government. https://www.gov.uk/government/publications/end-to-end -rape-review-report-on-findings-and-actions.

Hogue, Todd E. 1993. "Attitudes towards Prisoners and Sexual Offenders." *Issues in Criminological & Legal Psychology* 19:27–32.

Hohl, Katrin, and Elisabeth A. Stanko. 2015. "Complaints of Rape and the Criminal Justice System: Fresh Evidence on the Attrition Problem in England and Wales." *European Journal of Criminology* 12, no. 3 (May): 324–41. https://doi.org/10.1177%2F1477370815571949.

Hood, Roger, Stephen Shute, Martina Feilzer, and Aidan Wilcox. 2002. "Sex Offenders Emerging from Long-Term Imprisonment: A Study of Their Long-Term Reconviction Rates and of Parole Board Members' Judgements of Their Risk." *British Journal of Criminology* 42, no. 2 (March): 371–94. https://doi.org/10.1093/bjc/42.2.371.

Houge, Anette Bringedal, and Kjersti Lohne. 2017. "End Impunity! Reducing Conflict-Related Sexual Violence to a Problem of Law." *Law & Society Review* 51, no. 4 (December): 755–89. https://doi.org/10.1111/lasr.12294.

Hough, Mike, and Julian Roberts. 2017. "Public Opinion, Crime, and Criminal Justice." In *The Oxford Handbook of Criminology*, 6th ed., edited by Alison Liebling, Shadd Maruna, and Lesley McAra, 239–59. Oxford: Oxford University Press.

Hoyle, Carolyn, Naomi-Ellen Speechley, and Ros Burnett. 2016. *The Impact of Being Wrongly Accused of Abuse in Occupations of Trust: Victims' Voices*. Oxford: University of Oxford.

Hudson, Barbara. 1998. "Restorative Justice: The Challenge of Sexual and Racial Violence." *Journal of Law and Society* 25, no. 2 (June): 237–56. https://doi.org/10.1111/1467-6478.00089.

———. 2002. "Restorative Justice and Gendered Violence: Diversion or Effective Justice?" *British Journal of Criminology* 42, no. 3 (Summer): 616–34. https://doi.org/10.1093/bjc/42.3.616.

Hudson, Kirsty. 2005. *Offending Identities: Sex Offenders' Perspectives on Their Treatment and Management*. London: Willan.

Hughes, Everett Cherrington. 1958. *Men and Their Work*. Glencoe, IL: Free Press.

Hulley, Joanne L. 2016. "'While This Does Not in Any Way Excuse My Conduct . . .': The Role of Treatment and Neutralizations in Desistance from Sexual Offending." *International Journal of Offender Therapy and Comparative Criminology* 60, no. 15 (November): 1776–90. https://doi.org/10.1177%2F0306624X16668177.

Ievins, Alice. 2017. "SOTP: The View from the Inside." *Comparative Penology* (blog). https://www.compen.crim.cam.ac.uk/Blog/blog-pages-full-versions/aliceievinsblog2.

———. 2019. "Finding Victims in the Narratives of Men Imprisoned for Sex Offences." In *The Emerald Handbook of Narrative Criminology*, edited by Jennifer Fleetwood, Lois Presser, Sveinung Sandberg, and Thomas Ugelvik, 279–300. Bingley, UK: Emerald.

———. 2020a. "'Perfectly Individualized and Constantly Visible'? Lateral Tightness in a Prison Holding Men Convicted of Sex Offences." *Incarceration* 1 (1): 1–18. https://doi.org/10.1177/2632666320936433.

———. 2020b. "Power, Shame and Social Relations in Prisons for Men Convicted of Sex Offences." *Prison Service Journal* 251 (November): 3–10. https://www.crimeandjustice.org.uk/sites/crimeandjustice.org.uk/files/PSJ%20251%20November%202020%20%281%29.pdf.

———. 2022. "The Society of 'Sex Offenders.'" In *Power and Pain in the Modern Prison: The Society of Captives Revisited*, edited by Ben Crewe, Andrew Goldsmith, and Mark Halsey, 175–92. Oxford: Clarendon Press.

———. Forthcoming. "Taking the Long View: The Role of Shame and Guilt in Desistance." In *Criminology as a Moral Science*, edited by Anthony E. Bottoms and Jonathan Jacobs. Oxford: Hart.

Ievins, Alice, and Ben Crewe. 2015. "'Nobody's Better than You, Nobody's Worse than You': Moral Community among Prisoners Convicted of Sexual Offences." *Punishment & Society* 17, no. 4 (October): 482–501. https://doi.org/10.1177%2F1462474515603803.

Ievins, Alice, and Kristian Mjåland. 2021. "Authoritarian Exclusion and Laissez-Faire Inclusion: Comparing the Punishment of Men Convicted of Sex Offenses in England & Wales and Norway." *Criminology* 59, no 3 (August): 454–79. https://doi.org/10.1111/1745 -9125.12276.

Ievins, Alice, and Thea Reimer. Forthcoming. "Hope, Despair and Desistance: What Happens After People Are Imprisoned as 'Sex Offenders'?" In *Catholic Social Thought and Prison Ministry: Resourcing Theory and Practice*, edited by Elizabeth Phillips and Ferdia Stone-Davis. London: Routledge.

Ignatieff, Michael. 1989. *A Just Measure of Pain: The Penitentiary in the Industrial Revolution 1750–1850*. London: Penguin Books.

Independent Monitoring Board. 2012. *HMP Stafford, Annual Report, 1 May 2011 to 30 April 2012*. https://s3-eu-west-2.amazonaws.com/imb-prod-storage-10cod6bqkyovo/uploads /2015/01/stafford-2011–12.pdf.

———. 2014. *HMP Stafford, Annual Report, 1 May 2013 to 30 April 2014*. https://s3-eu-west-2 .amazonaws.com/imb-prod-storage-10cod6bqkyovo/uploads/2015/01/stafford-2013–14 .pdf.

Irwin, John, and Donald R. Cressey. 1962. "Thieves, Convicts and the Inmate Culture." *Social Problems* 10, no. 2 (Autumn): 142–55. https://doi.org/10.2307/799047.

Jacob, Jean Daniel, Marilou Gagnon, and Dave Holmes. 2009. "Nursing So-Called Monsters: On the Importance of Abjection and Fear in Forensic Psychiatric Nursing." *Journal of Forensic Nursing* 5, no. 3 (September): 153–61. https://doi.org/10.1111/j.1939–3938 .2009.01048.x.

Jarman, Ben. 2020. "Only One Way to Swim? The Offence and the Life Course in Accounts of Adaptation to Life Imprisonment." *British Journal of Criminology* 60, no. 6 (November): 1460–79. https://doi.org/10.1093/bjc/azaa036.

Johnson, Larissa Gabrielle, and Anthony Beech. 2017. "Rape Myth Acceptance in Convicted Rapists: A Systematic Review of the Literature." *Aggression and Violent Behavior* 34 (May): 20–34. https://doi.org/10.1016/j.avb.2017.03.004.

Jülich, Shirley. 2006. "Views of Justice among Survivors of Historical Child Sexual Abuse: Implications for Restorative Justice in New Zealand." *Theoretical Criminology* 10, no. 1 (February): 125–38. https://doi.org/10.1177%2F1362480606059988.

Kennedy, H. G., and D. H. Grubin. 1992. "Patterns of Denial in Sex Offenders." *Psychological Medicine* 22 no. 1 (February): 191–96. https://doi.org/10.1017/S0033291700032840.

Kim, Mimi E. 2018. "From Carceral Feminism to Transformative Justice: Women-of-Color Feminism and Alternatives to Incarceration." *Journal of Ethnic & Cultural Diversity in Social Work* 27 (3): 219–33. https://doi.org/10.1080/15313204.2018.1474827.

King, Roy D., and Kathleen McDermott. 1995. *The State of Our Prisons*. Oxford: Clarendon Press.

Kjelsberg, Ellen, and Liv Heian Loos. 2008. "Conciliation or Condemnation? Prison Employees' and Young Peoples' Attitudes towards Sexual Offenders." *International Journal of Forensic Mental Health* 7, no. 1 (May): 95–103. https://doi.org/10.1080/14999013.2008 .9914406.

Kotova, Anna. 2016. "'He's Got a Life Sentence, But I Have a Life Sentence to Cope with as Well': The Experiences of Long-Term Prisoners' Partners." PhD diss., University of Oxford.

Kotova, Anna, and Geraldine Akerman. 2022. "Navigating Moral Dimensions and Lateral Power—The Experiences of Men with Sexual Convictions and Histories of Sexual Abuse

Serving Sentences in a Therapeutic Community." *Incarceration* 3 (1): 1–17. https://doi
.org/10.1177/26326663221074263.

Kras, Kimberley R., and Brandy L. Blasko. 2016. "Pathways to Desistance among Men Convicted of Sexual Offenses: Linking Post Hoc Accounts of Offending Behavior and Outcomes." *International Journal of Offender Therapy and Comparative Criminology* 60, no. 15 (November): 1738–55. https://doi.org/10.1177%2F0306624X16668178.

Kruse, Anja Emilie. 2020. "The Who, the Why and the Wherefore: Explanations, Self-Change and Social Friction in Men's Narratives of Social Violations." PhD diss., University of Oslo.

Kruttschnitt, Candace, and Rosemary Gartner. 2003. "Women's Imprisonment." In *Crime and Justice: A Review of Research*, Vol. 30, edited by Michael Tonry, 1–81. Chicago: University of Chicago Press.

Kruttschnitt, Candace, and Rosemary Gartner. 2005. *Marking Time in the Golden State: Women's Imprisonment in California*. Cambridge: Cambridge University Press.

Lackenby, Joanne. 2018. "To Parole or Not to Parole? How Do Parole Board Members Make Decisions about Parole?" *Prison Service Journal* 237 (May): 32–35. https://www.crime
andjustice.org.uk/sites/crimeandjustice.org.uk/files/PSJ%20237%20May%202018%20
NEW.pdf.

Lacombe, Dany. 2008. "Consumed with Sex: The Treatment of Sex Offenders in Risk Society." *British Journal of Criminology* 48, no. 1 (January): 55–74. https://doi.org/10.1093/bjc
/azm051.

Lammy Review. 2017. *An Independent Review into the Treatment of, and Outcomes for, Black, Asian and Minority Ethnic Individuals in the Criminal Justice System*. September 2017.
https://assets.publishing.service.gov.uk/government/uploads/system/uploads/attach
ment_data/file/643001/lammy-review-final-report.pdf.

Lamont, Michèle, and Virág Molnár. 2002. "The Study of Boundaries in the Social Sciences." *Annual Review of Sociology* 28 (August): 167–95. https://doi.org/10.1146/annurev
.soc.28.110601.141107.

Laursen, Julie, and Ben Laws. 2017. "Honour and Respect in Danish Prisons: Contesting 'Cognitive Distortions' in Cognitive-Behavioural Programmes." *Punishment & Society* 19, no. 1 (January): 74–95. https://doi.org/10.1177%2F1462474516649175.

LeBel, Thomas P. 2012. "Invisible Stripes? Formerly Incarcerated Persons' Perceptions of Stigma." *Deviant Behavior* 33 (2): 89–107. https://doi.org/10.1080/01639625.2010.538
365.

Lees, Sue. 1993. "Judicial Rape." *Women's Studies International Forum* 16, no. 1 (January-February): 11–36. https://doi.org/10.1016/0277-5395(93)90077-M.

Leibrich, Julie. 1993. *Straight to the Point: Angles on Giving Up Crime*. Otago, NZ: University of Otago Press.

———. 1996. "The Role of Shame in Going Straight: A Study of Former Offenders." In *Restorative Justice: International Perspectives*, edited by Burt Galaway and Joe Hudson, 283–302. Monsey, NY: Criminal Justice Press.

Levine, Judith. 2002. *Harmful to Minors: The Perils of Protecting Children from Sex*. Minneapolis: University of Minnesota Press.

Levine, Judith, and Erica R. Meiners. 2020. *The Feminist and the Sex Offender: Confronting Sexual Harm, Ending State Violence*. London: Verso.

Liebling, Alison. 2000. "Prison Officers, Policing and the Use of Discretion." *Theoretical Criminology* 4, no. 3 (August): 333–57. https://doi.org/10.1177%2F1362480600004003005.

———. 2007. "Why Prison Staff Culture Matters." In *The Culture of Prison Violence*, edited by James M. Byrne, Don Hummer, and Faye S. Taxman, 105–22. Boston: Pearson Education.

———. 2013. "'Legitimacy under Pressure' in High Security Prisons." In *Legitimacy and Criminal Justice: An International Exploration*, edited by Justice Tankebe and Alison Liebling, 206–26. Oxford: Oxford University Press.

Liebling, Alison, assisted by Helen Arnold. 2004. *Prisons and Their Moral Performance: A Study of Values, Quality, and Prison Life*. Oxford: Oxford University Press.

Liebling, Alison, Helen Arnold, and Christina Straub. 2011. *An Exploration of Staff-Prisoner Relationships at HMP Whitemoor: 12 Years On*. Cambridge: University of Cambridge.

Liebling, Alison, and Ben Crewe. 2013. "Prisons beyond the New Penology: The Shifting Moral Foundations of Prison Management." In *The SAGE Handbook of Punishment and Society*, edited by Jonathan Simon and Richard Sparks, 283–307. London: Sage.

Liebling, Alison, Linda Durie, Annick Stiles, and Sarah Tait. 2005. "Revisiting Prison Suicide: The Role of Fairness and Distress." In *The Effects of Imprisonment*, edited by Alison Liebling and Shadd Maruna, 209–31. Cullompton, UK: Willan.

Liebling, Alison, and Deborah Kant. 2018. "The Two Cultures: Correctional Officers and Key Differences in Institutional Climate." In *The Oxford Handbook of Prisons and Imprisonment*, edited by John Wooldredge and Paula Smith, 208–34. Oxford: Oxford University Press.

Liebling, Alison, Ben Laws, Elinor Lieber, Katherine Auty, Bethany E. Schmidt, Ben Crewe, Judith Gardom, Deborah Kant, and Martha Morey. 2019. "Are Hope and Possibility Achievable in Prison?" *Howard Journal of Crime and Justice* 58, no. 1 (March):104–26. https://doi.org/10.1111/hojo.12303.

Liebling, Alison, David Price, and Guy Shefer. 2011. *The Prison Officer*. 2nd ed. London: Routledge.

Lindon, Giles, and Stephen Roe. 2017. *Deaths in Police Custody: A Review of the International Evidence*. London: Home Office.

Lord, Alex, and Phil Willmot. 2004. "The Process of Overcoming Denial in Sexual Offenders." *Journal of Sexual Aggression* 10, no. 1 (February): 51–61. https://doi.org/10.1080/13552600410001670937.

Lussier, Patrick, and Jay Healey. 2009. "Rediscovering Quetelet, Again: The 'Aging' Offender and the Prediction of Reoffending in a Sample of Adult Sex Offenders." *Justice Quarterly* 26, no. 4 (December): 827–56. https://doi.org/10.1080/07418820802593360.

Lynch, Mona. 1998. "Waste Managers? The New Penology, Crime Fighting, and Parole Agent Identity." *Law & Society Review* 32 (4): 839–70. https://doi.org/10.2307/827741.

MacKinnon, Catharine A. 2005. *Women's Lives, Men's Laws*. Cambridge, MA: Harvard University Press.

Madigan, Lee, and Nancy Gamble. 1991. *The Second Rape: Society's Continued Betrayal of the Victim*. New York: Lexington Books.

Mann, Natalie. 2012. "Ageing Child Sex Offenders in Prison: Denial, Manipulation and Community." *Howard Journal of Criminal Justice* 51, no. 4 (September): 345–58. https://doi.org/10.1111/j.1468-2311.2012.00705.x.

Mann, Ruth E. 2016. "Sex Offenders in Prison." In *Handbook on Prisons*, 2nd ed., edited by Yvonne Jewkes, Jamie Bennett, and Ben Crewe, 246–64. Abingdon, UK: Routledge.

Mann, Ruth E., Karl Hanson, and David Thornton. 2010. "Assessing Risk for Sexual Recidivism: Some Proposals on the Nature of Psychologically Meaningful Risk Factors." *Sexual Abuse* 22, no. 2 (June): 191–217. https://doi.org/10.1177%2F1079063210366039.

Marshall, William L., Dana Anderson, and Yolanda Fernandez. 1999. *Cognitive Behavioural Treatment of Sexual Offenders*. Chichester, UK: John Wiley & Sons.

Martin, Dianne L. 1998. "Retribution Revisited: A Reconsideration of Feminist Criminal Law Reform Strategies." *Osgoode Hall Law Journal* 36, no. 1 (Spring): 151–88. https://digitalcommons.osgoode.yorku.ca/ohlj/vol36/iss1/4/.

Maruna, Shadd. 2001. *Making Good: How Ex-Convicts Reform and Rebuild Their Lives*. Washington, DC: American Psychological Association.

Maruna, Shadd, and Heith Copes. 2005. "What Have We Learned from Five Decades of Neutralization Research?" In *Crime and Justice: A Review of Research*, Vol. 32, edited by Michael Tonry, 221–320. Chicago: University of Chicago Press.

Maruna, Shadd, and Ruth E. Mann. 2006. "A Fundamental Attribution Error? Rethinking Cognitive Distortions." *Legal and Criminological Psychology* 11, no. 2 (September): 155–77. https://doi.org/10.1348/135532506X114608.

Mathiesen, Thomas. 1965. *Defences of the Weak: A Sociological Study of a Norwegian Correctional Institution*. London: Tavistock.

Matza, David. 1969. *Becoming Deviant*. Englewood Cliffs, NJ: Prentice-Hall.

McAlinden, Anne-Marie. 2007a. *The Shaming of Sexual Offenders: Risk, Retribution and Reintegration*. Oxford: Hart.

———. 2007b. *Public Attitudes Towards Sex Offenders in Northern Ireland (full report): Report Prepared for the Northern Ireland Sex Offender Strategic Management Committee*. Belfast: Northern Ireland Office.

McCann, I. Lisa, and Laurie Anne Pearlman. 1990. "Vicarious Traumatization: A Framework for Understanding the Psychological Effects of Working with Victims." *Journal of Traumatic Stress* 3, no. 1 (January): 131–49. https://doi.org/10.1007/BF00975140.

McGlynn, Clare. 2010. "Feminist Activism and Rape Law Reform in England and Wales: A Sisyphean Struggle." In *Rethinking Rape Law: International and Comparative Perspectives*, edited by Clare McGlynn and Vanessa E. Munro, 139–53. Abingdon, UK: Routledge.

———. 2011. "Feminism, Rape and the Search for Justice." *Oxford Journal of Legal Studies* 31, no. 4 (Winter): 825–42. https://doi.org/10.1093/ojls/gqr025.

McGlynn, Clare, Julia Downes, and Nicole Westmarland. 2017. "Seeking Justice for Survivors of Sexual Violence: Recognition, Voice and Consequences." In *Restorative Responses to Sexual Violence: Legal, Social and Therapeutic Dimensions*, edited by Estelle Zinsstag and Marie Keenan, 179–91. Abingdon, UK: Routledge.

McGlynn, Clare, and Nicole Westmarland. 2019. "Kaleidoscopic Justice: Sexual Violence and Victim Survivors' Perceptions of Justice." *Social & Legal Studies* 28, no. 2 (April): 179–201. https://doi.org/10.1177%2F0964663918761200.

McGlynn, Clare, Nicole Westmarland, and Nikki Godden. 2012. "'I Just Wanted Him to Hear Me': Sexual Violence and the Possibilities of Restorative Justice." *Journal of Law and Society* 39, no. 2 (June): 213–40. https://doi.org/10.1111/j.1467-6478.2012.00579.x.

McNeill, Fergus. 2012. "Four Forms of 'Offender' Rehabilitation: Towards an Interdisciplinary Perspective." *Legal and Criminological Psychology* 17, no. 1 (February): 18–36. https://doi.org/10.1111/j.2044-8333.2011.02039.x.

Meiners, Erica R. 2016. *For the Children? Protecting Innocence in a Carceral State.* Minneapolis: University of Minnesota Press.

Merry, Sally Engle. 1990. *Getting Justice and Getting Even: Legal Consciousness among Working-Class Americans.* Chicago: University of Chicago Press.

Mews, Aidan, Laura Di Bella, and Mark Purver. 2017. *Impact Evaluation of the Prison-Based Core Sex Offender Treatment Programme.* London: Ministry of Justice. https://assets .publishing.service.gov.uk/government/uploads/system/uploads/attachment_data /file/623876/sotp-report-web-.pdf.

Miller, William Ian. 1997. *The Anatomy of Disgust.* Cambridge, MA: Harvard University Press.

Ministry of Justice. 2012. *The Criminal Injuries Compensation Scheme 2012.* London: Stationery Office. https://www.gov.uk/government/publications/criminal-injuries-compen sation-scheme-2012.

———. 2013. *Story of the Prison Population: 1993–2012 England and Wales.* London: Ministry of Justice. https://assets.publishing.service.gov.uk/government/uploads/system /uploads/attachment_data/file/218185/story-prison-population.pdf.

———. 2014. *Accredited Programmes, Annual Bulletin, 2013/14, England and Wales.* London: Ministry of Justice. https://assets.publishing.service.gov.uk/government/uploads /system/uploads/attachment_data/file/338517/accredited-programmes-annual-bulletin -2013-14.pdf.

———. 2018. *Offender Management Statistics Bulletin, England and Wales.* London: Ministry of Justice. https://assets.publishing.service.gov.uk/government/uploads/system /uploads/attachment_data/file/729211/OMSQ-2018-Q1.pdf.

———. 2022a. *Offender Management Statistics Bulletin, England and Wales.* London: Ministry of Justice. https://assets.publishing.service.gov.uk/government/uploads/system /uploads/attachment_data/file/1050241/OMSQ_Q3_2021.pdf.

———. 2022b. *Prison Population: 31 December 2021.* London: Ministry of Justice. https:// www.gov.uk/government/statistics/offender-management-statistics-quarterly-july-to -september-2021.

Morreall, John, ed. 1987. *The Philosophy of Laughter and Humour.* Albany: State University of New York Press.

Morris, Herbert. 1981. "A Paternalistic Theory of Punishment." *American Philosophical Quarterly* 18, no. 4 (October): 263–71. https://www.jstor.org/stable/20013924.

Mulholland, Ian. 2014. "Perrie Lectures 2013: Contraction in an Age of Expansion: An Operational Perspective." *Prison Service Journal* 211 (January): 14–18. https://www.crimean djustice.org.uk/sites/crimeandjustice.org.uk/files/PSJ%20211%20January%202014.pdf.

Murphy, Jeffrie G. 2012. *Punishment and the Moral Emotions: Essays in Law, Morality, and Religion.* Oxford: Oxford University Press.

Naughton, Michael. 2019. "Rethinking the Competing Discourses on Uncorroborated Allegations of Child Sexual Abuse." *British Journal of Criminology* 59, no. 2 (March): 461–80. https://doi.org/10.1093/bjc/azy037.

Nobles, Richard, and David Schiff. 2019. "Criminal Justice Unhinged: The Challenge of Guilty Pleas." *Oxford Journal of Legal Studies* 39, no. 1 (Spring): 100–23. https://doi.org /10.1093/ojls/gqy036.

Nussbaum, Martha C. 2004. *Hiding from Humanity: Disgust, Shame, and the Law.* Princeton, NJ: Princeton University Press.

———. 2021. *Citadels of Pride: Sexual Assault, Accountability, and Reconciliation*. New York: W. W. Norton.

O'Donnell, Ian. 2014. *Prisoners, Solitude, and Time*. Oxford: Oxford University Press.

O'Donnell, Ian, and Kimmett Edgar. 1999. "Fear in Prison." *Prison Journal* 79, no. 1 (March): 90–99. https://doi.org/10.1177%2F0032885599079001006.

Pali, Brunilda, and Karin Sten Madsen. 2011. "Dangerous Liaisons?: A Feminist and Restorative Approach to Sexual Assault." *Temida* 14, no. 1 (March): 49–65. https://doi.org/10.2298/TEM1101049P.

Palmer, Jerry. 1994. *Taking Humour Seriously*. London: Routledge.

Pearlman, Laurie Anne, and Karen W. Saakvitne. 1995. *Trauma and the Therapist: Countertransference and Vicarious Traumatization in Psychotherapy with Incest Survivors*. New York: W. W. Norton.

Philly Stands Up. 2012. "Accountability Road Map." *Abolitionist* 16 (Spring): 7–8. https://abolitionistpaper.wordpress.com/2012/02/06/issue-16-spring-2012/.

Pratt, John. 2008a. "Scandinavian Exceptionalism in an Era of Penal Excess: Part I: The Nature and Roots of Scandinavian Exceptionalism." *British Journal of Criminology* 48, no. 2 (March): 119–37. https://doi.org/10.1093/bjc/azm072.

———. 2008b. "Scandinavian Exceptionalism in an Era of Penal Excess: Part II: Does Scandinavian Exceptionalism Have a Future?" *British Journal of Criminology* 48, no. 3 (May): 275–92. https://doi.org/10.1093/bjc/azm073.

Priestley, Philip. 1980. *Community of Scapegoats: The Segregation of Sex Offenders and Informers in Prison*. Oxford: Pergamon Press.

Ricciardelli, Rosemary, and Mackenzie Moir. 2013. "Stigmatized among the Stigmatized: Sex Offenders in Canadian Penitentiaries." *Canadian Journal of Criminology and Criminal Justice* 55, no. 3 (July): 353–86. https://doi.org/10.3138/cjccj.2012.E22.

Ricciardelli, Rose, and Dale C. Spencer. 2018. *Violence, Sex Offenders, and Corrections*. Abingdon, UK: Routledge.

Rich, K. D. 1997. "Vicarious Traumatization: A Preliminary Study." In *Impact: Working with Sexual Abusers*, edited by Stacey Bird Edmunds, 75–88. Brandon, VT: Safer Society Press.

Richie, Beth E. 2012. *Arrested Justice: Black Women, Violence, and America's Prison Nation*. New York: New York University Press.

Rios, Victor M. 2011. *Punished: Policing the Lives of Black and Latino Boys*. New York: New York University Press.

Robinson, Gwen. 2008. "Late-Modern Rehabilitation: The Evolution of a Penal Strategy." *Punishment & Society* 10, no. 4 (October): 429–45. https://doi.org/10.1177%2F1462474508095319.

Rock, Paul. 1993. *The Social World of an English Crown Court: Witnesses and Professionals in the Crown Court Centre at Wood Green*. Oxford: Clarendon Press.

Rothman, David J. 1980. *Conscience and Convenience: The Asylum and Its Alternatives in Progressive America*. Boston: Little, Brown.

Rubin, Ashley T. 2015. "Resistance or Friction: Understanding the Significance of Prisoners' Secondary Adjustments." *Theoretical Criminology* 19, no. 1 (February): 23–42. https://doi.org/10.1177%2F1362480614543320.

———. 2021. *The Deviant Prison: Philadelphia's Eastern State Penitentiary and the Origins of America's Modern Penal System, 1829–1913*. Cambridge: Cambridge University Press.

Russell, Cherry. 1999. "Interviewing Vulnerable Old People: Ethical and Methodological Implications of Imagining Our Subjects." *Journal of Aging Studies* 13, no. 4 (Winter): 403–17. https://doi.org/10.1016/S0890-4065(99)00018-3.

Russell, Yvette. 2016. "Woman's Voice/Law's *Logos*: The Rape Trial and the Limits of Liberal Reform." *Australian Feminist Law Journal* 42, no. 2 (February): 273–96. https://doi.org/1 0.1080/13200968.2016.1257912.

Russo, Ann. 2013. "10 Strategies for Cultivating Community Accountability." *Prison Culture* (blog). September 16, 2013. https://www.usprisonculture.com/blog/2013/09/16/guest -post-strategies-for-cultivating-community-accountability-by-ann-russo/.

Sampson, Adam. 1994. *Acts of Abuse: Sex Offenders and the Criminal Justice System*. London: Routledge.

Sandberg, Sveinung. 2010. "What Can 'Lies' Tell Us about Life? Notes towards a Framework of Narrative Criminology." *Journal of Criminal Justice Education* 21, no. 4 (October): 447–65. https://doi.org/10.1080/10511253.2010.516564.

Sandbukt, Ingeborg Jenssen. 2021. "Reentry in Practice: Sexual Offending, Self-Narratives, and the Implications of Stigma in Norway." *International Journal of Offender Therapy and Comparative Criminology*. https://doi.org/10.1177%2F0306624X211049184.

Sanders, Teela. 2004. "Controllable Laughter: Managing Sex Work through Humour." *Sociology* 38, no. 2 (April): 273–91. https://doi.org/10.1177%2F0038038504040864.

Scheff, Thomas J. 1995. "Conflict in Family Systems: The Role of Shame." In *Self-Conscious Emotions: The Psychology of Shame, Guilt, Embarrassment, and Pride*, edited by June Price Tangney and Kurt W. Fischer, 393–412. New York: Guilford Press.

———. 2006. *Goffman Unbound! A New Paradigm for Social Science*. Boulder, CO: Paradigm.

Scheff, Thomas J., and Suzanne M. Retzinger. 1991. *Emotions and Violence: Shame and Rage in Destructive Conflicts*. Lexington, MA: Lexington Books.

Schinkel, Marguerite. 2014a. *Being Imprisoned: Punishment, Adaptation and Desistance*. Houndmills, UK: Palgrave Macmillan.

———. 2014b. "Punishment as Moral Communication: The Experiences of Long-Term Prisoners." *Punishment & Society* 16, no. 5 (December): 578–97. https://doi.org /10.1177%2F1462474514548789.

Schmucker, Martin, and Friedrich Lösel. 2015. "The Effects of Sexual Offender Treatment on Recidivism: An International Meta-Analysis of Sound Quality Evaluations." *Journal of Experimental Criminology* 11 (December): 597–630. https://doi.org/10.1007/s11292-015 -9241-z.

Schneider, Luisa T. 2020. "Sexual Violence During Research: How the Unpredictability of Fieldwork and the Right to Risk Collide with Academic Bureaucracy and Expectations." *Critique of Anthropology* 40, no. 2 (June): 173–93. https://doi.org/10.1177%2 F0308275X20917272.

Schwaebe, Charles. 2005. "Learning to Pass: Sex Offenders' Strategies for Establishing a Viable Identity in the Prison General Population." *International Journal of Offender Therapy and Comparative Criminology* 49, no. 6 (September): 614–25. https://doi.org /10.1177%2F0306624X05275829.

Scott, Susie. 2011. *Total Institutions and Reinvented Identities*. Houndmills, UK: Palgrave Macmillan.

Scully, Diana. 1990. *Understanding Sexual Violence: A Study of Convicted Rapists*. London: Harper Collins.

Sered, Danielle. 2019. *Until We Reckon: Violence, Mass Incarceration, and a Road to Repair*. New York: New Press.

Sexton, Lori. 2015. "Penal Subjectivities: Developing a Theoretical Framework for Penal Consciousness." *Punishment & Society* 17, no. 1 (January): 114–36. https://doi.org/10.1177%2F1462474514548790.

Sheldon, David. 2021. "Sex Offenders, Sex and the *Sub Rosa* Prison Economy." *Criminology & Criminal Justice* 21, no. 3 (July): 263–79. https://doi.org/10.1177%2F1748895819860875.

Sim, Joe. 1994. "Tougher than the Rest? Men in Prison." In *Just Boys Doing Business? Men, Masculinities and Crime*, edited by Tim Newburn and Elizabeth A. Stanko, 100–117. London: Routledge.

Simon, Jonathan. 1998. "Managing the Monstrous: Sex Offenders and the New Penology." *Psychology, Public Policy, and Law* 4, no. 1–2 (March–June): 452–67. https://psycnet.apa.org/doi/10.1037/1076-8971.4.1–2.452.

Skarbek, David. 2014. *The Social Order of the Underworld: How Prison Gangs Govern the American Penal System*. Oxford: Oxford University Press.

Skillen, A. J. 1980. "How to Say Things with Walls." *Philosophy* 55, no. 214 (October): 509–23. https://doi.org/10.1017/S0031819100049524.

Sloan, Jennifer Anne. 2016. *Masculinities and the Adult Male Prison Experience*. Houndmills, UK: Palgrave Macmillan.

Sparks, Richard, Anthony E. Bottoms, and Will Hay. 1996. *Prisons and the Problem of Order*. Oxford: Clarendon Press.

Stevens, Alisa. 2013. *Offender Rehabilitation and Therapeutic Communities: Enabling Change the TC Way*. London: Routledge.

———. 2016. *Sex in Prison: Experiences of Former Prisoners*. London: Howard League for Penal Reform.

Sturge, Georgina. 2020. *UK Prison Population Statistics*. Briefing Paper Number CBP-04334. London: House of Commons Library. https://commonslibrary.parliament.uk/research-briefings/sn04334/.

Sturge, Georgina, Joseph Robins, Yago Zayed, and Alexander Bellis. 2019. *The Spending of the Ministry of Justice*. Debate Pack Number CDP-2019–0217. London: House of Commons Library. https://commonslibrary.parliament.uk/research-briefings/cdp-2019–0217/.

Sullivan, Barbara. 2007. "Rape, Prostitution and Consent." *Journal of Criminology* 40, no. 2 (August): 127–42. https://doi.org/10.1375%2Facri.40.2.127.

Summers, Robert S. 1999. "Formal Legal Truth and Substantive Truth in Judicial Fact-Finding—Their Justified Divergence in Some Particular Cases." *Law and Philosophy* 18 (September): 497–511. https://link.springer.com/article/10.1023/A:1006327205902.

Sykes, Gresham M. (1958) 2007. *The Society of Captives: A Study of a Maximum Security Prison*. Princeton, NJ: Princeton University Press.

Sykes, Gresham M., and David Matza. 1957. "Techniques of Neutralization: A Theory of Delinquency." *American Sociological Review* 22, no. 6 (December): 664–70. https://doi.org/10.2307/2089195.

Tangney, June Price, and Ronda L. Dearing. 2002. *Shame and Guilt*. New York: Guilford Press.

Tangney, June P., Jeff Stuewig, and Logaina Hafez. 2011. "Shame, Guilt, and Remorse: Implications for Offender Populations." *Journal of Forensic Psychiatry & Psychology* 22 (5): 706–23. https://doi.org/10.1080/14789949.2011.617541.

Tasioulas, John. 2007. "Repentance and the Liberal State." *Ohio State Journal of Criminal Law* 4, no. 3 (Spring): 487–521. http://hdl.handle.net/1811/73044.

Tavuchis, Nicholas. 1991. *Mea Culpa: A Sociology of Apology and Reconciliation*. Stanford, CA: Stanford University Press.

Temkin, Jennifer, Jacqueline M. Gray, and Jastine Barrett. 2018. "Different Functions of Rape Myth Use in Court: Findings from a Trial Observation Study." *Feminist Criminology* 13, no. 2 (April): 205–26. https://doi.org/10.1177%2F1557085116661627.

Tewksbury, Richard. 2012. "Stigmatization of Sex Offenders." *Deviant Behavior* 33, no. 8 (July): 606–23. https://doi.org/10.1080/01639625.2011.636690.

Throness, Laurie. 2008. *A Protestant Purgatory: Theological Origins of the Penitentiary Act, 1779*. Aldershot, UK: Ashgate.

Thurston, Richard. 1996. "Are You Sitting Comfortably? Men's Storytelling, Masculinities, Prison Culture and Violence." In *Understanding Masculinities: Social Relations and Cultural Arenas*, edited by Máirtín Mac an Ghaill, 139–52. Buckingham, UK: Open University Press.

Topping, Alexandra, and Caelainn Barr. 2021. "Will Changes to How Law in England and Wales Treats Rape Bring Justice to Survivors?" *Guardian*, May 23, 2021. https://www.the guardian.com/society/2021/may/23/will-changes-to-how-law-in-england-and-wales -treats-rape-bring-justice-to-survivors?CMP=Share_iOSApp_Other.

Tracy, Jessica L., and Richard W. Robins. 2006. "Appraisal Antecedents of Shame and Guilt: Support for a Theoretical Model." *Personality and Social Psychology Bulletin* 32, no. 10 (October): 1339–51. https://doi.org/10.1177%2F0146167206290212.

Trivedi-Bateman, Neema. 2019. "The Combined Roles of Moral Emotion and Moral Rules in Explaining Acts of Violence Using a Situational Action Theory Perspective." *Journal of Interpersonal Violence* 36, no. 17–18 (September): 8715–40. https://doi .org/10.1177%2F0886260519852634.

Tynan, Rachel Rose. 2019. *Young Men's Experiences of Long-Term Imprisonment: Living Life*. Abingdon, UK: Routledge.

Ugelvik, Thomas. 2012. "Prisoners and Their Victims: Techniques of Neutralization, Techniques of the Self." *Ethnography* 13, no. 3 (September): 259–77. https://doi.org /10.1177%2F1466138111435447.

———. 2014. *Power and Resistance in Prison: Doing Time, Doing Freedom*. Translated by Stephen G. Evans. Houndmills, UK: Palgrave Macmillan.

Van Stokkom, Bas. 2002. "Moral Emotions in Restorative Justice Conferences: Managing Shame, Designing Empathy." *Theoretical Criminology* 6, no. 3 (August): 339–60. https:// doi.org/10.1177%2F13624806020060006.

Vaughn, Michael S., and Allen D. Sapp. 1989. "Less than Utopian: Sex Offender Treatment in a Milieu of Power Struggles, Status Positioning, and Inmate Manipulation in State Correctional Institutions." *Prison Journal* 69, no. 2 (October): 73–89. https://doi.org/10 .1177%2F003288558906900210.

Velotti, Patrizia, Carlo Garofalo, Federica Bottazzi, and Vincenzo Caretti. 2017. "Faces of Shame: Implications for Self-Esteem, Emotion Regulation, Aggression, and Well-Being."

Journal of Psychology 15, no. 2 (November): 171–84. https://doi.org/10.1080/00223980.2
016.1248809.

Von Hirsch, Andrew. 1993. *Censure and Sanctions*. Oxford: Clarendon Press.

———. 2003. "Punishment, Penance and the State: A Reply to Duff." In *Debates in Contemporary Political Philosophy: An Anthology*, edited by Derek Matravers and Jon Pike, 408–22. London: Routledge.

Wacquant, Loïc. 2009. *Punishing the Poor: The Neoliberal Government of Social Insecurity*. Durham, NC: Duke University Press.

Waddington, P. A. J., Doug Badger, and Ray Bull. 2005. "Appraising the Inclusive Definition of Workplace 'Violence.'" *British Journal of Criminology* 45, no. 2 (March): 141–64. https://doi.org/10.1093/bjc/azh052.

Waites, Matthew. 2016. "The Age of Consent and Sexual Consent." In *Making Sense of Sexual Consent*, edited by Mark Cowling and Paul Reynolds, 73–92. Abingdon, UK: Routledge.

Waldram, James B. 2007. "Everybody Has a Story: Listening to Imprisoned Sexual Offenders." *Qualitative Health Research* 17, no. 7 (September): 963–70. https://doi.org/10.1177%2F1049732307306014.

———. 2012. *Hound Pound Narrative: Sexual Offender Habilitation and the Anthropology of Therapeutic Intervention*. Berkeley: University of California Press.

Walker, Margaret Urban. 2006. *Moral Repair: Reconstructing Moral Relations After Wrongdoing*. Cambridge: Cambridge University Press.

Ware, Jayson, and Nicholas Blagden. 2020. "Men with Sexual Convictions and Denial." *Current Psychiatry Reports* 22. https://doi.org/10.1007/s11920-020-01174-z.

Warr, Jason. 2020. "'Always Gotta Be Two Mans': Lifers, Risk, Rehabilitation, and Narrative Labour." *Punishment & Society* 22, no. 1 (January): 28–47. https://doi.org/10.1177%2F1462474518822487.

Way, Ineke, Karen M. VanDeusen, Gail Martin, Brooks Applegate, and Deborah Jandle. 2004. "Vicarious Trauma: A Comparison of Clinicians Who Treat Survivors of Sexual Abuse and Sexual Offenders." *Journal of Interpersonal Violence* 19, no. 1 (January): 49–71. https://doi.org/10.1177/0886260503259050.

Williams, Bernard. 1993. *Shame and Necessity*. Berkeley: University of California Press.

Williams, Rowan. 2003. "Ministry in Prison: Theological Reflections." *Justice Reflections* 2: 1–16. http://www.justicereflections.org.uk/pdf-files/jr7.pdf.

Wilson, William. 2007. "What's Wrong with Murder?" *Criminal Law and Philosophy* 1 (May): 157–77. https://doi.org/10.1007/s11572-006-9017-7.

Winfree, L. Thomas, Jr., Greg Newbold, and S. Houston Tubb, III. 2002. "Prisoner Perspectives on Inmate Culture in New Mexico and New Zealand: A Descriptive Case Study." *Prison Journal* 82, no. 2 (June): 213–33. https://doi.org/10.1177%2F003288550208200204.

Wright, Serena, Ben Crewe, and Susie Hulley. 2017. "Suppression, Denial, Sublimation: Defending against the Initial Pains of Very Long Life Sentences." *Theoretical Criminology* 21, no. 2 (May): 225–46. https://doi.org/10.1177%2F1362480616643581.

Yates, Pamela M. 2009. "Is Sexual Offender Denial Related to Sex Offence Risk and Recidivism? A Review and Treatment Implications." *Psychology, Crime & Law* 15, no. 2–3 (March): 183–99. https://doi.org/10.1080/1068316080219090 5.

Zehr, Howard. 1990. *Changing Lenses: A New Focus for Crime and Justice*. Scottdale, PA: Herald Press.

Zhong, Shaoling, Morwenna Senior, Rongqin Yu, Amanda Perry, Keith Hawton, Jenny Shaw, and Seena Fazel. 2021. "Risk Factors for Suicide in Prisons: A Systematic Review and Meta-Analysis." *Lancet* 6, no. 3 (March): 164–74. https://doi.org/10.1016/S2468 -2667(20)30233-4.

Zijderveld, Anton C. 1968. "Jokes and Their Relation to Social Reality." *Social Research* 35, no. 2 (Summer): 268–311. https://www.jstor.org/stable/40969908.

Zinsstag, Estelle, and Marie Keenan, eds. 2017. *Restorative Responses to Sexual Violence: Legal, Social and Therapeutic Dimensions.* Abingdon, UK: Routledge.

INDEX

Abolitionism, 2, 5–6, 9, 31, 148, 153–56, 174–75n9. *See also* carceral feminism, critiques of

accountability, 4, 6, 153, 155, 174–75n9

adaptation. *See* prisoners' orientations to their sentence and typology

adjudications, or 'nickings', 68, 70–71, 120–21, 167n17

age and ageing, 26, 28, 113, 118

apologies, 20–21, 86, 148–49, 152, 156, 161n21

appeals, 79, 81, 90, 92, 97, 169n8. *See also* wrongful convictions

applications, or 'apps', 82, 113, 160n31

association, 25, 28–29, 74, 80, 97, 99, 106, 111, 121

attitudes to power. *See* compliance, resistance, and censoriousness

audiences of morally communicative punishment, 11, 13–14, 17, 36, 59, 174n4. *See also* morally communicative theories of punishment

'Bang up', 25, 80, 117, 168n28

Bedwatch, 25, 172n23

'Carceral feminism', 1–7, 31, 148; critiques of, 4–7, 31, 154, 157n5. *See also* rape law and law reform

change. *See* repentance

Clarke, Kenneth, 1–3, 5, 157n3,4

cognitive distortions, excuses, and justifications, 9, 17–18, 33–35, 52, 54–55, 73–74, 78–79, 83–86, 128–29, 152–53, 155, 167n25. *See also* institutional distortions and maintaining innocence

compliance, resistance, and censoriousness, 15, 23, 25–26, 28, 51, 53–54, 60–63, 67–72, 75–76, 78, 80–81, 89–91, 93–95, 99–102; and staff-prisoner relationships, 110–18, 121, 170n6, 172n22. *See also* complaints

complaints, 113, 116, 169–70n15, 171n16, 172n19

conditioning. *See* manipulation

Denial. *See* cognitive distortions, excuses, and justifications, maintaining innocence, social life among prisoners and collective denial, and wrongful convictions.

denunciation, 2, 6–7, 16, 19–21, 35, 37–39, 49, 73, 128, 143, 147–48, 153. *See also* morally communicative institutions and Stafford as a denunciatory institution

desistance, 5, 22, 45, 52, 164n13; and attitudes to the conviction, 17–18, 34, 52, 56, 66–67, 143, 152–53, 165n28, 168n35. *See also* treatment programs, effectiveness of

deterrence, 13, 72

disgust, 13, 44, 47–48, 62, 64–65, 82, 87, 94, 98, 130–31, 133, 138, 141, 145; from practitioners, 15, 107. *See also* stain, prison officers and contamination, and social relationships among prisoners and vicarious traumatization

Victims, 6, 11, 34, 147–48; and compensation, 91–92, 169n10; and experiences of the legal system, 1–5, 37, 54, 174n4; and prisoners' attitudes to, 21, 41, 49, 54, 59, 61–62, 64–65, 73, 77–78, 84–85, 87, 91–92, 97, 128, 138, 143; and their attitudes to justice, 148–50
Victims' Commissioner, 4, 158n9

Vulnerable Prisoners (VPs) and Vulnerable Prisoners' Units (VPUs), 24–25, 46, 82, 161–62n32, 170n6, 172n23,27. *See also* people convicted of sex offenses in prison

Women in prison, 12, 25, 158n12, 171n17
wrongful convictions, 169n3,8,9. See also appeals and maintenance of innocence.

Founded in 1893,
UNIVERSITY OF CALIFORNIA PRESS
publishes bold, progressive books and journals
on topics in the arts, humanities, social sciences,
and natural sciences—with a focus on social
justice issues—that inspire thought and action
among readers worldwide.

The UC PRESS FOUNDATION
raises funds to uphold the press's vital role
as an independent, nonprofit publisher, and
receives philanthropic support from a wide
range of individuals and institutions—and from
committed readers like you. To learn more, visit
ucpress.edu/supportus.